Putting the gospel first

PUTTING THE GOSPEL FIRST

The best of the Spring Harvest Word Alive Weeks

Edited by David Porter

CROSSWAY BOOKS
Leicester

CROSSWAY BOOKS
38 De Montfort Street, Leicester LE1 7GP, UK

Unless otherwise stated, Scripture quotations in this publication are from the Holy Bible, New International Version. Copyright © 1973, 1978, 1984 by International Bible Society. Used by permission of Hodder and Stoughton Ltd. All rights reserved. 'NIV' is a registered trademark of International Bible Society. UK trademark number 1448790.

The poem on page 47 is from *Gold Cord*, by Amy Carmichael, published by Christian Literature Crusade, Fort Washington, PA, USA: by permission of the Dohnavur Fellowship. Used by permission.

British Library Cataloguing-in-Publication Data
A catalogue record for this book is available from the British Library.

ISBN 1–85684–136–7

Set in Palatino
Photoset by Parker Typesetting Service, Leicester
Printed in Great Britain by Cox & Wyman Ltd, Reading

Contents

Editor's introduction   7

Basics for believers: an exposition of Philippians
D. A. Carson

   1. Put the gospel first! (Philippians 1:1–26)   9
   2. Adopt Jesus' death as a test of your outlook
      (Philippians 1:27 – 2:18)   26
   3. Emulate worthy Christian leaders (Philippians 2:19 – 3:21)   48
   4. Never give up the Christian walk (Philippians 4:1–23)   73

Four studies in Isaiah
David Jackman

   5. Know and trust your God (Isaiah 40)   97
   6. The servant solution (Isaiah 49)   113
   7. The good news about Jesus (Isaiah 52:13 – 53:12)   118
   8. Jerusalem, the Lord's delight (Isaiah 65)   144

The sins of half-heartedness: studies in Malachi
Roy Clements

   9. Doubt (Malachi 1:1–5)   161
  10. Apathy (Malachi 1:6 – 2:9)   176
  11. Infidelity (Malachi 2:10–16)   190
  12. Cynicism (Malachi 2:17 – 4:6)   207

The church in the modern world: Acts 16 – 20

  13. Acts 16   221
      Dick Dowsett
  14. Acts 17   229
      David Cook
  15. Acts 20   240
      Alec Motyer

Notes   249

Editor's introduction

The material in this book is a selection of ministry given at Word Alive, and consequently originated as spoken addresses. As editor, I have found it a joy and a privilege to work on this material once again. The editorial policy has been to preserve all the content and as much of the style as possible; I hope that something of the feel of the occasion itself has found its way on to the printed page.

In order to keep the book to an economic length, I have abridged the material slightly and have not always printed the whole of a Bible passage quoted by a speaker. However, no allusion to the Bible has been omitted, and references have been supplied. You will get the most from this book if you read it together with an open Bible, looking up each passage in its context, but I think all the speakers would agree that that is the best way to read any book of Bible exposition, abridged or not.

The expositions by Don Carson are largely his own revised, written version of the spoken ministry he gave in 1994. Those by David Jackman (given in 1995) are newly edited and abridged from transcripts. The expositions by Roy Clements were given in 1993 and appeared in *Word Alive: Bible Teaching at the Cutting Edge* (ed. David Porter, IVP, 1994), and the three expositions from Acts are from a series of five given at Word Alive 1994.

David Porter

BASICS FOR BELIEVERS
An exposition of Philippians
D. A. Carson

1
Put the gospel first!

Philippians 1:1–26

I would like to buy about three quid's worth of gospel, please. Not too much – just enough to make me happy, but not so much that I get addicted. I don't want so much gospel that I learn to really hate covetousness and lust; I certainly don't want so much that I start to love my enemies, cherish self-denial, and contemplate missionary service in some alien culture. I want ecstasy, not repentance; I want transcendence, not transformation. I would like to be cherished by some nice, forgiving, broad-minded people, but I myself don't want to love those from different races – especially if they smell. I would like enough gospel to make my family secure and my children well behaved, but not so much that I find my ambitions redirected, or my giving too greatly enlarged.

I would like about three quid's worth of gospel, please.

Of course, none of us is so crass as to put it that way. But most of us have felt the temptation to opt for a domesticated version of the gospel. In some ways, this temptation is perennial. But perhaps it is especially strong today, owing to a number of developments in the western world.

First, pressure has been building from the process of secularization. Secularization does not refer to some social impetus driving us toward the abolition of religion. Rather, secularization refers to the processes that squeeze religion to the periphery of life. The result is not that we abandon religion or banish the gospel; rather, religion is marginalized and privatized, and the gospel is rendered unimportant.

The evidence for this development is everywhere, but it can be most easily displayed by asking one question: what governs the national discourse? The answer, of course, is almost everything but the gospel: economics, politics, entertainment, sports, sleaze, who's 'in' and who's 'out'. There is relatively little moral discourse, and almost none that has to do with eternal perspectives – how to live in the light of death and the final judgment – despite the centrality of that theme in the teaching of Jesus. So when we insist on the supreme importance of the gospel, we find many in our society sceptical and dismissive. Unwittingly, partly to protect ourselves from others, partly because we ourselves are heavily influenced by the culture in which we live and move and have our being, we find ourselves formally espousing the gospel, and formally confessing that biblical religion is of infinite worth, while in reality we are no longer possessed by it. Or we maintain the faith by privatizing it: it becomes uncivilized to talk about religion in polite company. We buy our three quid's worth of gospel, but it challenges us very little.

Secondly, the sapping influences of self-indulgence throughout the Western world wield their power in the church. For many confessing Christians, it has become more important to be comfortable and secure than it is to be self-sacrificing and giving. Three quid's worth of gospel, please, but no more.

Thirdly, we are witnessing the rise of what some have called 'philosophical pluralism'. This is saying more than that many western nations, including Britain and America, are more diverse, more empirically pluralistic, than they have ever been. By almost any objective criteria, we boast a richer diversity of races, religions, moral values and forms of cultural heritage than any of our grandparents experienced in this country. In itself that is neither a good thing nor a bad thing: it is merely a brute fact, one that could be interpreted in quite different ways. By contrast, philosophical pluralism is the settled stance that insists that in most areas of human knowledge, and perhaps in all of them, knowledge of objective truth is impossible. Because it is impossible, it is wrong-headed, and perhaps immoral, to claim that any ideology or any religion is superior to another. Certainly no religion has the right to pronounce another wrong. That is the one 'wrong' thing. The sole heresy has become the view that there is such a thing as heresy.

In such a world, evangelism is easily written off as grotesque proselytizing. Quiet insistence that real truth exists is commonly written off as, at best, quaint nineteenth-century epistemology, and at worst, benighted bigotry. So once again, we find reasons to want only a little gospel: three quid's worth, perhaps, but we shouldn't overdo it.

Paul recognized the insidious evil of similar pressures in the Roman Empire of his day. Like modern Western culture, the Roman Empire had begun to decay. Like ours, it was prepared to use religion for political ends but unwilling to be tamed by it, settling slowly into cultured self-indulgence, proud of the diversity in the Empire and straining to keep it together by the demand for unhesitating loyalty to the Emperor. Pluralism of several kinds made it unpopular to say there is only one way of salvation. Indeed, vassal peoples normally swapped gods with the Romans: the Roman pantheon took on some of the new gods, while the newly subjugated people adopted some of the Roman deities. That way no god could become too presumptuous and challenge the might of Rome.

That is Paul's world when he writes to the Philippians. He had founded the church in the city of Philippi in AD 51 or 52, and visited it at least twice since then. At this point, however, he is writing from prison, probably in Rome about AD 61. So the church at Philippi is not more than ten years old. Paul perceives a variety of pressures lurking in the wings, pressures that could damage this fledgling Christian community. He cannot visit them, but he wants to encourage them to maintain basic Christian commitments and to be on guard against an array of dangers: temptations from within and seduction and opposition from without.

What a person says while unjustly incarcerated and facing the possibility of death is likely to be given more weight than if that person were both free and carefree. So the fact that Paul felt he had to write from prison to the Philippians to remind them of some Christian basics doubtless worked out, providentially, for their good.

What, then, is his burden as he addresses the Philippians? What is God telling us by his Spirit through these same words two thousand years later?

The first thing this book emphasizes is to *put the gospel first*. It will be helpful to trace this theme in four points.

Put the fellowship of the gospel at the centre of your relationships with believers (1:3–8)

As often in his letters, Paul begins with a warm expression of thanks to God for something in the lives of his readers. Here the grounds of his thanksgiving to God are three, though all three are tied to the same theme.

The *first* is their faithful memory of him. The NIV reads, 'I thank my God every time I remember you' (verse 3). But others offer 'I thank my God every time you remember me', or something similar. The original is ambiguous. For reasons I shan't go into, I think Paul is referring to their remembrance of him. Later on he will thank the Philippians for remembering him so warmly they sent funds to support him in his ministry. But here the vision is broader: he perceives that their interest in him is a reflection of their continued commitment to the gospel – and that is why he thanks God for them.

The point becomes explicit in the *second* cause of his thanksgiving: 'In all my prayers for all of you, I always pray with joy because of your partnership in the gospel from the first day until now' (verses 4–5). Their 'partnership in the gospel' injects joy into Paul's prayers of thanksgiving: 'I always pray *with joy*', he writes. The word rendered 'partnership' is more commonly translated 'fellowship' in the New Testament. What precisely does the word mean?

In common use 'fellowship' has become somewhat debased. If you invite a pagan neighbour to your home for a cup of tea, it is friendship; if you invite a Christian neighbour, it is fellowship. If you attend a meeting at church and leave as soon as it is over, you have participated in a service; if you stay for tea and crumpets afterward, you have enjoyed some fellowship. In modern use, then, fellowship has come to mean something like warm friendship with believers.

In the first century, however, the word commonly had commercial overtones. If John and Harry buy a boat and start a fishing business, they have entered into a fellowship, a partnership. Intriguingly, even in the New Testament the word is often tied to fiscal matters. Thus when the Macedonian Christians send money to help the poor Christians in Jerusalem they are entering into fellowship with them.

The heart of true fellowship is self-sacrificing conformity to a shared vision. Both John and Harry put their savings into the fishing boat. Now they share the vision that will put the fledgling company on its feet. *Christian* fellowship, then, is self-sacrificing conformity to the gospel. There may be overtones of warmth and intimacy, but the heart of the matter is this shared vision of what is of transcendental importance, a vision that calls forth our commitment. So when Paul gives thanks, with joy, because of the Philippians' 'partnership in the gospel' or 'fellowship in the gospel', he is thanking God for the fact that these brothers and sisters in Christ, from the moment of their conversion ('from the first day until now', Paul writes), rolled up their sleeves and got involved in the advance of the gospel. They continued their witness in Philippi, they persevered in their prayers for Paul, they sent money to support him in his ministry – all testifying to their shared vision of the importance and priority of the gospel. That is more than enough reason for thanking God.

There is a *third* basis for Paul's thanks to God for them. It is nothing less than God's continuing work in their lives. 'I thank my God', Paul begins in verse 3, and now adds, '. . . being confident of this, that he who began a good work in you will carry it on to completion until the day of Christ Jesus' (verse 6). This is almost a definition of what a real Christian is. The New Testament affords not a few examples of people who made professions of faith that were spurious, as evidenced by the fact that they did not endure, they did not persevere. For example, at the end of John 2 many people believed in Jesus' name when they saw the miraculous signs he was doing. 'But Jesus would not entrust himself to them' (Jn. 2:24), we are told; he knew their faith was not genuine. A few chapters later, to those who had made profession of faith Jesus declared, 'If you hold to my teaching, you are really my disciples' (Jn. 8:30–31). Or as Hebrews 3:14 puts it, 'We have come to share in Christ if we hold firmly till the end the confidence we had at first.' In the parable of the sower Jesus depicts some who 'hear the word and at once receive it with joy. But since they have no root, they last only a short time. When trouble or persecution comes because of the word, they quickly fall away' (Mk. 4:16–17). Speedily they receive the word; speedily they fall away. The most promising of the crop in this case proves fickle: they start by showing signs of life, but never produce any fruit.

Not so the Philippians. Paul is convinced they will persevere, and the reason is that God is preserving them. Paul gives thanks to God because he is entirely confident, as he has observed the Philippians, that God did indeed begin a 'good work' in them (theirs was no spurious conversion), and the God who begins a good work finishes it.

It is worth pausing to reflect on the fact that as Paul gives thanks his stance is not mechanical or merely ritualistic. Look at verse 4: 'In all my prayers for all of you, I always pray *with joy* . . . .' His words remind us of what John says in his third epistle: 'I have no greater joy than to hear that my children are walking in the truth' (3 Jn. 4). Implicitly, such an apostolic stance asks us what gives us our greatest joy. Is it personal success? Some victory for our children? Acquisition of material things? '*I have no greater joy*', John writes, 'than to hear that my children are walking in the truth.' Paul reflects exactly the same attitude. Paul adds, 'It is right for me to feel this way about all of you, since I have you in my heart' (1:7). Probably this was written against the background of Stoic influence that was cautious about whole-life commitments, especially if they involved the 'passions'. Be cool; do not be vulnerable; do not get hurt. But that was not Paul's way. 'It is right for me to feel this way about all of you', Paul insists, regardless of what the contemporary culture says. 'I have you in my heart': my whole life and thought are bound up with you.

Paul's circumstances will not affect his joyful and prayerful regard

13

for the Philippian believers. 'Whether I am in chains or defending and confirming the gospel' (verse 7), he insists, he will adopt the same stance. The clause could be taken in either of two ways: (1) 'whether I am in chains or brought before the court'; or (2) 'whether I am in chains or freed again and defending and articulating the gospel'. Either way, Paul delights to remind them, 'all of you share in God's grace with me' (1:7).

So strongly does he want the Philippians to recognize his devotion to them that Paul puts himself under an oath: 'God can testify how I long for all of you with the affection of Christ Jesus' (1:8). The purpose of the oath is not because without it he might lie. Rather, he puts himself under an oath so that the Philippians might *feel* the passion of his truthfulness, in exactly the same way that God puts himself under an oath in the epistle to the Hebrews: the point is not that otherwise God might lie, but that God wants to be believed (Heb. 7:20–25). So Paul: '*God is my witness* how I long for all of you with the affection of Christ Jesus.'

Here is no mere professionalism. Nor is this an act, a bit of showmanship to 'turn them on' to the apostle. Rather, it is something that repeatedly bubbles through Paul's arguments. It recurs, for example, in chapter 4: 'Therefore, my brothers, you whom I love and long for, my joy and crown, that is how you should stand firm in the Lord, dear friends!' (4:1).

From both Paul's example and from the Philippians' example, then, we must learn this first point: the fellowship of the gospel, the partnership of the gospel, must be put at the centre of our relationships with other believers. That is the burden of these opening verses. Paul does not commend them for the fine times they had shared watching games in the arena. He doesn't mention their literature discussion groups, or the excellent meals they had had, although undoubtedly they had enjoyed some fine times together. What lies at the centre of all his ties with them, doubtless including meals and discussion, is this passion for the gospel, this partnership in the gospel.

What ties us together? What do we talk about when we meet, even after a church service? Mere civilities? The weather? The FA Cup draw? Our careers and our children? Our aches and pains?

None of these topics should be excluded from the conversation of Christians, of course. In sharing all of life, these things will inevitably come up. But what must tie us together as Christians is this passion for the gospel, this fellowship in the gospel. On the face of it, nothing else is strong enough to hold together the extraordinary diversity of people who constitute many churches: men and women, young and old, blue collars and white collars, the healthy and the ill, the fit and the flabby, people from different races, with different incomes, different levels of education, different personalities. What holds us together? It is the gospel, the good news that in Jesus God himself has reconciled us to himself. This brings about a precious God-centredness that we share with other believers.

This means that in our conversations we ought regularly to be sharing in the gospel: delighting in God, sharing with one another what we have been learning from his Word, joining in prayer for the advance of the gospel (not least in the lives of those to whom we have been bearing witness), encouraging one another in obedience and maturing discipleship, bearing one another's burdens and growing in self-sacrificial love for one another for Christ's sake.

In short, we must put the gospel first. And that means we must put the fellowship of the gospel at the centre of our relationships with fellow believers.

Put the priorities of the gospel at the centre of your prayer life (1:9–11)

Already in verse 4 Paul has insisted that whenever he prays for the Philippians he does so with joy and thanksgiving. Now he gives us the content of his prayers for them: 'And this is my prayer: that your love may abound more and more in knowledge and depth of insight, so that you may be able to discern what is best and may be pure and blameless until the day of Christ, filled with the fruit of righteousness that comes through Jesus Christ – to the glory and praise of God.'

This is stunning. Paul's petitions reflect the priorities of the gospel. Observe three features of this prayer.

First, Paul prays that the love of the Philippians 'may abound more and more'. Paul provides no specific object. He does not say, '. . . that your love *for God* may abound more and more', or '. . . that your love *for one another* may abound more and more'. I suspect he leaves the object open precisely because he would not want to restrict his prayer to one or the other. From a Christian point of view, growing love for God must be reflected in love for other believers (see 1 Jn. 5:1). However wonderful this congregation has been, however faithful in its love even for the apostle himself, Paul prays that their love may abound more and more.

Secondly, what Paul has in mind is not mere sentimentalism or the rush of pleasure spawned, for example, by a large conference. 'I pray', Paul writes, 'that your love may abound more and more *in knowledge and depth of insight*.' The kind of love that Paul has in mind is the love that becomes more knowledgeable. Of course, Paul is not thinking of any kind of knowledge. He is not hoping they will learn more and more about nuclear physics or sea turtles. What he has in mind is knowledge *of God*; what he wants them to enjoy is insight into his words and ways, and thus how to live in their light.

His assumption, evidently, is that you really cannot grow in your knowledge of God if you are full of bitterness or other self-centred sins. There is a moral element in knowing God. Of course, a person might memorize Scripture or teach Sunday School somewhere or earn a degree in theology from the local seminary or divinity faculty, but that is not necessarily the same thing as growing in the knowledge of God and gaining insight into his ways. Such growth requires repentance; it demands a lessening of our characteristic self-focus. To put it positively, it demands an increase in our love, our love for God and our love for others.

Just as knowledge of God and his Word serves as an incentive to Christian love, so love is necessary for a deepening knowledge of God. The reason is that it is exceedingly difficult to advance in the Christian way on only one front. Christians cannot say, 'I will improve my prayer life but not my morality', 'I will increase in my knowledge of God but not in my obedience', 'I will grow in love for others but not in purity or in my knowledge of God'. They cannot do it. The Christian life embraces every facet of our existence. All of our living and doing and thinking and speaking is to be discharged in joyful submission to God and to his Son, our Saviour.

So if Paul prays that the Philippians' love 'may abound more and more', he quickly adds, 'in knowledge and depth of insight'.

Thirdly, for Paul this prayer has a further end in view. He lifts these petitions to God (he tells the Philippians) 'so that you may be able to discern what is best and may be pure and blameless until the day of Christ'. Clearly, Paul does not want the Philippian believers to be satisfied with mediocrity. He cannot be satisfied, in a fallen world, with the *status quo*. He wants these believers to move on, to become more and more discerning, proving in their own experience 'what is best'. He wants them to pursue what is best in the knowledge of God, what is best in their relationships with other believers, what is best in joyful obedience – for ultimately what he wants from them is perfection: he prays that they 'may be pure and blameless until the day of Christ'.

For Paul, this is not an idolatrous prayer. For some people, of course, it could become just that. For perfectionists, perfection, at least in some arenas where they excel, becomes a kind of fetish, even a large idol. But this is not the case with Paul. The excellence for which he prays, for himself and for others, is further defined in verse 11: 'being filled with the fruit of righteousness that comes through Jesus Christ'. Moreover, none of this will be allowed simply to enhance our reputations – for sad to say, some people are more interested in a reputation for holiness and excellence than in holiness and excellence. But all such petty alternatives are swept aside in Paul's final constraint: his prayer is offered up 'to the glory and praise of God' (1:11).

That is what Paul prays for. It takes only a moment's reflection to see that all of these petitions are gospel-centred. These are gospel prayers, *i.e.* they are prayers offered to advance the work of the gospel in the lives of the Philippian believers. And, by asking for gospel fruit in their lives, the *ultimate* purpose of these petitions is to bring glory to the God who redeemed them.

How much do such petitions feature in our praying?

When was the last time you prayed that the brothers and sisters in Christ in your congregation would abound in love more and more in knowledge and depth of insight so that they might discern the best things and prove them in their own experience, being filled with the fruit of righteousness, to the glory and praise of God?

What *do* you pray for? Thank God that some do pray along these lines. But many of us devote most of our praying, in private and in public, to personal matters largely removed from gospel interests: our mortgages, physical safety, good health, employment for ourselves or someone else. Doubtless these and countless other concerns are legitimate subjects for prayer: after all, we serve a God who invites us to cast *all* our cares on him because he cares for us (1 Pet. 5:7). But where is our gospel focus? Read through the letters of Paul and copy out his prayers. Ask yourself what it is he asks for. Observe how consistently most of his petitions are gospel-related. Are we being faithful to Scripture if most of our petitions are not?

Put the gospel first. And that means you must put the priorities of the gospel at the centre of your prayer life.

Put the advance of the gospel at the centre of your aspirations (1:12–18a)

The flow of Paul's argument is remarkable.

Apparently some of his critics thought Paul had let the side down rather badly by getting himself arrested. If as is likely he is writing from prison in Rome, he is awaiting trial before the Emperor – and Paul is in this situation because Paul himself has appealed to the Emperor (Acts 26). One can easily imagine the reasoning of Paul's critics. Depending on how this case turns out, Paul's appeal to the Emperor could bring Christianity into bad odour. Paul is constantly rushing headlong into things where a wiser, cooler head would have been cautious. Why did he have to go up to Jerusalem and get himself arrested anyway? He knew how much he was held in contempt there. Surely there had to be a better way.

But Paul has few regrets: 'Now I want you to know, brothers, that what has happened to me has really served to advance the gospel' (1:12). That is what he cares about: not his own comfort, but the advance of the gospel. He offers two reasons in defence of his judgment.

First, his arrest and imprisonment in Rome have meant that the full praetorian guard has heard that he has been arrested for Christ's sake: '. . . it has become clear throughout the whole palace guard and to everyone else that I am in chains for Christ' (1:13). Because the full praetorian guard, when it was up to full strength, numbered close to nine thousand troops, many commentators wryly protest that nine thousand soldiers could not have been cycled in to guard Paul so that all of them could have heard his witness. Surely this must be hyperbolic, or a reference to some small detachment of the guard. But Paul's reference to 'the whole palace guard' probably has a simpler explanation. Paul proved to be such an extraordinary prisoner, and his witness so telling, that stories about him circulated very quickly. It was not that each of the praetorian soldiers took a turn guarding Paul and therefore heard his story from his own lips. Rather, every soldier who was assigned this duty doubtless heard the gospel and perhaps something of his testimony. Paul was neither a hardened criminal nor a suave 'white collar' swindler. Instead of protesting his innocence or gauging his chances of impressing Caesar's court, he spent his time talking about a Jew called Jesus, crucified at the eastern end of the Mediterranean and (if Paul was to be believed) somehow risen from the dead. And according to this prisoner, not only will this Jesus be our Judge on the last day, but the only hope anyone has of being accepted by God is by trusting this Jesus. In short, Paul was proving to be such an extraordinary prisoner that stories began to circulate about him around the palace – and not only stories about him, but the gospel story as well. And that, Paul insists, is wonderful. There has been an advance in the circulation of the gospel because I am in chains.

There is a second reason Paul insists that his incarceration has advanced the gospel: 'Because of my chains, most of the brothers in the Lord have been encouraged to speak the word of God more courageously and fearlessly' (1:14). A whiff of persecution sometimes puts backbone into otherwise timid Christians. Older readers of these pages will remember the five Wheaton College graduates in the 1950s who lost their lives in an attempt to bring the gospel to the Auca Indians. Among the excellent unforeseen results was the very high number of Wheaton graduates who year after year for the next decade or two offered themselves for missionary service. Because of the death of the 'Auca five', many were 'encouraged to speak the word of God more courageously and fearlessly'.

Nevertheless, Paul is a realist. He squarely faces the fact that not every consequence of his imprisonment was rosy in every respect. 'It is true', he writes, 'that some preach Christ out of envy and rivalry, but others out of good will. The latter do so in love, knowing that I am put here for the defence of the gospel. The former preach Christ out of selfish ambition, not sincerely, supposing that they can stir up trouble for me while I am in chains. But what does it matter? The important thing is that in every way, whether from false motives or true, Christ is preached. And because of this I rejoice' (1:15–18a).

Who are these curious preachers who 'preach Christ' but who do so out of the most astonishing motives? It is important to recognize that they are not heretics – that is, they are not preaching 'another Christ' or 'another gospel' that is really no gospel at all. As for those who proclaim some 'gospel' other than the apostolic gospel, let them be 'anathema': we would say, 'May they be damned' (see Gal. 1:8–9). The issues are too serious to play around with that kind of pluralism. Those who preach 'another Jesus' are 'false apostles' and must not be given the ear of the church (2 Cor. 11:4, 13–15). So Paul is not open to commending every preacher who offers some show of piety and who preaches 'Jesus': he wants to know *which* Jesus. We must constantly ask if the Jesus being pushed is the Mormon Jesus, or the Jehovah's Witnesses' Jesus, or the naturalistic, liberal Jesus, or the health, wealth and prosperity Jesus. Or is it the biblical Jesus?

So the fact that Paul can offer these preachers a sort of back-handed compliment shows that they are not heretics, dangerous false teachers. If they had been, Paul would have exposed them. The preachers to whom Paul makes reference here are a different sort: they propound the true gospel, but sometimes do so for the strangest mix of motives. In this case, the people Paul has in mind are those who must be understood to lie behind verse 12. They think that Paul has done damage to the cause by getting himself arrested. Probably they magnify their own ministry by putting Paul down. We can imagine their pompous reflections: 'It really is sad that so great a man as Paul has frittered away his gospel opportunities simply because he is so inflexible. After all, I and many others manage to remain at large and preach the gospel: one must assume that Paul has a deep character flaw that puts him in the path of trouble. *My* ministry is being blessed, while *he* languishes in prison.' Thus the more they speak, the more their own ways are justified, and the more Paul is made to look like a twit.

How does Paul handle this? Is he wounded?

Doubtless he has feelings like everyone else. But he is a man of deep principle, and he perceives that whether by preachers like this, or by preachers who align themselves with the apostle, the gospel is getting out – and that is more important than whether or not he himself achieves universal respect in the church. Not only can he say, 'But what does it matter? The important thing is that in every way, whether from false motives or true, Christ is preached' (1:18), but he can add, 'And because of this I rejoice' (1:18).

Paul's example is impressive, and clear: put the advance of the gospel at the centre of your aspirations. Our own comfort, our bruised feelings, our reputations, the misunderstanding of our motives – all of these are insignificant in comparison with the advance and splendour of the gospel. As Christians we are called upon to put the advance of the gospel at the very centre of our aspirations.

What are your aspirations? To make money? To get married? To travel? To see your grandchildren grow up? To find a new job? To retire early?

None of these is inadmissible; none is to be despised. The question is whether these aspirations become so devouring that the Christian's *central* aspiration is squeezed to the periphery, or choked out of existence entirely.

I recall a Christian some years ago who always gave the same response when he was asked the numbing vocational question, 'What do you do?'

Invariably he replied, 'I'm a Christian.'

'Yes, but I didn't ask about your religion; I asked what you *do*.'

'I'm a Christian.'

'Do you mean that you are in vocational ministry?'

'No. I'm not in vocational ministry. But I'm a Christian, full time.'

'But what do you do *vocationally*?'

'Oh. Vocationally. Well, I'm a Christian full time, but I pack pork to pay expenses.'

At one level, of course, his standard response was slightly perverse. Moreover, in God's universe all morally good and useful work is honourable and not to be dismissed as of marginal importance. Whether it's packing pork or writing computer programs or baking a pie or changing a baby's nappy, we are to offer our work up to God. We are his, and all we say and do, including our work, must be offered up for his glory and his people's good. But having insisted on that point, there are some elements of what we do that are more directly tied to the gospel than are others. Some things we do, and only some things, have direct eternal significance.[1] As the apostle preserves gospel priorities in his prayers, so he preserves them in his aspirations. We must do the same.

In quite a lot of Western evangelicalism, there is a worrying tendency to focus on the periphery. I have a colleague in the Missions Department at Trinity Evangelical Divinity School whose analysis of his own heritage is very helpful. Dr Paul Hiebert laboured for years in India before returning to the United States to teach. He springs from Mennonite stock, and analyses his heritage in a fashion that he himself would acknowledge is something of a simplistic caricature, but a useful one nonetheless. One generation of Mennonites believed the gospel, and held as well that there were certain social, economic, and political entailments. The next generation assumed the gospel, but identified with the entailments. The following generation denied the gospel: the entailments were everything.

Assuming this sort of scheme for evangelicalism, one suspects that large swathes of the movement are lodged in the second step, with some drifting toward the third.

What we must ask one another is this: what is it in the Christian faith that makes you excited? What consumes your time? What turns you on? Today there are endless subgroups of confessing Christians who invest enormous quantities of time and energy in one issue or another: abortion, home schooling, the defence of a particular Bible version, pornography issues, women's ordination (for or against), economic injustice, a certain style of worship, and much more. The list varies from country to country, but not a few countries have a full agenda of urgent, peripheral demands. Not for a moment am I suggesting we should not think about such matters and throw our weight behind some of them. But when such matters devour most of our time and passion, each of us must ask, in what fashion am I confessing the centrality of the gospel?

This is not a subtle plea for a denuded gospel, a merely privatized gospel, a gospel without social ramifications. We wisely re-read the accounts of the Evangelical Awakening and the extraordinary ministries of Howell Harris, George Whitefield, the Wesley brothers, and others. We rightly remind ourselves how under God their converts led the fights to abolish slavery, reform the penal code, begin trade unions, transform prisons, free the children from servitude in the mines. All of society was transformed because soundly converted men and women saw that life must be lived under God and in a manner pleasing to him. But virtually without exception these men and women put the gospel first. They were gospel people; they revelled in it, preached it, cherished Bible reading and exposition that were Christ-centred and gospel-centred – and from that base moved out into the broader social agendas. In short, they put the gospel first, not least in their own aspirations. Not to see this priority means we are not more than a generation away from denying the gospel.

It may be that God has called you to be a homemaker or an engineer or a chemist or a ditch digger; it may be that you will take some significant role in, say, the rising field of bioethics. But although the gospel directly affects how you will discharge your duties in each case, none of these is to displace the gospel that is central to every thoughtful Christian. You will put the gospel first in your aspirations. Then you will be able to endure affliction and persecution and even misunderstanding and misrepresentation from other Christians. You will say with Paul, 'I want you to know . . . that what has happened to me has really served to advance the gospel' (1:12).

So here is Paul's third point: put the advance of the gospel at the centre of your aspirations.

Put the converts of the gospel at the centre of your principled self-denial (1:18b-26)

Once again it is the flow of Paul's thought that is so striking. Paul has just declared that he will rejoice if Christ is preached (1:18a). But that is not the only source of Paul's rejoicing, wonderful as it is. 'Yes, I will continue to rejoice', Paul hastens on, 'for I know that through your prayers and the help given by the Spirit of Jesus Christ, what has happened to me will turn out for my deliverance' (1:18b–19). In this context 'deliverance' does not mean release from imprisonment, but something more important: his ultimate vindication, whether in life or in death. This will come about through their prayers: that is, owing not least to their prayers and the consequent 'help given by the Spirit of Jesus Christ', Paul will be so faithful that he will be entirely vindicated before God in the end. That Paul wants above all else to be found faithful is made clear by verse 20: 'I eagerly expect and hope that I will in no way be ashamed, but will have sufficient courage so that now as always Christ will be exalted in my body, whether by life or by death.'

Thus Paul's driving concern is not that he should be released from jail, or that if he must die he should have a relatively painless departure, but that he should do nothing of which he would some day be ashamed. He wants courage, so that Christ may be exalted in his body, 'whether by life or by death' (1:20). He wants to hear Christ's blessed 'Well done!' on the last day. And he openly solicits the prayers of God's people in Philippi that he might be strengthened toward that end.

Almost as if he feels he must articulate and defend this vision of what is important, Paul summarizes his values: 'For to me, to live is Christ and to die is gain' (1:21). In the context, 'to live is Christ' surely means that for Paul to keep on living here means ministry, Christ-centred ministry, Christ-empowered ministry, Christ's presence in his ministry. To die is to bring that ministry to an end, but even so there is only gain: the ministry is not an end in itself, and it is now swallowed up in the glorious delight of the unshielded presence of the exalted Jesus himself.

What can you possibly do with Christians like that? Kill them? You simply cannot hush them up; Christ means too much to them, the gospel is too central for them. As for Paul, it is not in his power to choose between service here and departing to be with Christ, between living and dying, between being released from prison for more gospel ministry and paying the ultimate price, thus being released into the presence of the exalted Christ. Yet suppose he *could* choose: what would he do? 'I do not know!' (1:22b), he frankly admits – that is, he has no word from the Lord as to what is going to happen and therefore what he ought to choose under such hypothetical circumstances. 'I am torn between the two: I desire to depart and be with Christ, which is better by far; but it is more necessary for you that I remain in the body' (1:23–24) – that is, that he be acquitted before the imperial court and released from prison, and therefore free to continue his apostolic ministry to the benefit of the Philippians and others.

What is striking about Paul's evaluation is how deeply it is tied to the well-being of other believers, rather than his own. Even in this respect, Paul is imitating his Master. 'Convinced of this', *i.e.* 'convinced that my remaining alive will be best for you', 'I know that I will remain, and I will continue with all of you for your progress and joy in the faith' – or, better translated, 'I know that I expect to remain and expect to continue with all of you for your progress and joy in the faith.'[2] And even this progress in faith that Paul covets for the Philippians, he construes as a cause for their joy: '. . . so that through my being with you again your joy in Christ Jesus will overflow on account of me' (1:26).

The lesson to be learned is startlingly clear: put the converts of the gospel at the centre of your principled self-denial. Paul's deepest hopes for his own immediate future turn neither on the bliss of immediately gaining heaven's portals, nor on returning to a fulfilling ministry and escaping the pangs of death, but on what is best for his converts. So often we are tempted to evaluate alternatives by thinking through what seems best *for us*. How often do we raise as a first principle what is best *for the church*? When faced with, say, a job offer that would take us to another city, or with mortal illness that calls forth our diligent intercession, how quickly do we deploy Paul's criterion here established: *what would be the best for the church? What would be the best for my brothers and sisters in Christ?*

There is a kind of asceticism that is frankly idolatrous. Some people gain a kind of spiritual 'high' out of self-denial. But the self-denial that is motivated by the spiritual good of others is unqualifiedly godly. That is what Paul displays.

Here, then, is the burden of this passage: put the gospel first. In particular:

(1) put the fellowship of the gospel at the centre of your relationships with believers;

(2) put the priorities of the gospel at the centre of your prayer life;

(3) put the advance of the gospel at the centre of your aspirations;

(4) put the converts of the gospel at the centre of your principled self-denial.

Put the gospel first.

Brothers and sisters in Christ, such a valuation of the gospel ought not to be the exception among us, but the rule. We are talking about the good news that reconciles lost men and women to the eternal God. We are confessing the gospel: that God himself has provided a redeemer who died, the just for the unjust, to bring us to himself. Without this gospel we are cut off, without hope in this world or the next, utterly undone. Compared with this good news, what could possibly compete? Put the gospel first.

One remembers what an ageing Christian said to John G. Paton in the last century when Paton was planning to go as a missionary to the South Sea Islands. 'You'll be eaten by cannibals,' Paton was warned.

Paton replied, 'Mr. Dickson, you are advanced in years now and your own prospect is soon to be laid in the grave, there to be eaten by worms; I confess to you, that if I can but live and die serving and honouring the Lord Jesus, it will make no difference to me whether I am eaten by Cannibals or by worms; and in the Great Day my resurrection body will arise as fair as yours in the likeness of our risen Redeemer.'[3]

Put the gospel first. 'Only one life, 'twill soon be passed; Only what's done for Christ will last.'

Put the gospel first.

2

Adopt Jesus' death as a test of your outlook

Philippians 1:27 – 2:18

What does the cross achieve? Why does it occupy so central a place in the minds of the New Testament writers?

The Bible gives many wonderfully rich answers to such questions. I would like to begin this chapter by sketching a few of them. It will prove helpful to think about the cross from various perspectives, before we examine exactly what the passage before us has to contribute to a comprehensive theology of the cross.

God's perspective

What does the cross look like to God?

If we ask that question of contemporary writers, immediately we are embroiled in various disputes, even a dispute about the translation of a word. Perhaps it will clarify the issues a little if we lightly trace out one such argument.

According to 1 John 2:2, believers have an Advocate with the Father, Jesus Christ, the Righteous One. And he (according to the Authorized Version) is the 'propitiation' for our sins. What does that mean? The NIV declares that Jesus is the 'atoning sacrifice' for our sins. What does this change in wording signify? The issue is crucially important if we are to grasp how God views the cross.

'Propitiation' is that act by which God becomes 'propitious', that is, favourable. For centuries the church happily used the term. The cross is the place, the event, the sacrifice, by which God becomes favourable or propitious to us poor sinners. The cross, in other words, was the place of propitiation; it was the means by which God was propitiated, his anger assuaged and appeased. But about sixty years ago it became out of vogue to speak of propitiation. The argument went something like this. 'Propitiation' sounds too much like pagan sacrifice. In animistic cultures, the aim of many of the sacrifices offered to various spirits and deities is to win their approval – in short, to propitiate them. You don't want the storm gods to be angry. You certainly want the appropriate deity to ensure that the crops will be good, or that your wife has a fat baby, or that your husband comes home safely from his hunting expedition in the jungle. So you offer the spirits the prescribed sacrifices and thereby try to win their favour. You are performing an act of propitiation. In this model, human beings are the subjects, and they propitiate the gods, who are the objects of this action.

But if that model prevails, it was argued, how can one reasonably think of the cross as an act of propitiation? In the cross, human beings do not offer up a sacrifice to appease God. Far from it: God himself is the subject, the one who loves the world so much as to send his Son (Jn. 3:16). He initiates the action; he sends his own Son to be the sacrifice. So how can the sacrifice propitiate him, when he initiated the act of sacrifice? So we must not think of the cross as an act of *propitiation*, but as an act of *expiation* – that is, the cross has nothing to do with making God favourable (since God is already so favourable to this broken world that he has sent his beloved Son), and has everything to do with cancelling sin.

No sooner was this argument put forth than objections appeared. How can we dispense with the notion of propitiation, in the light of the many biblical passages that speak of the wrath of God? If God is wrathful on account of our sin, if he is truly angry, then that which removes his anger is that which propitiates him. In other words, we cannot get away from the notion of propitiation as long as the Bible talks about the wrath of God. It is a fearful thing to fall under that wrath. What sets aside that wrath is the cross: Jesus takes our punishment, and we go free. Propitiation must not be set aside.

The new voices replied to the effect that the only way we can reconcile passages that speak of the wrath of God with passages that tell us that God loved the world so much that he sent his Son is by recognizing that the 'wrath' of God must be understood in impersonal terms. In this view, the 'wrath of God' is merely a metaphorical way of talking about the terrible yet inevitable results of sin. If you do bad things, bad things ensue. That is the way God has constructed the universe: in that sense, the bad things that follow your evil can be traced, however indirectly, to God. But God himself, they argued, cannot be thought of as personally angry: how could that be, when this God, in love, sent his Son while we were yet sinners?

But the traditional voices would not be silenced. The new view that wants to ban propitiation simply does not take sin and wrath seriously enough. It is not true that doing bad things always works out in impersonal judgment: sometimes wicked people get away with horrible sins, and even prosper because of them. Unless one holds that God personally responds in judgment to balance the books, it is terribly naïve to think that impersonal judgment prevails

27

with justice. Besides, in the few places in the Bible where the word traditionally rendered 'propitiation' is found, the surrounding context is, repeatedly, the wrath of God. Granted this link, how can one responsibly say that God's wrath is nothing more than the inevitable *and impersonal* outworking of evil? As soon argue that the love of God is also impersonal, and nothing more than the inevitable outworking of good! The entire conception of God is drifting from biblical theism to thoroughly unbiblical deism.

And so the debate goes on. A lot of ink has been spilled on this question. But some of that debate is misguided, because it attempts to drive wedges between truths that the Bible joins together. In particular, the Bible insists that God is simultaneously angry and loving. What the Bible says about propitiation cannot be grasped unless this point is understood.

In the Bible, God's wrath is a function of his holiness. His wrath or anger is not the explosion of a bad temper, of a chronic inability to restrain his irritability, but of just and principled opposition to sin. God's holiness is so spectacularly glorious that it *demands* that he be wrathful with those of his creatures who defy him, slight his majesty, thumb their noses at his words and works, and insist on their own independence when every breath they breathe, not to say their very existence, depends on his providential care. If God were to gaze at sin and rebellion, shrug his shoulders, and mutter, 'Well, I'm not too bothered. I can forgive these people. I don't really care what they do', surely there would be something morally deficient about him. Should God care nothing for Hitler's outrages? Should God care nothing about my rebellion and your rebellion? If he acted this way, he would ultimately discount his own significance, sully his own glory, besmirch his own honour, and soil his own integrity.

That is why, in Scripture, God is sometimes portrayed as blister-ingly angry. Moreover, it is important that we reject the common evangelical cliché on this subject: 'God hates the sin but loves the sinner.' The second part may be true, but, as cast, this antithesis is fundamentally mistaken, and is clearly refuted by Scripture. For example, fourteen times in the first fifty psalms alone the texts insist that God 'hates' sinners, 'abhors' those who tell lies, and so forth.

But the glorious truth about God is that although he is angry with us, in his very character he is a God of love. Despite his anger as he perceives our anarchy, anger that is a necessary function of his holiness, God is a loving God, and so he provides a means of forgiving sins *that will leave the integrity of his glory unsullied*. He comes to us in the person of his Son. His Son dies as the propitiation of our sins: that is, he dies to ensure that God becomes favourable toward us in precisely those areas where God has been standing over against us in judgment and wrath. But because God himself is the One who has provided the sacrifice, this is quite unlike pagan propitiation. In pagan propitiation, as we have seen, *we* offer the sacrifices and the gods are propitiated. By contrast, in the Bible God is both the origin and the object of the propitiating sacrifice. He provides it by sending his Son to the cross; at the same time, the sacrifice satisfies God's own honour, and his righteous wrath is turned away without his holiness being impugned.

Much of this is summarized in another letter written by Paul: 'God presented Jesus as a propitiation [NIV 'sacrifice of atonement'] in his blood. He did this to demonstrate his justice, because in his forbearance he had left the sins committed beforehand unpunished – he did it to demonstrate his justice at the present time, so as to be just and the one who justifies those who have faith in Jesus' (Rom. 3:25–26). Observe how Paul repeatedly insists that God sent his Son to the cross 'to demonstrate his justice' – not simply to save us, but *to demonstrate his justice*, as well as to be the One who justifies those who have faith in his Son. It is the cross that unites God's love and his perfect holiness.

Sometimes poetry says this better than prose:

Love in the Deity stretches conceptions of men;
Love seems not love which permits our full measure of
  hate.
Promise of judgment in ages beyond seems too late.
Where is God's love when the wretched are wretched
  again?
Holiness absolute stands far removed from our ken,
Either its brightness so alien it seems to frustrate,
Blindingly brilliant, or else its rich glories abate,
Fading in mist as the distance seems too much to mend.
  One place remains where this love and this holiness meet,
  Mingling in poetic measures with no verbal dross.
  Symbol of holiness pure, justice without defeat,
  Coupled with unbounded love, stands the stark, ugly
    cross.

Lord God of hosts, in the worship surrounding your throne
Questions once clamouring give place to hushed homage
  alone.

That is one of the ways, at least, that God looks at the cross.

29

Christ's perspective

Here, too, many things could be said. But one of the great and neglected themes about what the cross means to the Son is the obedience of the Son. This theme surfaces with special strength in the epistle to the Hebrews and in the gospel of John. There we repeatedly learn that the Father sends and the Son goes; the Father commissions and the Son obeys. The Son always does what pleases the Father (Jn. 8:29). The most staggering commission the Father gives to the Son is to go to the cross to redeem a race of rebels. And the Son knows that that is the commission given him: Jesus came, he insists, not to be served, but to serve, and to give his life as a ransom for many (Mk. 10:45). But knowledge of the commission he had received did not make obedience easy: Gethsemane and the cross were faced with an agony of intercession, characterized by the repeated petition, 'Yet not what I will but what you will' (Mk. 14:36).

Thus the cross for Jesus was not only the means by which he sacrificed himself, the just for the unjust, to bring us to God, but also the high point of his unqualified obedience to his heavenly Father. That point is alluded to in the passage before us: . 'And being found in appearance as a man, he humbled himself and became *obedient* to death – even death on a cross!' (2:8).

The devil's perspective

One of the most important chapters in the New Testament for understanding the devil's perspective on the cross is Revelation 12. There Satan is portrayed as full of rage because he has been banished from heaven and knows that his time is short. He has not been able to crush Jesus, so he vents his rage on the church. He is the 'accuser of the brothers' who simultaneously wants to vex their consciences and accuse God of ungodliness because he, God, accepts such miserable sinners as these. But believers, we are told, defeat Satan on the ground of 'the blood of the Lamb' – an unambiguous reference to the cross. What does this mean?

What is meant, of course, is that these believers escape the accusations of Satan himself, whether in their own minds and consciences or before the bar of God's justice, because they make instant appeal to the cross. They sing with full attention and deep gratitude the wonderful words,

> Nothing in my hands I bring,
> Simply to thy cross I cling.

Before that appeal, Satan has no retort. God *has* retained his honour while redeeming a rebel brood. We *can* be free from guilt – both objective guilt before a holy God and subjective awareness of guilt – not because we ourselves are guiltless but because Jesus 'himself bore our sin in his body on the tree, so that we might die to sins and live for righteousness; by his wounds you have been healed' (1 Pet. 2:24).

Imagine the first Passover, just before the exodus. Mr Smith and Mr Jones, two Hebrews with remarkable names, are discussing the extraordinary events of the previous weeks and months. Mr Smith asks Mr Jones, 'Have you sprinkled the blood of a lamb on the two doorposts and on the lintel over the entrance to your dwelling?'

'Of course', replies Mr Jones. 'I've followed Moses' instructions exactly.'

'So have I', affirms Mr Smith. 'But I have to admit I'm very nervous. My boy Charlie means the world to me. If the angel of death passes through the land tonight, as Moses says, taking out all the firstborn in the land, I just don't know what I'll do if Charlie dies.'

'But that's the point. He won't die. That's why you sprinkled the lamb's blood on the doorposts and on the lintel. Moses said that when the angel of death sees the blood, he will "pass over" the house so protected, and the firstborn will be safe. Why are you worried?'

'I know, I know', splutters Mr Smith, somewhat irritably. 'But you have to admit that there have been some very strange goings-on these last few months. Some of the plagues have afflicted only the Egyptians, of course, but some of them have hit us, too. The thought that my Charlie could be in danger is terribly upsetting.'

Rather unsympathetically, Mr Jones replies, 'I really can't imagine why you're fretting. After all, I have a son, too, and I think I love him just as much as you love your Charlie. But I am completely at peace: God promised that the angel of death would pass over every house whose door is marked by blood in the way he prescribes, and I take him at his word.'

That night the angel of death passed through the land. Who lost his son, Mr Smith or Mr Jones?

The answer, of course, is – neither. For God's promise that the angel of death would simply 'pass over' and not destroy was not made conditional on the intensity of the faith of the residents, but only on whether or not they had sprinkled blood on the doorposts and on the lintel. In both cases the blood was shed, the houses marked; in both cases the firstborn son was saved.

So with us, who have come to trust Christ and his cross-work on our behalf. The promise of deliverance, the assurance that we are accepted by almighty God, is not tied to the intensity of our faith, or to the consistency of our faith, or to the purity of our faith, but to the object of our faith. When we approach God in prayer, our plea is not that we have been good that day, or that we have just come from a Christian meeting full of praise, or that we try harder, but that Christ has died for us. And against that plea, Satan has no riposte.

For the truth of the matter is that the cross marks Satan's defeat. And Satan knows it. That is what the cross means to him.

Sin's perspective

Sin is not a living thing, of course; one cannot suppose that sin literally has a perspective. But the category is useful, even if metaphorical, because it helps us see what the cross achieved with respect to sin.

The answer to that question is highly diverse in the Bible, because sin can be thought of in so many ways. Sin can be thought of as a debt: I owe something I cannot pay. In that case the cross is seen as the means by which the debt is paid. One sometimes reads on Christmas cards the two-line poem,

> He came to pay a debt he did not owe
> Because we owed a debt we could not pay.

That is exactly right. That is what the cross achieved.

Sin can also be thought of as a stain. In that case the dirt is removed by the death of Christ. Or sin is offence before God. In that case we insist that the cross expiates our sin, it cancels it and thus removes it. But regardless of what foul imagery is used to depict odious sin, the cross is the solution, the sole solution.

Our perspective

Here, too, many complementary things could be underlined. The cross is the high-water mark of the demonstration of God's love for his people. It is a symbol of our shame, and of our freedom. It is the ultimate measure of how serious our guilt is, and the comforting assurance that our guilt has been dealt with. In the New Testament, the cross is tied to many of the most important words and concepts: justification, sanctification, the gift of the Spirit, the dawning of the kingdom.

But in the New Testament the cross also serves as the supreme standard of our behaviour. That theme is perhaps most dramatically drawn, in the New Testament, by the apostle Peter in his first letter. But it is also the primary point that Paul makes here: 'Your attitude should be the same as that of Christ Jesus', Paul writes (2:5) – and then he presses on to the cross.[4]

Although the passage before us runs from 1:27 to 2:18, there is little doubt that the core section is 2:6–11. We shall see not only that it is important for what it says about Jesus and his cross, but that its thought controls the surrounding paragraphs.

There is at least some evidence, albeit disputed, that this passage preserves some early Christian hymn. That is why the NIV sets out the text in poetic lines. Some have criticized these lines because in Greek they do not seem to scan as poetry very well. One remembers the limerick:

> There once was a poet from Japan
> Whose poems could not possibly scan.
>> When told this was so,
>> He replied, 'Yes, I know;
> That is because I always try to squeeze as many words into
> the last line as I possibly can.'

It would be unfair to accuse Paul of this particular deviation. Nevertheless one must remember that Greek poetry, like its contemporary English counterpart, can break forms for the sake of effect.

It is possible that this hymn (if hymn it be) is older than the letter to the Philippians, and that just as Paul quotes the Old Testament (and on occasion can even quote pagan lines), so there is no reason why he should not here draw on some hymn of the church. If that is what Paul has done, he may also have adapted it.

Alternatively, he may have written the entire passage himself (just as I have sometimes written poetry to illustrate or adorn some prose piece I have written). Either way, by deploying these lines here, they have been preserved in an apostolic writing judged canonical, and thus have come down to us for our edification.

This great passage can most usefully be broken down into two parts.

Verses 6–8

Verse 5 tells us that our attitude should be the same as that of Christ Jesus, whose attitude in his own indescribably remarkable self-denial is the theme of the first part of this passage. 'Being in very nature God, [he] did not consider equality with God something to be grasped': there are two important elements to understanding these opening words. First, the words 'being in very nature God', more literally 'being in the *form* of God', do not precisely address the distinction between essence and function much loved in the western world. The passage is not quite saying that he was in very essence God, still less that he merely functioned as if he were God (which would surely be a shocking thing to say anyway, granted who the God of the Bible is). The word used is a subtle shading of both ideas. In the next verse it appears again: Jesus empties himself and takes 'the very nature of a servant', more literally 'the *form* of a servant' (2:8). Clearly in this latter context it is not merely ontology, mere essence, mere being, that is being claimed: Jesus lives and acts and functions as a servant.

The idea, then, is that Christ Jesus began, shall we say, in the mode of existence of God himself, but took on the mode of existence of a servant. This 'mode of existence' of God embraces both essence and function: he enjoyed real equality with God, and he becomes a real servant. That is why the second line of verse 6 insists that Jesus 'did not consider equality with God something to be grasped', or, perhaps, better, something to be exploited, something to be deployed for his own advantage. Rather, he 'made himself nothing' and took 'the mode of existence of a servant.'

Secondly, the opening expression, both in Greek and in English, is slightly ambiguous: '*being* in very nature God' could be understood in one of two ways. It could be understood concessively: '*although* he was in very nature God', he took on the form of a servant. Or it could be understood causally: '*because* he was in very nature God', he took on the form of a servant. On the whole, the latter better suits the context. The eternal Son did not think of his status as God as something which gave him the opportunity to get and get and get. Instead, his very status as God meant he had nothing to prove, nothing to achieve. And precisely because he is one with God, one with this kind of God, he 'made himself nothing', and gave and gave and gave.

He 'made himself nothing': What does that mean? Literally translated, the original reads, 'He emptied himself.' But the expression does not mean he emptied himself *of something*. For example, it is not as if he emptied himself of his deity, for then he would not longer be God. Nor did he empty himself of the attributes of his deity (though that has been argued), for the result would be the same. An animal that waddles like a porcupine, and has the quills of a porcupine, and in general all the attributes of a porcupine, is a porcupine. If you take away all the attributes of a porcupine, whatever you have left is not a porcupine. Likewise, if the Son is stripped of the attributes of deity, it is difficult to see how he can in any meaningful sense still claim to be deity.

In fact, the expression 'he emptied himself', far from meaning he emptied himself *of something*, is idiomatic for 'he gave up all his rights' or the like. He emptied *himself*; hence NIV's '[he] made himself nothing' – not literally nothing, of course, for then he would not be here. He abandoned his rights; he became a nobody. In particular, Paul tells us in the next line that Jesus became a servant, a slave. That is of course the defining characteristic of slaves: from many points of view, they are nobodies. They might represent certain wealth to their owners, and they might have certain cherished skills. But they have no rights; they are nobodies. By contrast, the eternal Son has always had all the rights of deity; he was one with God. But precisely because of this, he did not perceive his equality with God something to be exploited, but became a nobody. He 'made himself nothing, taking the very nature of a slave'.

It is important to recognize that Paul does not tell us that Christ exchanged one form for another. Paul is not saying that Jesus was God, gave that up, and became a slave instead. Rather, without ever abandoning who he is, he adopts the mode of existence of a slave. To do this, he (literally) becomes 'in human likeness' (2:7): the idea is not that he merely becomes *like* a human being, a reasonable facsimile but not truly human. Rather, it means that he becomes a being fashioned in this way – a human being. He was always God; he now becomes something he was not, a human being. 'And being found in appearance as a man, he humbled himself and became obedient to death – even death on a cross!' (2:8).

It is very hard for us today to hear the shocking overtones of the words Paul uses, because the cross has become for us such a domesticated symbol. Today many women and some men dangle crosses from their ears. Our bishops hang crosses around their necks. Our buildings have crosses on the spires, or stained wooden crosses are backlit with fluorescent lights. Some of our older church buildings are actually built in cruciform, and no-one is shocked.

Suppose you were to place in a prominent position in your church building a fresco of the massed graves of Auschwitz. Would not everyone be horrified? But in the first century, the cross had something of that symbolic value. Scholars have gone through every instance of the word 'cross' and related expressions that have come down to us from about the time of Jesus, and shown how 'crucifixion' and 'cross' inevitably evoke horror. Of the various forms of Roman execution, crucifixion could be used only for slaves, rebels and anarchists; it could never be used for a Roman citizen, unless with the express sanction of the Emperor. Crucifixion was considered too cruel – so shameful that the word itself was avoided in polite conversation.

But here is Paul, bold as brass, insisting that the Lord Christ whom we serve, precisely because he is that kind of God, makes himself a nobody, becomes in fact a slave (becoming a human being as part of this process), and then humbles himself yet further and obeys his heavenly Father by dying – by dying the odious, revolting death of the cross, reserved for public enemies and the dregs of the criminal justice system. The language is *meant* to shock. Jesus died on a *cross*!

I believe it was W. H. Auden who penned the lines,

> Only the unscarred, overfed,
> Enjoy the verbal event of Calvary.

Verses 9–11

The second part of this 'hymn' (if hymn it be) treats the Son's vindication. 'Therefore', Paul writes – because of his self-emptying, because of his obedience, because of his death on the cross – therefore 'God exalted him to the highest place and gave him the name that is above every name, that at the name of Jesus every knee should bow, in heaven and on earth and under the earth, and every tongue confess that Jesus Christ is Lord, to the glory of God the Father' (2:9–11). Here, in magnificent summary, are the Father's approval and vindication of the Son.

When Paul says that God gave Jesus 'the name that is above every name', he is saying much more than that the Father simply 'renames' him or the like. In the ancient world, names were more than convenient labels. What is meant here is that God assigns Jesus a 'name' that reflects what he has achieved and that acknowledges who he is. Probably the 'name' that Paul has in mind is 'Lord' – and inevitably this title brings with it echoes of many Old Testament passages. In Isaiah, God declares, 'I am the LORD; that is my name!' (Is. 42:8). The Hebrew is 'I am YAHWEH': God is the Eternal One, the God who discloses himself through his covenantal name (*cf.* Ex. 3:14). But when that Hebrew word was rendered in Greek, it was commonly translated simply 'Lord' (*Kyrios*). Jesus has achieved this same 'lordship', this same status with his Father, over the whole broken universe – not because there was no sense in which he had it before, but because there is a sense in which he now achieves it, for the first time, as the God-man, as the crucified and risen Redeemer. That the New Testament should quote Isaiah 42 on this matter is particularly significant, for the context shows that this honour belongs to God alone: 'I am the LORD; that is my name! *I will not give my glory to another or my praise to idols*' (Is. 42:8). To give such a title to Jesus, therefore, is tantamount to confessing Jesus' deity, but now as the triumphant, once-crucified and now reigning, resurrected God-man.

One cannot help but be reminded of Jesus' teaching in the gospel of John: the Father has determined that all should honour the Son even as they honour the Father (Jn. 5:23). Every knee in heaven and on earth and under the earth shall bow *to him*. Here, too, the language is drawn from Isaiah, and once again the context of the passage is presupposed. In Isaiah 45 God declares:

> Turn to me and be saved,
>   all you ends of the earth;
>   for I am God, and there is no other.
> By myself I have sworn,
>   my mouth has uttered in all integrity
>   a word that will not be revoked:
> Before me every knee will bow;
>   by me every tongue will swear.
> They will say of me, 'In the LORD alone
>   are righteousness and strength.'
> All who have raged against him will come to him and be
>   put to shame.
> But in the LORD all the descendants of Israel
>   will be found righteous and will exult. (Is. 45:22–25)

Once again, the implications for who Jesus is, if such words as these are unhesitatingly applied to him, are staggering. To confess that Jesus Christ is Lord, using the language of this passage in Isaiah ('Before me every knee will bow'), is a transparent ascription of deity to Jesus Christ. Yet even so, Jesus is distinguished from God the Father: it is *God* who has exalted Jesus to the highest place. Moreover, the confession that 'Jesus Christ is Lord' is 'to the glory of God the Father' (2:10,11). Some of the rudiments of what would later be called the doctrine of the Trinity are coming together in a passage like this.

Not for a moment can this passage be used to support universalism, the view that every single person in the entire world will finally be saved. In the Isaiah 45 passage, everyone confesses that in the LORD alone are righteousness and strength; everyone bows the knee. Nevertheless, 'All who have raged against him will come to him and be put to shame' (45:24). So here in Philippians 2 every tongue will confess that Jesus Christ is Lord, but it does not follow that every tongue will confess Jesus Christ as Lord out of happy submission. The text promises that Jesus has the last word, that he is utterly vindicated, that in the end no opposition against him will stand. There will not be universal salvation; there will be universal confession as to who he is.

That means that either we repent and confess him by faith as Lord now, or we will confess him in shame and terror on the last day. But confess him we will.

Perhaps you have talked to someone about the Lord Jesus, only to be rebutted in the following terms: 'Look, I'm pleased if you think this Jesus helps you. If he makes you feel better and enables you to cope and find some sort of significance in life, I'm happy for you. But frankly, I don't need your religion. I like you as a friend, but if this friendship is going anywhere, not to put to fine a point on it, you and this Jesus will have to keep off my back.'

What do you say?

One of the things you must say, sooner or later, and only in the kindest possible way, is something like this: 'You *are* a friend, and I wouldn't want to lose your friendship. But I have to insist that the Jesus I talk about is not some sort of personalized therapy. The Jesus I am talking about made you. You owe him. And one day you will have to give an account of your life to him. Every knee will bow to him sooner or later, whether in joy or in shame and fear. Not to see this is already a mark of horrible lostness from which only he can enable you to escape.'

In other words, the claim that is being made is not of a Jesus who is domesticated, easily marginalized, psychologically privatized, remarkably sanitized, merely personal. He is one with God, yet he died on the cross to redeem us to himself. Elsewhere Paul insists that all things were made by him and for him (Col. 1:16). Now he insists that the Father has vindicated him in his humiliation and sacrifice, and every knee will bow before him.

This is a wonderful passage. Unqualified divine majesty unites with the immeasurable divine self-sacrifice. And now, Paul insists, 'Your attitude should be the same as that of Christ Jesus' (2:5).

Indeed, that is what the surrounding paragraphs tease out. We may summarize their arguments in the following three points:

We are called not only to believe on Christ but also to suffer for him (1:27–30)

We must begin by recognizing how important conduct is for the apostle. '*Whatever happens*', Paul writes, 'conduct yourselves in a manner worthy of the gospel of Christ' (1:27). The words 'Whatever happens' are the NIV's attempt to render the thought in the Greek's peculiar expression, 'Only this' or 'This one thing': the idea is that whatever else may be mandated, whatever pressures may be brought to bear, 'whatever happens', certain things are central – and they focus on conduct.

The initial description of the conduct is staggering: 'conduct yourselves *in a manner worthy of the gospel of Christ*'. Clearly the standard is immensely high. But what exactly do these words mean?

Certainly they are not suggesting that we ourselves become worthy of the gospel, as if Christ sets up a standard and then somehow by dint of effort we become worthy of it and gain its benefit. The gospel is the good news that Christ died and rose again for sinners. By the death and resurrection of his Son, by the power of the Spirit whom he has sent, God has transferred us out of the kingdom of darkness and into the kingdom of the Son he loves (Col. 1:13). Already we have received the Spirit as the down-payment of the promised inheritance, and one day we shall enjoy the inestimable glories of the new heaven and the new earth. To conduct ourselves 'in a manner worthy of the gospel of Christ' therefore does not suggest we should try harder in order to secure something, but argues that because something has already been secured for us we should try harder out of gratitude and out of frank recognition that this is what the gospel has saved us for. We are to be diligent to live up to the good news that we have received, the good news that has saved us.

The verb 'conduct yourselves' was sometimes used in the ancient world to refer to conduct becoming faithful citizens. The Greeks were to 'conduct themselves as citizens' in such and such a fashion. There may be some corporate overtones in these words when they are applied to the conduct of believers in the church, in this citizenship of the kingdom.

But we must primarily ask, 'What conduct does Paul have in mind that is worthy of the gospel?' The next lines flesh out what is expected. The kind of conduct that Paul wants is the consistent kind that acts the same way whether an apostle is looking over your shoulder or not: 'whether I come to see you or only hear about you in my absence', Paul writes (1:27). The conduct that he wants to discover consistently displayed in them is that they 'stand firm in one spirit, contending as one man for the faith of the gospel without being frightened in any way' by those who oppose them (1:27–28). This unity, this standing firm in one spirit, this 'contending as one man for the faith of the gospel', serves as a double sign: 'This is a sign to them that they will be destroyed, but that you will be saved – and that by God' (1:28). In other words, your change in character, your united stand in defence of the gospel, your ability to withstand with meekness and without fear the opposition that you must endure, constitute a sign. That sign speaks volumes, both to the outside world and to the Christian community. It is a sign of judgment against the world that is mounting the opposition; it is a sign of assurance that these believers really are the people of God and will be saved on the last day.

So conduct worthy of the gospel is in the first instance a corporate unity and steadfastness in defence of the gospel that cheerfully, meekly, and without fear withstands all opposition and boldly promotes the gospel. To put it bluntly, conduct worthy of the gospel is above all conduct that promotes the gospel. What could be more appropriate? The most appropriate way to live, in response to the glorious good news that has saved and transformed you, is to behave in such a way, with other believers, that you actively contend for the faith. Such conduct will prove to be a sign of assurance for you, and a sign of impending judgment to those who will not hear.

Paul then adds a few lines that identify an intrinsic connection between this conduct and the gospel of the cross for which they are to contend. Paul tells the Philippians, 'For it has been granted to you on behalf of Christ not only to believe on him but also to suffer for him' (1:29). Their call to suffer on behalf of the gospel has been *granted* to them: it is a gracious gift from God! Not only have they enjoyed the privilege of coming to faith, they currently enjoy the privilege of suffering for Christ – 'not only to believe on him', Paul writes, 'but also to suffer for him'.

That is not the way we normally think of suffering, not even the suffering of persecution. But it is what Paul says. *If their salvation has been secured by the suffering of another on their behalf, their discipleship is to be demonstrated in their own suffering on his behalf.*

Of course, our suffering for Christ is not *exactly* the same as Christ's suffering for us. His suffering is the suffering of the God-man, the suffering of the one who enjoyed equality with God, the suffering that secured the forgiveness of others, the suffering of a guiltless victim. Our suffering for Christ cannot add to the atoning significance of his suffering.

Nevertheless, we are called to suffer like him, and for him. Do you recall what Jesus tells his disciples in Mark 8? 'If anyone would come after me, he must deny himself and *take up his cross* and follow me' (Mk. 8:34). This language, too, is shocking. To first-century ears, it does not mean that we must all learn to put up with a wart or a disappointment or an obstreperous mother-in-law or an impending mathematics exam: 'We all have our crosses to bear!' No, to first-century ears this means you must take the cross-member on your beaten shoulders, and stagger to the place of crucifixion, and there be executed in blistering agony and shame. To take up your cross means you have passed all point of possible reprieve, all point of hope that you will once again be able to pursue your own interests: you are on your way to death, a dishonourable death at that. So for Jesus' disciples to take up their cross, even to take up their cross *daily* (Lk. 9:23), is to say, in spectacularly metaphorical terms, that they are to come to an end of themselves, no matter how costly that death, in order to follow Jesus.

This lies at the heart of all Christian discipleship. Every time and every place that we refuse to acknowledge this is so, we sin against Christ and need to confess the sin and return to basics. We are to take up our cross daily.

In many parts of the world, this stance includes a willingness to endure overt persecution for Jesus' sake. That is what the Philippians were called to face. In this they were simply following apostolic example: Paul gently reminds them, 'You are going through the same struggle you saw I had, and now hear that I still have' (1:30). Indeed, when the original apostolic band faced their first beating, they left the court 'rejoicing because they had been counted worthy of suffering disgrace for the Name' (Acts 5:41). Doubtless many of us in the West have been relatively cocooned from such outright opposition. But that is not the way it is in many parts of the world.

Missiologists who plot these things tell us that the greatest period of gospel expansion has been the last century and a half. That same century and a half has witnessed more Christian martyrs than the previous eighteen hundred years combined. And it is not at all impossible, if present trends continue in the West, that opposition to the gospel will extend beyond family disapproval, trouble at work, condescension from intellectual colleagues and the like, to concrete persecution.

But learning to take up our cross daily, learning to suffer cheerfully for Jesus' sake, certainly extends beyond physical persecution. One does not have to be a Christian very long before one discovers that there are countless occasions when we are called to put aside self-interest for the sake of Christ. *And in large measure it is the example of Christ and his sufferings that will empower us to tread this path.*

Several years ago I was asked to interview for a video-taping Dr Carl F. H. Henry and Dr Kenneth S. Kantzer. These two American theologians have been at the heart of not a little of the evangelical renaissance in the western world, especially but not exclusively in America. Each was about eighty years of age at the time of the video-taping. One has written many books; the other brought to birth and nurtured one of the most influential seminaries in the Western world. They have both been connected with Billy Graham, the Lausanne movement, the assorted Congresses on Evangelism, the influential journal *Christianity Today*, and much more. The influence of these Christian leaders extends to the countless numbers of younger pastors and scholars whom they helped to shape, not only by their publications and public teaching but by the personal encouragement at which both excelled. Both men gave lectures for the video cameras before several hundred theological students, and then I interviewed them. Toward the end of that discussion, I asked them a question more or less in these terms: 'You two men have been extraordinarily influential for well-nigh half a century. Without wanting to indulge in cheap flattery, I must say that what is attractive about your ministries is that you have retained integrity. Both of you are strong, yet neither of you is egotistical. You have not succumbed to eccentricity in doctrine, or to individualistic empire-building. In God's good grace, what has been instrumental in preserving you in these areas?'

Both spluttered in deep embarrassment. And then one of them ventured, with a kind of gentle outrage, 'How on earth can anyone be arrogant when standing beside the cross?'

That was a great moment, not least because it was so spontaneous. These men had retained their integrity precisely because they knew their attitude should be the same as that of Jesus Christ (2:5). They knew they had been called not only to believe in Christ but also to suffer for him. If their Master had viewed equality with God not as something he would exploit for personal advantage but as the basis for the humiliating path to the cross, how could they view influential posts of Christian leadership as something they should exploit for personal advantage?

We are called not only to believe on Christ but also to suffer for him.

We are called not only to enjoy the comforts of the gospel but also to pass them on (2:1–4)

That is the burden of the opening lines of chapter 2. One cannot fail to observe that Paul's argument is quite overtly an appeal to experience. The argument, in brief, is this. If you have experienced a number of important and delightful Christian blessings, then there is an entailment: you must act in such and such a manner. To put it another way, Paul argues that if they have enjoyed certain wealth of experience, then this precious treasure becomes a mandate to specific conduct.

What, then, is this experience to which the apostle makes appeal? And what conduct does he expect?

The appeal to experience is bound up with a series of 'If . . .' clauses in 2:1: 'If you have any encouragement from being united with Christ, if any comfort from his love, if any fellowship with the Spirit, if any tenderness and compassion . . .' In other words, if being Christians has brought them any encouragement, any comfort in times of pain or loneliness as they have basked in the assurance that they are loved by God himself and loved by other believers, if any sense of fellowship or partnership arising from the Spirit's common work in the family of God, if any fresh experience of tenderness and compassion, *then* (verse 2), 'make my joy complete by being like-minded, having the same love, being one in spirit and purpose'.

In other words, Paul asks us if there have been times in our lives when as believers we have sensed God close to us; when we've been aware of his love in tremendous, scarcely describable ways; when we have revelled in the sense of belonging to the fellowship of God's people; when we've received wonderful encouragement as a 'benefit' of the fact that we are Christians. This is, quite bluntly, an appeal to experience. But if these facets of normal Christian living have been part of your experience, you must recognize that a great deal of that experience has come about because other Christians have mediated God's grace to you. They have loved you, cherished you, encouraged you, made you feel part of the partnership of the redeemed. What this means for *you* as a Christian is that you owe the same to others. And if you recognize this point and live by it you will excite the apostle's joy: '. . . then [he writes] make my joy complete by being like-minded [*i.e.* adopting the same stance as those who have ministered to you], having the same love [*i.e.* as that shown to you], being one in spirit and purpose [*i.e.* the entire church is to reflect this same precious, Christ-honouring, God-fearing, self-denying, other-edifying stance]'. And in case this is not cast in terms that are sufficiently practical, Paul spells his point out: 'Do nothing out of selfish ambition or vain conceit, but in humility consider others better than yourselves. Each of you should look not only to your own interests, but also to the interests of others' (2:3–4).

What is this if it is not a principled taking up of one's cross, dying to self-interest for the sake of others?

43

> It takes more grace than I can tell
> To play the second fiddle well.

That is what Paul is saying. Others have ministered to you, not least because, as Christians, for Christ's sake and out of care for you they chose to play second fiddle. Now it is your turn. 'Selfish ambition' and 'vain conceit' must go. Self-denying interest in the welfare of others must be our watchword.

For Paul, the issue is finally one of attitude. And the person who has perfectly manifested exactly the right attitude is the Lord Jesus Christ: 'Your attitude should be the same as that of Christ Jesus . . .' (2:5) – whose example is then set forth in the bold lines of the verses that follow (2:6–11).

The point Paul is making, then, is that we have been called not only to enjoy the comforts of the gospel but also to pass them on. If you have received personal benefit from the gospel at the hands of other believers, then maintain the tradition: treat others in such a way that they receive them too. After all, we profess to trust and follow one whose entire mission was characterized by self-denial: in obedience to his heavenly Father he gave and gave and gave. Your attitude, writes Paul, should be the same as his: give and give and give.

Do we not say as much to our young people sometimes? They go through self-conscious phases in which they think that everyone is staring at them, and that no-one likes them. If they fall into a pattern of self-pity in this regard, sooner or later we say to them, 'Look, stop your whining. To whom have you shown yourself a friend? Those who would have friends must show themselves friendly. Have you looked around your classroom and found the students who are loneliest, most commonly rejected, alone – and tried to befriend them? Why not? Why do you think everyone should be friendly to you when you make no effort to befriend others?'

Of course, all such arguments, as useful as they are, are narrowly pragmatic. Paul's argument is far stronger. *We* owe love and encouragement to others because we *have* received so much; above all, we owe this kind of character and stance to others because we profess to follow Christ Jesus, and that, supremely, is *his* character and stance. It is always deeply disturbing to find some professed Christians, members of the church, who think only of what they get. What a pathetically Christ-denying attitude! Give and give and give. We are called not only to enjoy the comforts of the gospel but also to pass them on.

We are called not only to early steps of faith and obedience, but to an entire life of working out our salvation (2:12–18)

Note how these verses begin: 'Therefore, my brothers . . .' (2:12). In other words, Paul is now drawing logical connections from the hymn of praise he has just offered up to Christ. There are at least two logical links in the connections he draws. First, 'every knee shall bow' (2:10): *therefore* we do well to live in the light of the fact that we shall all bow before Christ on the last day and give an account to him. But more importantly, Christ Jesus, after terrible suffering, was finally vindicated. So shall we be. He obeyed and endured to the end, and was finally vindicated. '*Therefore* . . . continue to work out your salvation with fear and trembling' (2:12).

It is vitally important to grasp the connection between God's sovereignty and our responsibility in verses 12 and 13. The text does not say, 'Work to acquire your salvation, for God has done his bit and now it is all up to you.' Nor does it say, 'You may already have your salvation, but now perseverance in it depends entirely on you.' Still less does it say, 'Let go and let God. Just relax. The Spirit will carry you.' Rather, Paul tells us to work out our salvation with fear and trembling, *precisely because* it is God working in us 'both to will and to act according to his good purpose' (2:12–13). Nor is God working merely to strengthen us in *our* willing and acting. Paul's language is stronger than that. God himself is working in us both to will and to act: he works in us at the level of our wills and at the level of our doing. But far from this being a *dis*incentive to press on, Paul insists that this is an incentive. Assured as we are that God works in this way in his people, we should be all the more strongly resolved to will and to act in ways that please our Master.

For reasons too complex to probe here, a great deal of western thought has gone wrong at precisely this point. We have expended huge quantities of energy pitting God's sovereignty against human responsibility, when the Bible insists that these things belong together. That is true, for example, with respect to election. Many untutored Christians think that any notion of election must be a *dis*-incentive to evangelism. Not so for Paul, according to Luke: at one of the apostle's discouraging periods of life and ministry, God encourages him by assuring him that he is to preach on and endure precisely because God already 'has' many people in the city of Corinth, and thus they are bound to be called forth at the right time by the preaching of the Word (Acts 18:9–10).

45

So also here: God's continuous, gracious, sovereign work in our lives becomes for us an incentive to press on with fear and trembling. And once again, Paul will not let us escape with a merely theoretical point. As in 2:1–4, where he moves from the general exhortation to the specific shape of the command, so he moves here from the general exhortation (2:12–13) to concrete content. If we want to know just what that concrete content is, just what Paul means when he tells us to work out our salvation with fear and trembling, we shall be left in no doubt. He makes three brief points.

(1) 'Do everything without complaining or arguing', Paul writes, 'so that you may become blameless and pure, children of God without fault in a crooked and depraved generation, in which you shine like stars in the universe as you hold out the word of life' (2:14–16a). In other words, Christian contentment, a theme that the apostle takes up later in this epistle, stands out in a selfish, whining, self-pitying world. As Christians 'hold out the word of life', there must not be a trace of self-pity, but a life characterized by sincere gratitude and godly praise.

(2) Moreover, this kind of perseverance is undertaken, at least in part, so as to delight Christian leaders: this, too, is a theme that is about to be developed further, in that the next chapter and a half focus on the importance of emulating the right kind of Christian leaders. So Paul says here that the way the Philippian leaders live, with cheerful godliness as they hold out the word of life, is a commitment undertaken 'in order that I may boast on the day of Christ that I did not run or labour for nothing' (2:16b).

(3) Finally, such Christian perseverance is a form of Christian sacrifice that makes the leaders' sacrifice a complementary capstone to theirs. The argument is subtle, but it is very important. Paul writes, 'But even if I am being poured out like a drink offering on the sacrifice and service coming from your faith, I am glad and rejoice with all of you' (2:17). In this metaphor, the actions of the Philippians constitute the primary 'sacrifice'. They give themselves to Christ, and commit themselves to pleasing him, whatever the cost. Then, if Paul has to give up his life, his sacrifice is merely a kind of libation poured out on top of their sacrifice. Such a libation is meaningless unless it is poured out on a more substantial sacrifice. But their Christian living is that sacrifice; Paul's martyrdom, should it occur, or the pains and sufferings and persecutions he faces as an apostle, are the complementary drink offering poured over theirs. Paul says, in effect, 'If I suffer, or even lose my life, in a sacrifice poured out on top of your principled self-denial, I am *delighted*. What I do not want is to die a martyr's death without any corresponding fruit in your life. As it is, whatever small sacrifice I am called upon to make is but a

complementary capstone to the sacrifice that all Christians are called to make. In this I will rejoice. So you too should rejoice and be glad with me' (cf. 2:18).

So we are called not only to early steps of faith and obedience, but to an entire life of working out our salvation. This will be characterized by self-denying contentment; by a conscious effort to please mature Christian leaders; and by a cheerful sacrifice that ratifies and endorses the work that more mature Christian leaders have poured into our lives. And all of this is nothing more than learning the entailments of following a crucified Messiah.

In short, we must adopt Jesus' death as a test of our outlook.

One of the great Christian poets of this century was Amy Carmichael, one of whose compositions captures many themes in this chapter:

> From prayer that asks that I may be
> Sheltered from winds that beat on Thee,
> From fearing when I should aspire,
> From faltering when I should climb higher,
> From silken self, O Captain, free
> The soldier who would follow Thee.
>
> From subtle love of softening things,
> From easy choices, weakenings
> (Not thus are spirits fortified,
> Not this way went the Crucified),
> From all that dims Thy Calvary,
> O Lamb of God, deliver me.
>
> Give me the love that leads the way,
> The faith that nothing can dismay,
> The hope no disappointments tire,
> The passion that will burn like fire.
> Let me not sink to be a clod:
> Make me Thy fuel, Flame of God.

Adopt Jesus' death as a test of your outlook.

3
Emulate worthy Christian leaders

Philippians 2:19 – 3:21

When I was an undergraduate at McGill University thirty years ago, reading chemistry and mathematics, another Christian student and I began an evangelistic Bible study in my room in the men's dorm where we were living. We were both a little nervous, and didn't want to be outnumbered. So we invited only three unbelievers, expecting that not more than one or two would show up. It was rather distressing when all three put in an appearance. I had never done anything like this before. Within a few weeks, sixteen students squeezed into my little room, and still only two of us were believers. Doubtless some Christian observers thought it was going exceedingly well; as for me, I was exceedingly frightened. The Bible study engendered all kinds of private discussions, and I soon discovered I was out of my depth.

Mercifully, there was a chap on campus called Dave, a rather brusque graduate student who was known to be wonderfully effective in talking to students about his faith and about elementary biblical Christianity. I was not the only one who on occasion brought our friends and contacts for a little chat with Dave.

On the particular occasion I have in mind, I brought two of the undergraduates from the Bible study down the mountain to Dave's rooms. He was pressed for time, and, as usual, a bit abrupt, but he offered us coffee and promptly turned to the first student.

'Why have you come to see me?' he asked.

The student replied along these lines: 'Well, you know, I've been going to this Bible study and I realize I should probably learn a bit more about Christianity. I'd also like to learn something of Buddhism, Islam, and other world religions. I'm sure I should broaden my perspectives, and this period while I am a university student seems like a good time to explore religion a little. If you can help me with some of it, I'd be grateful.'

Dave stared at him for a few seconds, and then said, 'I'm sorry, I don't have time for you.'

I just about dropped my jaw. The student thus addressed was equally nonplussed, and blurted out, 'I beg your pardon?'

Dave replied, 'I'm sorry, I don't mean to be rude, but I only have so much time. I'm a graduate student with a heavy programme myself. If you have a dilettante's interest in Christianity, I'm sure there are people around who could spend a lot of time and energy showing you the ropes. I can introduce you to some of them, and give you some books. When you're really interested in Christ, come and see me again. But under the present circumstances, I don't have time.'

He turned to the second student. 'Why did you come?'

After listening in on the rebuff administered to the first student, the second may have been a bit cowed. But gamely he ploughed on. 'I come from what you people would call a liberal home. We don't believe the way you do. But it's a good home, a happy home. My parents loved their children, disciplined us, set a good example, and encouraged us to be courteous, honourable, and hard-working. And for the life of me I can't see that you people who think of yourselves as Christians are any better. Apart from a whole lot of abstract theology, what have you got that I haven't?'

This time I held my breath to see what Dave would say. Once again he stared at his interlocutor for a few seconds, and then he simply said, 'Watch me.'

I suppose my mouth dropped open again. The student, whose name was Rick, said something like, 'I'm sorry, I don't understand.'

Dave answered, 'Watch me. Come and live with me for a month, if you like. Be my guest. Watch what I do when I get up, what I do when I'm on my own, how I work, how I use my time, how I talk with people, what my values are. Come with me wherever I go. And at the end of the month, you tell me if there is any difference.'

Rick did not take Dave up on his invitation, at least not in exactly those terms. But he did get to know Dave better, and in due course Rick became a Christian, married a Christian woman, and the two of them, by this time medical doctors, practised medicine and lived their faith both in Canada and overseas.

'Watch me.' At the time I worried about the sheer arrogance that such an invitation seemed to capture. At the same time, my mind recalled the words of the apostle Paul: 'Follow my example, as I follow the example of Christ' (1 Cor. 11:1).[5] Sober observation and reflection assure us that much Christian character is as much caught as taught – that is, it is picked up by constant association with mature Christians.

The general importance of learning by a kind of existential mimicry is well established at every level. Why do Canadian children grow up speaking with Canadian accents? Why is it that if you are reared in Yorkshire you sound like a Yorkshireman, and if you grow up in Dallas you sound like a Texan? We all know the answer: people grow up imitating those around them. For exactly the same reason, parents are concerned that their children have the right kind of friends, because they know that children copy children. If all their friends are violent or vulgar or uncouth, the odds are much greater that their own children will be violent or vulgar or uncouth. This is no less true in the teen years. At that point, the unconscious habit of copying Mummy and Daddy weakens. And yet, thinking themselves to be wonderfully independent, all these teenagers become terribly eager to copy their peers. But they are still imitating *someone*.

Even television operates in this way. It provides a kind of vicarious friendship. In some ways, it might be judged better than a friend: it never talks back – or if, with the advent of interactive television, it does talk back, you can always switch it off. But if you watch thousands of violent deaths before the age of eighteen, it is bound to affect your personality. If you watch sexual promiscuity day in and day out, then even if at one level of your mind you conclude that promiscuity is immoral, in fact your tolerance levels have been subtly altered. You are no longer shocked. And for many people, television provides a sort of moral 'bottom line': they have no other dominating reference point. Multiply such influence by the millions of people who watch, and the effect in society is inevitable: massive moral decline. That is why some wise parents, if they have a TV at all, limit how much they and their children watch, and when they permit their children to watch they insist that one parent or the other be present, not least so that the content can be talked about and evaluated afterward.

But mimicry is not restricted to the secular arena. It is no less important in our Christian pilgrimage. How did you learn to pray? If you were reared in a Christian home, doubtless you learned to pray by hearing your parents pray. Perhaps, too, they taught you some very simple prayers to be prayed at bedtime: 'Now I lay me down to sleep . . .' or 'Gentle Jesus, meek and mild. . . .' If you spring from a very conservative Christian home, where the Authorized Version exposed you to archaic English, your first public prayer, perhaps when you were six or eight years old, probably sounded like this: 'We thank Thee, blessed God, that in Thy mercy Thou hast vouchsafed to us Thy grace through the merits of Thy Son and our Saviour, Jesus Christ.' But if you were not converted until your third year at university, in a UCCF or Navigators or Campus Crusade group, and you spring from a home that never brought you to church at all, your first public prayer probably sounded something like this: 'We just wanna thank you, Jesus, for being here.' In *both* cases you learned to pray by listening to others.

Modelling, modelling: it takes place all the time, whether we take it into account or not. This is true even of adults. Of course, we enjoy a wider range of choices of people after whom we want to pattern our lives, but the modelling goes on. That is why advertising works. Companies spend billions of pounds a year selling toothpaste or a car or a stereo system visually linked to some beautiful blonde or some amazing hunk. The companies would not do this if they did not think it worked. We may not be so naïve as to think, 'If only I used that toothpaste, I would look like that, too!' Yet at some deep level, advertisements must work for most of us, or companies would not pay their billions to produce them.

Some of our habits of imitation are frankly amusing. When I was still a young preacher, and still single, my mother, who was my best critic until my wife came along, one day asked me, after a sermon, where I had picked up my grotesque leer. I assured her I did not have a clue what she was talking about. She told me that sometimes in full flow I would pause, lean over the pulpit, drop my bottom lip, and leer. Once I thought about it, I realized where I had picked the habit up. Another minister, who had befriended me, taken me aside weekly and taught me the rudiments of intercessory prayer, had the same habit. I revered that man, and on him the facial contortion looked, in my eyes at least, thoughtful and reflective. Probably he was entirely unaware of his mannerism. But sure enough, I had picked it up, and on me it came across as nothing but leering at the congregation.

How, then, shall new Christians learn to talk Christianly, think Christianly, evaluate society Christianly, live in families Christianly, learn to witness, learn to give, learn to develop godly habits of life? Of course, much is said on all these topics in Scripture: many believers will find their lives shaped simply by reading and re-reading Scripture. Nor would I want to minimize the powerful, inner work of the Holy Spirit. But the Spirit most commonly uses means. And those means include the modelling that more experienced Christians offer.

Perhaps I should pause and comment on one element of this challenge, an element that affects what I do every week. There was a time when the majority of those who came to our seminaries and theological colleges to offer themselves for the ministry sprang from Christian homes. Many of them were themselves children of the manse or of the mission field. This is today decreasingly the case. Our students come from all sorts of colourful backgrounds. Many were converted only in their twenties. Most were never inculturated in a particular ecclesiastical heritage; some of them come from broken homes, and not a few of them once took drugs. How on earth can we be expected to prepare them for pastoral ministry, if we restrict ourselves to whatever we can put into their lives in the classroom? Oh, they are genuinely Christians, all right – but many of them are carrying so much emotional baggage, and they are so inexperienced in mature ecclesiastical cultures, that three years in a seminary classroom are not going to resolve all the issues. Seminaries and theological colleges can do some things extremely well. But they must not be seen as pastors' finishing schools: a great deal of the polish must be administered *within the context of the local church*. In that context pastoral apprentices learn much more of living, ministering, preaching, interacting graciously with obstreperous people, bearing one another's burdens, praying fervently, weeping with those who weep and laughing with those who laugh, *by observing how mature Christians excel in all of these areas*.

So the question is not *whether* we shall learn from others by conscious and unconscious mimicry, but *what* we shall learn, and *from whom* we shall learn it. And that question is massively addressed in the passage before us. It is implicit throughout the passage, and it becomes explicit at discrete points: *e.g.* 3:17, 'Join with others in following my example, brothers, and take note of those who live according to the pattern we gave you.' A verse like this is not narrowly doctrinal: it is existential, it concerns how you live. Similarly, part of the reason Paul describes Timothy and Epaphroditus at the end of chapter 2, and is so self-revealing about his own motives and habits in chapter 3, is that he is concerned to establish and reinforce good models. He is not stooping to cheap flattery of his colleagues, nor is he indulging in self-congratulation. His aim is to provide clear Christian examples that younger and less experienced Christians ought to emulate. For if they do not have such models, or if they are not encouraged to follow them, they are likely to follow poor or misleading or even dangerous examples.

So whom should we follow? Which Christians should be our models?

Emulate those who are interested in the well-being of others, not their own (2:19–21)

Paul's opening words regarding Timothy constitute a wonderful accolade: 'I hope in the Lord Jesus to send Timothy to you soon, that I also may be cheered when I receive news about you. I have no-one else like him, who takes a genuine interest in your welfare' (2:19–20). One of the reasons Paul is sending Timothy is that when Timothy returns Paul will find out how the Philippians are getting on (2:19). But the other reason is that Timothy himself reflects Paul's attitude exactly: he 'takes a genuine interest in your welfare' (2:20). When Paul says, 'I have no-one else like him', he probably does not mean that he knows no other Christians anywhere who exhibit the same kind of maturity, but that of the helpers he has with him at the moment Timothy is outstanding: none of the others can touch him in this particular, the transparent interest Timothy takes in the well-being of others.

There are many different styles of leadership. Some leaders live to be admired, to be praised. Without ever being so crass as to say so, they give the impression that the church exists and flourishes primarily because of their gifts, and the least the church can do in return is offer constant adulation. But that is not Timothy's attitude. He lives for them; he is genuinely interested in their well-being.

Of course, in the light of the letter so far, this is nothing other than a sign that Timothy follows not only Paul but Jesus. Although Christ Jesus enjoyed equality with God, he did not think of such equality as something to be exploited, but adopted the form of a servant. He became a human being, a man, and then obediently went to his odious death on the cross. Those who follow Jesus Christ inevitably learn to cast self-interest and self-comfort and self-focus to one side. Paul knows that as a general rule 'everyone looks out for his own interests, not those of Jesus Christ' (2:21). But Timothy has eclipsed that narrow snare.

So whom will you follow? Which contemporary Christians will serve you well as good models? Emulate those who are interested in the well-being of others, not their own. Be on the alert for Christians who really do exemplify this basic Christian attitude, this habit of helpfulness. They are never the sort who strut their way into leadership with inflated estimates of their own importance. They are the kind who cheerfully pick up after other people. They are not offended if no-one asks after them; they are too busy asking after others. They are the kind who are constantly seeking to do good spiritually, to do good materially, to do good emotionally. They are committed to the well-being of others. Watch them. Watch how they act, how they talk, how they react. Talk with them; learn their heartbeat. Imitate them. Emulate those who are interested in the well-being of others, not their own.

Emulate those who have proved themselves in hardship (2:22–30)

Paul reminds the Philippians that they 'know that Timothy has proved himself, because as a son with his father he has served with me in the work of the gospel' (2:22). The analogy is a lovely one. In the ancient world, before the industrial revolution, most sons ended up doing vocationally what their fathers did. If your father is a farmer, the chances are very high that you will become a farmer; if your father is a baker, most likely you will become a baker. And your primary apprenticeship is to your father: it is your Dad who teaches you the tricks of the trade, who gradually teaches you all he knows, and, step by step, increases your load of knowledgeable responsibility.

The image is less forceful for us today, not only because most of our children will not follow the vocational path followed by their parents, but because most of our children do not really see us at work. In the ancient world, children observed their parents working, and learned the trade by working alongside them. But my children do not accompany me to the seminary where I teach. Only rarely do they accompany me when I go somewhere to preach. They cannot share with me endless hours in the library or in my study; unless it takes place at the dinner table, they cannot listen in on the counsel I am expected to give to many who come to see me. So even if one of my children were to end up in vocational ministry, not much of their training would be grounded in working beside me. And so it is for most of us.

But Paul's analogy is based on the ancient model. Timothy has learned his Christianity and his first steps in Christian ministry from Paul, as a son learns from his father. Timothy has enjoyed Paul as his spiritual father, his mentor. In that context he has been tested: he 'has proved himself', Paul writes. So Paul is entirely at ease about sending him: 'I hope, *therefore*, to send him as soon as I see how things go with me' (2:23). Timothy will serve as a kind of forerunner to Paul, who hopes to come along shortly himself: 'And I am confident in the Lord that I myself will come soon' (2:24).

Then there is Epaphroditus (2:25–30). This paragraph of Scripture shows Paul to be a leader characterized by deep empathy and compassion. Wonderfully tender lines are found in verse 29, where Epaphroditus is held up as a man to be honoured: 'Welcome him in the Lord with great joy, and honour men like him'.

The circumstances are more or less clear. The opening words

suggest that Epaphroditus was himself from Philippi. 'I think it is necessary to send *back* to you Epaphroditus, my brother': Epaphroditus had been the messenger of the Philippians to Paul, a messenger 'sent to take care of my needs' (2:25), Paul writes. Epaphroditus had borne their financial gift to the apostle (4:10, 14–18); probably he had also supported Paul by his own hard work once he was on site. But now Paul wants to send him back to Philippi. That is what Epaphroditus wants, too, and Paul recognizes the fact: 'For he longs for all of you and is distressed because you heard he was ill' (2:26). That is a remarkable assessment. Epaphroditus was not distressed because he was ill, but because he knew by now that his Philippian brothers and sisters in Christ had heard he was ill. Epaphroditus was distressed because he feared his fellow believers would be distressed on his account.

However much Paul applauds the attitude of Epaphroditus, he will not let him get away with downplaying the seriousness of the illness. The apostle carefully lays out the gravity of the trauma through which the Philippian emissary has passed: 'Indeed he was ill, and almost died' (2:27). If he survived, it was a singular mercy from God, a mercy not only to Epaphroditus, but also to Paul, who was thus spared a profound sorrow (2:27). Paul can scarcely imagine what he would have done if Epaphroditus had been taken from him. 'Therefore I am all the more eager to send him, so that when you see him again you may be glad and I may have less anxiety' (2:28) – that is, my mind will be relieved if he reaches home safely and you enjoy a happy reunion.

Those, in brief, are the circumstances that lie behind this paragraph. But note how Paul casts the matter. He refers to Epaphroditus in the most collegial manner ('my brother, fellow worker and fellow soldier', 2:25), and then concludes *with an exhortation to the Philippians to hold up such leaders as Christians to be honoured and emulated*. 'Welcome him in the Lord with great joy', Paul writes, 'and honour men like him, because he almost died for the work of Christ, risking his life to make up for the help you could not give me' (2:29–30). In short: emulate those who have proved themselves in hardship, not the untested upstart and the self-preening peacock.

One should also ponder Paul's choice of one particular word in this paragraph. Epaphroditus, Paul says, risked his life 'to make up for the *help* you could not give me'. The word here rendered 'help' is a strange one in this context. It is a word that might more commonly be rendered 'religious service' or the like, a word that would be used in the context of discussing worship. But what might Paul be meaning when he says that Epaphroditus risked his life to make up for the 'religious service' that the Philippians themselves could not render?

In recent years, the western church has produced quite a few books and discussions on the nature of Christian worship. Some want worship to become more liturgical. They are usually the people who do not themselves belong to liturgical traditions. Others want worship to become much less liturgical: they are usually the believers who belong to liturgical traditions. The 'grass on the other side of the fence' syndrome works in this debate as efficiently as in other debates. For some people, worship means pipe organs; for others, it means guitars and synthesizers. For some, it means sonorous hymns written at least a century or two ago, and preferably longer; for others, it is not truly Spirit-driven and fresh unless it is characterized by no musical composition more than twenty years old. When people ask what worship is, charismatics tend to begin with 1 Corinthians 12 and 14, musicians tend to begin with David's choirs, sacramentalists begin with 1 Corinthians 11 and other references to the Lord's Supper, and New Testament specialists tend to begin by trying to identify hymn fragments in the New Testament. For many of us, worship is what you do *before* the sermon, but certainly does not include the sermon itself. Thus we carefully distinguish between the 'worship leader' and the preacher: the worship leader doesn't preach and the preacher doesn't lead in worship. After the sermon, if you sing a little more you have returned to worship. But few have tried to construct a genuinely biblical theology of worship.

An exception is a recent book by David Peterson,[6] who rightly points out that under the old covenant, worship, along with all the vocabulary associated with it (sacrifice, prayer, adoration, praise, service, priest), is primarily bound up with the tabernacle and then with the temple. But when one turns to the new covenant, the worship terminology is not so narrowly constrained. Worship terminology is not restricted to, say, the Lord's Supper, or to the public meetings of the church. What is remarkable about worship terminology under the new covenant is that *it characteristically touches all of life*. The well-known passage at the beginning of Romans 12 is a case in point: 'Therefore, I urge you, brothers, in view of God's mercy, *to offer* yourselves as *living sacrifices,* holy and pleasing to God – this is your spiritual act of worship' (Rom. 12:1). In the New Testament, all genuine believers constitute a royal priesthood. In Romans 15 worship is bound up with evangelism. Jesus himself taught that worship is no longer bound up with the cultic in one geographical location or another, whether Jerusalem with its temple or the mountains of Gerizim and Ebal in Samaria (Jn. 4). No, the Father seeks those who will worship him in spirit and in truth. Here, as elsewhere, worship embraces all of life and every location. Worship is the consistent offering of all of one's life and time and energy and body and resources to God; it is profound God-centredness. There is a sense in which true Christians should never be *not* worshipping.

So well-instructed Christians must never suggest that they come together to worship, if by this they mean that during the rest of the week they have not been worshipping and now they gather on Sunday morning at 11:00 a.m. primarily to discharge their obligation to worship. For the Christian, worship embraces all of life. But, you reply, does this mean that Christians *do not* or *should not* worship when they come together? That is what some have suggested: Christian corporate meetings are *not* for worship but primarily for instruction. But that, too, misses the point. It is not that we worship all week and refuse to worship when we come together! Rather, when we gather together, we worship corporately, as we have been worshipping individually all week. This corporate worship includes corporate praise, mutual edification, instruction in the Word and Christian truth, celebration of Christ's death in the memorial that he left behind for that purpose. Thus the sermon itself is not *un*-worship; it is part of our corporate worship, both a sign of it and a profound incitement to it.

This is at least part of the structure of New Testament thought about worship. Once this material has been properly absorbed, it may be useful to discuss pipe organs and guitars. But before absorbing what the Bible has to say on the subject of worship, such discussion is likely to be premature.

In the context of these new-covenant emphases on worship, the reason Paul chooses the particular word that he does when he addresses the Philippians becomes reasonably clear. Epaphroditus almost died for the work of Christ, 'risking his life to make up for the *religious service* you could not give me' (2:30). The Philippian believers would very much have wanted to help Paul personally. All such help he viewed as 'religious service' – part and parcel of their God-centred living, their God-centred service, their God-centred offering of themselves as a continuous sacrifice to God. Whether their help was money, or prayers, or moral encouragement, or concrete evangelism, or some other assistance offered to the apostle, Paul saw it as an element of their service, their worship. And if they were too far away to perform such service personally, then they were happy to send an emissary, whose 'religious service', whose 'worship', was at the risk of his very life. There is nothing to suggest that this risk of life and limb was the result of persecution: probably Epaphroditus fell ill because of some very ordinary bug. But on the other hand, he would not have caught the bug if he had remained comfortably at home on the shores of the Aegean. It was his commitment to help Paul and further the gospel that brought him to Rome, a trip that almost cost him his life – and all of this is bound up with 'religious service', worship if you will, that is simultaneously a help to Paul and an offering to God. And very little of what Epaphroditus brought Paul had much to do with Sunday morning at 11:00 a.m.

Such a view of worship is not designed to depreciate what we do corporately on Sunday morning. It is designed, rather, to ensure that all of life is lived in faithful and delighted obedience to the gospel of God, with the result that what we do corporately when we come together on Sunday morning, or any other time, is the overflow of our experience of God, and a place to be refreshed in the joy of the Lord as we think through his Word, express our praise and thanksgiving, and deepen our links of love with him and with one another. But the point to recognize is that under the terms of the new covenant, worship is bound up with all of life. We live holistically under the grace of God. Either we are God-centred in all that we do, or we are not. If we are, then God's words and ways are precious to us, and all of our living is offered in worship; if we are not, we are in rebellion against God, and nothing that we do is true worship.

The reason this excursus is important to my main point is that mature Christian living is inextricably bound up with this attitude of self-sacrificial service offered up to God, not least in the promotion of the gospel and for the good of other believers. Emulate those who have proved themselves in hardship, not the untested upstart and the self-promoting peacock.

I well remember a Christian leader who a number of years ago used to give this advice to younger Christians: 'One of the most important things in Christian leadership', he would solemnly intone, 'is never to admit any weaknesses. If you admit weaknesses, others will exploit them to your detriment.' Astonishing! Surely there are many areas in which Christians *must* acknowledge their weaknesses. Isn't that Paul's policy, when in 2 Corinthians 12 he insists he has learned to 'boast' of his weaknesses so that Christ's strength might be made perfect in him?

Indeed, in the same passage, Paul circumscribes what he says about his own spiritual experiences, precisely because he is fearful that people will think too much of him. If he must be assessed, he wants to be judged by what he says and does in the public arena, not by laying claim to spiritual experiences no-one else can test (2 Cor. 12:5–6). What is remarkable is the way Paul's stance differs from our own. Many Christians today, even Christian leaders, go through life fearful that people will think too little of them. They quickly become irritable if someone, especially a junior, is praised more than they. But Paul goes through life fearful that people will think too much. Follow a leader like that! He has been tested by hardship, and he is not an untested upstart or a self-promoting peacock. Emulate such leaders.

Emulate those whose constant confidence and boast are in Christ Jesus and in nothing else (3:1–9)

Paul begins, according to most of our English versions, with the words 'Finally, my brothers . . .' There have been a lot of jokes levelled at preachers because of that 'Finally'. One child allegedly asked his Dad what the preacher meant when he said 'Finally', and his father muttered in reply, 'Nothing.' Some critics, eager to be sceptical about the Bible, argue that this word proves that this letter was not written at one time by the apostle, but is a pastiche of sources, one of which ended up with this paragraph beginning with 'Finally'. Some clumsy editor slapped the paragraph into this location, and the result is nonsense.

In fact, our common translations have made things unnecessarily difficult for us. The Greek word used here often served, at this late period of Greek, as a loose connective particle, like our 'So then'. What Paul is doing is picking up the theme of rejoicing he introduced in 2:17–18. There he insists that as he is prepared to offer himself as a kind of drink offering poured out on *their* self-sacrifice, he is glad and rejoices with all of them, and he wants them to rejoice with him. In the following verses, he has told of two helpers, Timothy and Epaphroditus, who have similarly displayed this willingness to suffer for the sake of others, a stance which, ironically, brings joy. 'So then, my brothers', Paul now writes (3:1), 'rejoice in the Lord!'

That sounds very much like a transitional comment. In the verses that follow, although Paul will warn against some false teachers in the strongest language, the issues still turn, in part, on this willingness to put aside what the world and self-interest might choose, in order to pursue knowledge of Christ. But from Paul's perspective, this is so wonderful a privilege that what starts off as self-abnegation turns out to be exactly what the thoughtful Christian wants to do anyway, simply because there is nothing better and finer and more enjoyable than knowing Jesus Christ.

Paul has told the Philippians these things before. That is why he now says, 'It is no trouble for me to write the same things to you again, and it is a safeguard for you' (3:1). The 'same things' to which Paul refers are probably not things that Paul has already said in this letter, since there is no really close parallel between these next verses and what Paul has already written in this epistle. Probably what Paul is referring to is what he has earlier taught them. A little review in spiritual matters is entirely salutary.

So he embarks on this review. 'Watch out for those dogs, those men who do evil, those mutilators of the flesh. For it is we who are the circumcision, we who worship by the Spirit of God, who glory in Christ Jesus, and who put no confidence in the flesh' (3:2–3). This is strong language. Almost certainly Paul is referring to a recurring problem in the churches that he founds. There were many devout Jews who were prepared to believe that Jesus was the promised Messiah, but who thought that for Gentiles to accept this Jewish Messiah they would have to become Jews first. That means they would have to be circumcised and take on responsibility for observing the law of Moses. In other words, they think of Christianity as Judaism plus a little extra, almost as a sect of Judaism.

Paul does not share their view. He insists that they are misreading the Hebrew Bible, what we call the Old Testament. The old-covenant Scriptures do not establish eternal structures of religious observance that are capped by the coming of Jesus. Rather, they anticipate his coming, they look forward to his coming, they announce his coming – but it is his coming that is the ultimate hope. In this view, although the temple in the Old Testament had many functions, one of its most important functions was in pointing to him who would *be* the 'temple', i.e. the supreme place of sacrifice and the supreme meeting-place between God and his people (Jn. 2). The priesthood of the old covenant looks forward to the one, supreme high priest 'after the order of Melchizedek' (Heb. 5 – 7). The sacrifices ultimately anticipate one who would shed his own blood, not the blood of bulls and goats that can never finally take away sin (Heb. 9:11–28). The Passover not only looked back to the blessed night when the angel of death 'passed over' the homes of those who put the blood of the Passover lamb on the two doorposts and on the lintel, but it looks forward to Christ our passover lamb who was sacrificed for us (1 Cor. 5:7), as Paul himself argued.

For many conservative Jews, the sign of entrance into the covenant was circumcision. That is why circumcision was such a crucial issue for them. If Gentiles had to become Jews before they became Christians, then they had to be circumcised before they became Christians. To put it the other way round: when Jews told Gentile Christians they had to be circumcised before they could be real and proper Christians, they were saying, in effect, that Gentiles could not really enjoy the blessings of the gospel, the blessings of Christ Jesus, until they had undergone the rite of circumcision, and solemnly pledged themselves to live under the ancient Jewish law. But Paul's point is that those who argue in this way do not really understand what the Old Testament Scriptures say about circumcison. Already in the Old Testament, the biblical writers make clear that circumcision of the heart is more important than literal circumcision (*e.g.* Dt. 10:16; 30:6; Je. 9:25; Ezk. 44:9). Paul agrees, but he goes a step further: under the terms of the new covenant inaugurated by the Lord Jesus, circumcision of the flesh is no longer the sign of entrance into the covenant community. The distinguishing feature of a Christian, of a new covenant believer, is that he or she has undergone 'circumcision of the heart, by the Spirit, not by the written code' (Rom. 2:29).

That is the background to the challenge that Paul faces. Very often after he has preached the gospel in some town or city and then moved on to the next needy place, other Jews have dogged his path and tried to convince his new converts that if they are to view themselves as Christians at all they must submit to circumcision and thus signal that they are prepared to take on the law of Moses. Whether such people have arrived in Philippi and are beginning to trouble the church, or, alternatively, Paul fears that their arrival is impending and dangerous, he takes the opportunity to warn the Philippian Christians about them and thus to arm them with sound information so that they will be able to withstand the assault.

'Watch out for those dogs, those men who do evil, those mutilators of the flesh' (3:2). Paul's point is that although many conservative Jews spoke of themselves as 'the circumcision', and of Gentiles as unclean 'dogs', in reality by rejecting Jesus Christ they are themselves the 'dogs' – and their vaunted circumcision is nothing more than mutilation if it claims prerogatives for itself beyond its proper place in redemptive history. In particular, if it relativizes Christ and fails to see that he is the *fulfilment* of Old Testament types and models, it is positively 'evil'. For in fact 'it is we who are the circumcision' (3:3) – not, of course, the circumcision of the flesh, but that of the changed life and heart brought about by the gospel. It is 'we who worship by the Spirit of God, who glory in Christ Jesus, and who put no confidence in the flesh' (3:3).

Paul is not saying these things out of barely suppressed jealousy, as if he were frustrated because he himself enjoyed none of the privileges of status, training and discipline that were a godly part of the heritage of the old covenant. Far from it: Paul himself, if he were so minded, could cheerfully boast about the many forms of religious 'confidence' that he himself enjoyed. 'If anyone else thinks he has reasons to put confidence in the flesh, I have more' (3:4), Paul writes – and then lists what he has in mind, the kinds of things that would fly very well in some conservative Jewish circles in the first century.

For a start, he himself had been 'done' on the eighth day of his life: he was circumcised, a full-blooded Jew, covenantally belonging to the people of Israel. Not only so, he sprang from the tribe of Benjamin, one of only two tribes that did not rebel against the Davidic dynasty. Culturally, he was a 'Hebrew of the Hebrews': though born in Tarsus and thoroughly acquainted with Graeco-Roman culture, he was steeped in the language and culture of his racial and religious heritage, receiving his educational formation in Jerusalem. So far as the various Jewish 'sects' or parties were concerned, and their varied stances on how far the law of Moses was to be observed, he was brought up a Pharisee: strict, disciplined, informed, widely respected. Nor was he a Pharisee in name only: he understood the claims of the fledgling Christian community well enough to realize that they could not be ignored, and went after them with persecuting zeal. In fact, as for the full sweep of righteousness under the law (a better rendering of the Greek than NIV's 'legalistic righteousness'), Paul was, quite frankly, 'faultless' (3:6). By this he does not mean he had attained sinless perfection. Far from it: the law provided the remedies for sin, prescribing certain sacrifices, teaching earnest young Jews to look to the God who was addressed each 'day of atonement' by the high priest who sprinkled the blood of animals in the Most Holy Place, to atone both for the his own sins and for the sins of the people. Paul followed the entire pattern of religious life carefully. He was utterly exemplary.

'But whatever was to my profit', Paul writes, 'I now consider loss for the sake of Christ' (3:7). Everything in the credit column has been transferred to the debit column; Christ alone stands in the credit column.

And then, fearing perhaps that his point has still not been made with sufficient force, Paul resorts to even stronger language. 'What is more', he writes, 'I consider everything a loss compared to the surpassing greatness of knowing Christ Jesus my Lord, for whose sake I have lost all things' (3:8). And lose them he did. He was written off by his erstwhile friends and intellectual peers. He lost the security of a home, becoming a constant traveller with no fixed abode. The kinds of sufferings he endured make for an astonishing list (see 2 Cor. 11:23–29). Yet none of this is uttered by way of complaint. We would be misrepresenting Paul in the worst possible way if we were to conclude that these lines betray an apostle who sometimes indulges in a little pity-party. Regarding the things that were taken away from him, Paul calmly asserts, 'I consider them rubbish, that I may gain Christ and be found in him, not having a righteousness of my own that comes from the law, but that which is through faith in Christ – the righteousness that comes from God and is by faith' (3:9).

Here, then, Paul exposes his fundamental values. On one side stands everything the world has to offer, including the privileged world of learned and disciplined Judaism. On the other stands Jesus Christ, and 'the righteousness that comes from God and is by faith'. Paul insists there is no contest: Jesus and the righteousness from God that Jesus secures are incomparably to be preferred.

We should pause a moment to reflect on why Paul would make this judgment. The word 'righteousness' could equally be rendered 'justification', and often is. Despite the criticisms voiced by some critics, the word regularly means, in Paul's letters, that God on account of the death of his Son declares certain people 'just' or 'righteous'. Paul quickly and allusively makes three points about this 'justification' or 'righteousness'. (1) It 'comes from God': that is, it is God's gift, secured because God sent his own Son to die for sinners. (2) It is 'by faith': that is, it is secured 'through faith in Christ'. The means of receiving it is faith, and the object of that faith is Christ. (3) This 'righteousness' is set over against whatever Paul could achieve by observing the law – as he puts it, 'a righteousness of my own that comes from the law' (3:9). Paul does not think that those under the old covenant were not really obligated to abide by its stipulations, or that no-one in those days could be right before God. Rather, now that Christ Jesus has come, in fulfilment of the law, he sees the legal requirements of the law in a new way. He holds that even under the old covenant men and women were saved by God's grace, appropriated through faith – but that such faith manifested itself, under the old covenant, in terms of obedience to that covenant. Paul is not depreciating obedience. He is insisting that many Jews, including himself in his pre-Christian days, had come to think of the law in a way that was never intended. Instead of seeing the law as one of the preparations for the righteousness from God that would be secured by the coming and death of the Messiah, the law had increasingly become the basis for being 'righteous' before God. That is why some people, as we have seen, urged that Gentiles had to commit themselves to keeping the whole law, symbolized by submitting themselves to circumcision, before they could properly become Christians (see on 3:2–3, above). Paul will not have it: as far as he is concerned, everything else is rubbish in comparison with gaining Christ, with receiving this righteousness from God that is by faith.

Paul understands that justification is God's work – secured by Christ's death and appropriated by faith. God looks at me through the death of his Son and he declares me just. Paul recognizes that in God's universe, the most important thing is to know God. In a flow of history that inevitably runs toward the judgment, the great judgment in which only God's verdict matters, to be declared righteous by this Creator God, this Judge, is infinitely more precious than anything else one can imagine. It is infinitely more important than having all the laurels – ecclesiastical, academic, societal, financial, personal – in the world. Since that righteousness from God turns absolutely, at this point in redemptive history, on gaining Christ and being found in him (3:8–9), that is what Paul wants above all things. Everything else is just rubbish.

In the flow of the chapter, then, Paul makes these points, at least in part, to insist that the Philippian believers emulate those whose constant confidence and boast are in Christ Jesus, and in nothing else. Most who read these pages, I suspect, will not be greatly tempted to boast about their Jewish ancestry and ancient rights of race and religious heritage. But we may be tempted to brag about still less important things: our wealth, our status, our education, our emotional stability, our families, our political or industrial successes, our denominational alignments – or even over which version of the Bible we use. Be careful of people like that. They tend to see everyone else but those in their little group as somehow inferior. Somewhere along the way they inadvertently – or even maliciously! – imagine that faith in Christ Jesus and delight in him are a little less important than they ought to be.

Look around instead for those whose constant confidence is Jesus Christ, whose constant boast is Jesus Christ, whose constant delight is Jesus Christ. Jesus is the centre of their worship, the centre of their gratitude, the centre of their love, the centre of their hope. After that, doubtless we shall sometimes need to argue about relatively peripheral matters. But in the first instance, emulate those whose constant confidence and boast are in Christ Jesus, and in nothing else.

Emulate those who are continuing to grow spiritually, not those who are stagnating (3:10–16)

Verse 10 is often cited by Christians today. What is astonishing is that it was first written by an apostle who had known Christ for almost thirty years. 'I want to know Christ', Paul writes – though of course he *does* know him. What he means is that he wants to know him better and better. If you love someone then you know that person, at least in measure. But your love for that person ensures you want to know that person more and more. A good marriage uncovers to the eyes of one spouse more and more about the other spouse, as long as that marriage endures.

That is the way Paul views Jesus. The riches bound up in him are unending. We shall spend all eternity getting to know him better, and we shall discover that knowing him is knowing God, and the exploration is eternal and inexhaustible. And already, during our pilgrimage here, it is our delight, as it is our duty, to know Jesus Christ better and better.

In particular, Paul says, 'I want to know Christ and the power of his resurrection and the fellowship of sharing in his sufferings, becoming like him in his death' (3:10). What does that mean?

In Paul's usage, the 'power of his resurrection' is the power of God that raised Jesus from the dead. According to Paul, that same 'incomparably great power' (Eph. 1:19), the power that raised Jesus from the dead, is the power that is at work in us to make us holy, to make us a fit place for Jesus to dwell in, to enable us to grasp the limitless dimensions of God's love for us (Eph. 3:14–19), to strengthen us so that we shall have great endurance and faith and lives constantly characterized by thanksgiving (Col. 1:11–12). It takes extraordinary power to change us to become like that. In fact, it takes nothing less than the power of God that raised Jesus from the dead. What the apostle wants, then, is not power so that we might be thought powerful, but power so that we might be conformed to the will of God. Only the power that brought Jesus back from death will do.

That is not all Paul wants. He wants 'the fellowship of sharing in [Christ's] sufferings' (3:10). Here again is the word 'fellowship' or 'partnership' that we considered in the first chapter. Paul wants to identify with Christ in his sufferings, to participate in those sufferings, to know Christ better by experiencing sufferings just as Jesus did. After all, this is the apostle who had earlier written, 'For it has been granted to you on behalf of Christ not only to believe on him, but also to suffer for him' (1:29). Clearly Paul is not the sort of leader who is prepared to tell his converts how to suffer but is unwilling to suffer himself.

We must see that there is no trace of spiritual masochism in this. Certainly Paul does not want to suffer simply because he likes to suffer, as if suffering gives him a kind of perverted joy, so he wants to suffer. Rather, Paul understands that the Master was 'a man of sorrows, and familiar with suffering' (Is. 53:3), and he feels it is part of knowing that Master that he should follow him. That means 'becoming like him in his death' (3:10) – that is, just as Jesus had been crucified, so also Paul wants to take up his cross and follow him. For the privilege of knowing that Master better, no suffering is too great.

Is it not obvious how adoption of the same stance would transform our witness and values? If Philippians 3:10 were our watchword, or if we like the first apostles learned to rejoice under persecution because we had been counted worthy of suffering disgrace for the Name (Acts 5:41), inevitably our own perspectives would change when we faced a whiff of opposition. We might say, 'Thank God! He is finally entrusting me with a little bit of persecution. I want more of it, if it means I may know Christ better.'

One reason Paul adopts this stance is that he holds the end in view: he wants to know Christ in these ways, he says, 'and so, somehow, to attain to the resurrection from the dead' (3:11). By this wording he does not mean to inject doubt as to whether or not he will himself attain the resurrection from the dead. The word 'somehow' in the original probably suggests that Paul is uncertain as to the timing and circumstances of this experience. Might it come to him in his lifetime, so that he receives a transformed, resurrection body without passing through death? We know from his first letter to the Thessalonians that that is what Paul teaches will befall those believers who are alive when Jesus returns (1 Thes. 4:13–17). Or will he die and then rise from the dead? Either way, 'somehow', he will 'attain to the resurrection from the dead'. And in Paul's mind, attaining that glorious end, the final resurrection, the new heaven and the new earth, the home of righteousness, is bound up with persevering in the knowledge of Jesus Christ. So for knowledge of Christ, Paul yearns.

In other words, Paul is not stagnating. And it is this attitude, more than any other, that ensures that when Paul tells us we are to imitate him (3:17; 1 Cor. 11:1) he is not setting himself up as a guru who has already 'arrived'. If Paul knows that he is a model to be imitated, he also knows that he is a model in transition to greater glory. If he wants to be followed, he wants to be followed not least in this, that he himself is still following hard after Jesus. He is pressing on. He does not think of himself as having already been made perfect. Indeed, he explicitly disavows the suggestion: 'Not that I have already obtained all this, or have already been made perfect, but I press on to take hold of that for which Christ Jesus took hold of me' (3:12). What he is aiming for is the attainment of the very purpose for which Christ called him. Anything less would be a betrayal of that calling.

As if the one disavowal is not enough, Paul repeats himself: 'Brothers, I do not consider myself yet to have taken hold of it. But one thing I do: Forgetting what is behind and straining toward what is ahead, I press on toward the goal to win the prize for which God has called me heavenward in Christ Jesus' (3:13–14). Refusing to stand on past triumphs, Paul eagerly strains forward to the glories to come.

Not for a moment is Paul suggesting that his stance is unique, or one that is expected only of apostles. Far from it: 'All of us who are mature should take such a view of things' (3:15). This is how *any* mature Christian should think. And by implication, those who are immature should think this way, too: that is, they should become mature in order to think this way. That is why Paul adds, 'And if on some point you think differently, that too God will make clear to you' (3:15). And meanwhile, all Christians without exception should at least live up to the level of what they already know: 'Only let us live up to what we have already attained' (3:16).

The implications are staggering. Christians should never be satisfied with yesterday's grace. It is a shocking thing for Christians to have to admit that they have grown little in their knowledge of Jesus Christ. As Paul would later exhort Timothy, we are to be diligent in the Christian responsibilities laid on us, so that others may see our progress (1 Tim. 4:15). That includes both 'life' and 'doctrine' (1 Tim. 4:16).

Obviously these things apply with special urgency to preachers and teachers of the gospel. If you have been on the same plateau of both knowledge ('doctrine') and experience ('life') for the past twenty years, there is something dreadfully wrong. It is mandated of all of us that we grow: 'All of us who are mature should take such a view of things' (Phil. 3:15). It is not that we leave old truths and steps of holiness behind, but that new truths and applications of old truths open up before our eyes, and shape our knowledge and our living so powerfully that others see the improvement. Our sins become less and less excusable: those who are most saintly are invariably most deeply aware of how sinful they are, and how odious sin is to God. Holiness becomes more and more attractive.

The glories of the world to come make all the glories of this world fade into dull greys by way of comparison.

Sadly, not all believers, not even all Christian leaders, adopt this stance that Paul views as normal and normative. So look around carefully, and emulate those who are continuing to grow spiritually, not those who are stagnating. Beware of those who project an image of smug self-satisfaction; imitate those who imitate Christ.

Emulate those who eagerly await Jesus' return, not those whose mind is on earthly things (3:17–21)

Verse 17 is transitional: it applies as well to what precedes as to what follows. Clearly, it brings to a focus what precedes. In case we have not discerned that Paul has talked so much about his own attitude toward growth and maturity precisely because he wants others to follow his pattern, he now makes the point explicitly: 'Join with others in following my example, brothers, and take note of those who live according to the pattern we gave you' (3:17). The 'others' to whom Paul refers are probably those in other churches. Paul's point is that he is not laying on the Philippians some special responsibility. If they follow Paul, they are doing no more than what Christians in other churches he has planted are doing. They are lining themselves up with other Christians in other centres. And since Paul cannot be everywhere at once, then they should carefully take note of Christians in their own number who live according to the pattern that Paul gave to the Philippian believers, and let them be their guide.

There are two unavoidable implications in this verse. (1) Part of what Paul taught new converts was how to live. He speaks of 'the pattern we gave you', which in the context clearly means the 'pattern of life (what we would call the "lifestyle") we gave you'. (2) Once again, the apostle assumes that many such elements in Christian discipleship are more easily caught than taught. That is why the Philippians are told to look around them for models, models who are clearly approximating to the apostolic model, and to follow them.

Equally clearly, verse 17 leads on to the thought of the last few verses of this chapter. By insisting that some of the believers make excellent models for others to follow, he implies that some others do not. 'For, as I have often told you before and now say again even with tears, many live as enemies of the cross of Christ' (3:18). But exactly who are these people?

It is hard to be certain and precise about their identity, but we can draw some reasonable inferences. They are probably not self-confessed unbelievers, for (1) it is unlikely that Paul would find himself in tears over complete unbelievers who were dangerously likely to lead the Philippian believers astray; (2) in the context, Paul is contrasting the model he and other mature Christians provide with what these people are doing – and it is unlikely that the Philippian Christians would be tempted to model themselves after people who didn't at least make a claim to being Christian; and (3) the expression 'enemies of the cross of Christ' may suggest people who claim to be believers but who are in reality 'fifth-column' enemies. The expression would surely be unlikely if it referred to all unbelievers without distinction, and if instead it referred to strong unbelievers who actively opposed the gospel, then we return to the second point: it is difficult to imagine why the Philippians would be tempted to follow them.

It appears, then, that these people make some sort of profession of Christian faith, and draw away some, but in reality they are 'enemies of the cross of Christ'. Every generation produces some of these shysters. They are not to be confused with Christian preachers whose motives may sometimes be mixed, like those Paul mentions in 1:15–16. Nor are they to be confused with pagans or others who make no pretence of faith in Christ, but whose opposition to the gospel may become very intense. Rather, they talk a good line, dupe the unwary and the undiscerning, parade themselves as Christian leaders, and perhaps even exhibit a good deal of 'power'. But what is missing, judging by Paul's expression, is a focus on the cross like his own: Paul wants to know more both of the power of Christ's resurrection *and of the fellowship of sharing in his sufferings, becoming like him in his death* (3:11). Enemies of the cross of Christ never adopt that stance.

Doubtless who these people are was clear both to Paul and to the Philippians. Paul adds enough details to enable the first readers to make a clear identification: 'Their destiny is destruction' – that is, they are not real believers, however much they say otherwise. Further, 'their god is their stomach, and their glory is in their shame': far from being drawn to suffering for Christ's sake, they are endlessly drawn to creature comforts. They please themselves; their god is located no higher than their belly. The kinds of things they really value, far from being inspiring and glorious and worthy of emulation, are downright shameful. In brief, 'their mind is on earthly things' (3:19). It is not that they focus on explicitly wicked things. But if all of their values and cherished goals are tied to what belongs to this world and this earth, and no part of them breathes, with the passion of Paul, 'somehow, to attain to the resurrection from the dead' (3:11), they are to be pitied. Certainly they are to be avoided, so far as any modelling is concerned.

Paul's vigorous denunciation is not callous or spiteful. He issues it 'even with tears' (3:18). He is grieved to find professing Christian leaders who in fact are idolaters ('their god is their belly') and wretchedly lost ('their destiny is destruction'). We are reminded of the tears of Christ, whom Paul is emulating. When Jesus denounces the religious charlatans of his day, he ends up in grief as he looks over the city (Mt. 23). For our part, we must not become people who denounce but who do not weep. Neither may we become people who weep but who never denounce. Too much is at stake both ways.

In any case, Paul insists that genuine Christians cannot adopt the stances of these enemies of Christ. By contrast with them, Paul insists, 'our citizenship is in heaven. And we eagerly await a Saviour from there, the Lord Jesus Christ, who, by the power that enables him to bring everything under his control, will transform our lowly bodies so that they will be like his glorious body' (3:20–21). Paul insists in the strongest terms that genuine Christianity, the kind that he wants imitated, lives in the light of Jesus' return. It is Christianity that joins the church in every generation, crying, 'Amen. Come, Lord Jesus!' (Rev. 22:20).

In short, it is Christianity that is *preparing* for heaven, for that is where our true home is, our true citizenship, our true destiny. Only that stance is sufficient to make Paul's attitude toward suffering sensible and reasonable. If cheerful identification with Christ and his sufferings in this world finally issues in the spectacular glory of the Lord's return and the splendour that follows, then we, too, are vindicated, in a fashion somewhat analogous to the way that Christ was vindicated (see on 2:6–11).

Genuine spirituality cannot long outlive an attitude that is homesick for heaven, that lives with eternity's values in view, that eagerly awaits Jesus' return, that anticipates the day when Christ himself will 'bring everything under his control' and 'will transform our lowly bodies so that they will be like his glorious body' (a theme Paul treats more fully in 1 Corinthians 15). Thoughtful Christians will not see themselves first of all as citizens of the United Kingdom or the US or Canada or Pago Pago. We are citizens of heaven. Only that citizenship has enduring significance. Happy the believer whose epitaph was the couplet:

> Of this blessed man let this praise be given:
> Heaven was in him before he was in heaven.

Emulate those who eagerly await Jesus' return, not those whose mind is on earthly things.

I conclude. Cotton Mather, an American Puritan of great influence and learning in his day, wrote:

> Examples do strangely charm us into imitation. When holiness is pressed upon us we are prone to think that it is a doctrine calculated for angels and spirits whose dwelling is not with flesh. But when we read the lives of them that excelled in holiness, though they were persons of like passions with ourselves, the conviction is wonderful and powerful.

But of course, there is a sting in the tail of all that I have written in this chapter. I have cast it all in terms of our responsibility to emulate worthy Christian leaders, and then followed the text in discovering the characteristics of these worthy Christian leaders. But if we Christians are responsible for finding suitable examples whom we might properly emulate, *then of course when we do so we shall become suitable examples whom others will emulate.*

Not all ministry in the church is verbal; not all ministry is prominent. But all Christians are called upon to set a standard of talk and life that influences a new generation of converts in a godly and Christ-honouring way.

In some senses, the needs are becoming more urgent. There are rising numbers of Christian families that have given no thought to family devotions. Who will model for them what is to be done? Homes are ripped apart by divorce: which Christian parents will model for a new generation of young people, sometimes brought up with little love or with confusing models, what a Christian marriage looks like? It is common knowledge that abusive people are often the offspring of abusive people: will we not simultaneously proclaim the gospel and model what generous, self-denying, content, Christian homes look like? Christians used to be known as those who know how to die well: will we not show a new generation of believers how to die, how to grieve, how to trust, how to disagree with another believer without turning belligerent and while still cherishing forbearance and humility? Will we show by our example how to stand up for righteousness in our society? Did we not learn to pray by listening to others? Whom, then, have we taught to pray? Whom have we taught the rudiments of self-discipline?

Yes, we must emulate those who are interested in the well-being of others, and not their own; but we must be such people ourselves. Yes, we must emulate those who have proved themselves in hardship, not the untested upstart and the self-promoting peacock; but we must become such people. Yes, we must emulate those whose constant confidence and boast are in Christ Jesus, and nothing else; but that must be our boast, too. Yes, we must emulate those who are continuing to grow spiritually, not those who are stagnating; but of course, if we do, we shall grow ourselves. Yes, we must emulate those who eagerly await Jesus' return, not those whose mind is on earthly things; but then our minds will be on heavenly things, no less than theirs. And we shall look out on a new generation whom we may influence for Jesus' sake. That is the mandate: to go and make disciples.

Brothers and sisters in Christ, we are called to emulate worthy Christian leaders. We are called to be worthy Christian leaders whom others will emulate.

God help us.

4

Never give up the Christian walk

Philippians 4:1–23

In working through Paul's letter to the believers in Philippi, we have summarized his argument in several simple formulas:

1. Put the gospel first.
2. Adopt Jesus' death as a test of your outlook.
3. Emulate worthy Christian leaders.

And now,

4. Never give up the Christian walk.

But why should this last imperative be made the summary of Philippians 4? There are at least three reasons.

First, the burden of the first verse is to 'stand firm', and this verse is transitional, pointing both backwards to what we have already examined, and forward to the chapter ahead. Paul writes, 'Therefore, my brothers, you whom I love and long for, my joy and crown, that is how you should stand firm in the Lord, dear friends!' The evidence that this verse points backward is clear enough: '*Therefore*, my brothers . . .': that is, in the light of the themes just articulated, especially in the light of 3:17 ('Join with others in following my example . . .'), *therefore* stand firm. Indeed, Paul injects a tender, emotional element: 'my brothers', he addresses them, 'you whom I love and long for, my joy and crown'. He has warned them about false leaders, bad examples. Watch out for those who parade a pseudo-Christianity that may for a while take you in. Beware of those whose god is their belly and whose end is destruction. Do not be deceived by them. Imitate instead those worthy Christian leaders who make much of the cross, and whose spiritual life is vital, growing, and constantly focused on Jesus Christ. In particular, in the light of the Lord's impending return, when he will even transform our bodies, *therefore* stand firm.

So the way 4:1 points backward is clear enough. But there is also a word in this verse that almost certainly points forward. If I were rendering the verse in a crassly literal way, part of it would read '*thus* stand firm in the Lord' (rendered '*that is how* you should stand firm in the Lord' in the NIV). The word I have rendered 'thus' regularly points forward. For example, a literal rendering of John 3:16 reads, 'For God *thus* loved the world that he gave his one and only Son': the word 'thus' points forward to the supreme evidence that God loved the world. So also here in Philippians 4:1: '*thus* stand firm' – that is, stand firm in the way I am about to prescribe. Stand firm; never give up the Christian walk.

Secondly, many of the themes in Philippians 4 have already been treated in Philippians 1 – 3. But in this last chapter of Paul's letter, these themes are recast in such a way as to foster perseverance and endurance. This will become abundantly clear as we work our way through the chapter. So this becomes an additional reason for treating the chapter under this theme.

Thirdly, most importantly of all, we cannot help but see that many of the specific injunctions in this chapter are calculated to foster perseverance. What Paul offers is not simply doctrinal content (though that is important) or simple orders designed to elicit some sort of explicitly Christian behaviour, but attitudinal commands aimed at fostering whole-life, long-lasting commitment to the one true God.

We may put it this way. What kind of exhortation will best help Christians persevere in the way of Christ? Should we encourage one another to recite the creeds and read our Bibles more? Certainly we should – but we must also acknowledge that one can treat the Bible coldly, or merely as an object of academic pursuit (in much the same way as others study Shakespeare). Shall we foster obedience to specific commandments? Yes, doubtless we all need encouragement along those lines from time to time. Yet some obedience is merely formal; other kinds of obedience sink into a pathetic brand of legalism.

So the kinds of things Paul chooses to emphasize in his closing chapter are these: integrity in relationships, fidelity toward God, quiet confidence in him, purity and wholesomeness in thought, godliness in heart attitude. In every area, Paul wants to foster firmness, stability, endurance, perseverance, faithfulness before God – before the God who has disclosed himself so wonderfully and climactically in Jesus Christ, his Son.

The burden of Philippians 4, then, is this: never give up the Christian walk. We may usefully unpack this theme and discover seven components.

Resolve to pursue like-mindedness with other true believers (4:2–3)

The concrete case immediately before Paul concerns two women, Euodia and Syntyche, who cannot seem to get along. What is shocking in this situation is that these two are not peripheral people known for their bad tempers and wagging tongues, and for little else. No, they are women who have worked with Paul in the cause of the gospel (4:3). They have been at the forefront of evangelism: they 'have contended at my side in the cause of the gospel', Paul writes. There is no hint of heresy or immorality in them; they simply cannot get on. So what does Paul do?

First, he pleads with them. Isn't that wonderful? He does not begin with heavy-handed authority. He does not cite his apostolic credentials and tear a strip off them. Indeed, for all that the appeal is personal and impassioned, it is not calculated to shame them. There are important lessons to be learned here for those who are called to mediate in contemporary personality conflicts within the church.

Secondly, Paul asks the person who is to receive this letter to intervene and help the two women sort it out. Sometimes frictions between believers become so severe that the wise course is for a third party to mediate between the two sides and try to help each side see things from the other's perspective, and think through what faithful Christian attitudes should be in such circumstances. Who the person is in this case we do not know. When a letter was sent to the entire local church, as this letter was, doubtless it had to be sent more specifically to an individual who would read it to the whole church. Certainly Paul and the Philippian church knew who this individual was, but we do not. It is reasonable to assume that this person was an elder, a pastor; it may even have been Luke. But we cannot be certain. In fact, it is even possible that the word rendered 'yoke-fellow' is a proper name (though there is no independent attestation of such a name in the ancient world). In that case, by referring to the man as (literally) 'true Yoke-fellow', Paul is resorting to a pun: Mr Yoke-fellow in name and true yoke-fellow in action, as you are yoked together with me in the cause of the gospel. But whoever this person is, Paul asks him to intervene.

Thirdly, the substance of Paul's plea to the women, and the aim of the intervention he wants from his 'loyal yoke-fellow', is that the two women 'agree with each other in the Lord.' The verb translated 'to agree with' is a common one in Philippians, appearing no fewer than ten times in these four short chapters. What exactly is Paul asking for?

(1) This is not an appeal for unity at the expense of truth. Paul does not say, 'Regardless of what is coming between you, bury the hatchet. Do not ever let doctrine stand in the way of unanimity. Doctrine does not matter; just love one another, and that will be

enough.' The Paul who thinks doctrinal matters can draw a line between the person who is reconciled to God and the person who is anathema (Gal. 1:8–9) is unlikely to be slipping into relativistic sentimentality here. When fundamental gospel interests are at stake, it is sometimes necessary to divide. But that is not what is going on here in Philippi.

(2) In the light of the argument of Philippians as a whole, this is not a hopeless demand for perfect agreement on every subject. Paul is not saying to Euodia and Syntyche, 'Ladies, on every single point of doctrine and life I expect you to thrash out your differences and arrive at perfect agreement.' For when the verb is used elsewhere, the appeal is broader and deeper. Recall, after all, Paul's argument at the beginning of Philippians 2. 'If you have any encouragement from being united with Christ, if any comfort from his love, if any tenderness and compassion, then make my joy complete *by being like-minded* [same verb], *having the same love, being one in spirit and purpose*' (2:1–2). In other words, Paul is appealing for a mental attitude that adopts the same basic direction as other believers, the same fundamental aim, the same orientation and priorities. This is a *gospel* orientation.

Some honest differences of opinion among genuine believers could be resolved if they would take the time to sort out *why* they are looking at things differently, if they would take their views and attitudes and submit them afresh, self-critically, to the Scriptures. But many disputes will not be resolved because those who are quarrelling will neither take the time nor deploy the energy to study the Scriptures together. In some cases, neither side *wants* to be corrected or sharpened: both sides are so convinced they are right that mere facts will not correct them, and in any case all they want to do is win. In that frame of mind, they easily forget that it is always inappropriate at best, and frankly sinful at worst, to try to manipulate believers into changing their minds. You know the kind of comments I have in mind: 'Your stance hurts my feelings. Don't you trust me?' Emotional blackmail is never a mark of godliness. It is never a sign of Christian maturity when, under the guise of preserving good relations, Christians try to manipulate others. Usually what is being exposed is a rather embarrassing immaturity. Where there are disagreements of principle, argue them out. Take out your Bibles, think things through, find out why you are disagreeing, be willing to be corrected.

But in *every* case, whether you can reach agreement on this detail or that, identify what takes absolute priority, and begin with that. Focus on what you have in common. Make sure you agree over the gospel. Work hard to develop perfect agreement on matters of greatest importance: the gospel, the Word of God, the glory of Christ, the good of God's people, the beauty of holiness, the ugliness of sin, especially your own. Personal differences should never become an occasion for advancing your party, for stroking bruised egos, for resorting to cheap triumphalism, for trimming the gospel by appealing to pragmatics. Focus on what unites you: the gospel, the gospel, the gospel. Be like-minded; think the same things; agree with one another. Work hard and humbly on these central issues, and in most instances the peripheral matters will take care of themselves. Resolve to pursue like-mindedness with other believers. This will ennoble and strengthen all sides, so that you will never abandon the Christian walk.

Resolve always to rejoice in the Lord (4:4)

Paul writes, 'Rejoice in the Lord always. I will say it again: Rejoice!' (4:4). Of course, Paul has already introduced this theme into his letter. In the first chapter, Paul assured his readers, 'In all my prayers for all of you, I always pray *with joy* because of your partnership in the gospel' (1:4). The theme recurs in chapter 2: Paul is ready to be poured out as a kind of drink offering, a sacrifice on top of all their sacrifices – and if this should transpire he would be glad and rejoice with them, and expect them to be glad and rejoice with him (2:17– 18). The same theme is picked up in chapter 3: 'So then, my brothers, rejoice in the Lord!' (3:1). And now it returns once more, and in a most emphatic form.

Doubtless the Philippians could not read many such exhortations from the apostle without remembering that Paul had been a prime example of this virtue when he had first preached the gospel among them. According to Acts 16, he and Silas were arrested and thrown into prison. Beaten, bruised, their feet in stocks, they displayed not a whiff of self-pity. Far from it: they began a midnight chorus of praise. Now Paul finds himself in prison again. He is not writing this epistle from a chalet in the south of France, or taking a few minutes out from the happy pleasures of paddling in the waters off Tenerife. He is under arrest. And what does he say? 'Hang in there, brothers and sisters, as I am trying to hang on myself'? Not a chance! 'Rejoice in the Lord. I will say it again: Rejoice!'

In one sense, this injunction is so self-evidently right that it is embarrassing that we should have to be reminded of it. Surely all redeemed men and women will want to rejoice in the Lord. Our sins have been forgiven! We have been declared righteous, because another has borne our guilt. We have received the gift of the Spirit, the down-payment of the promised inheritance that will be ours when Jesus comes again. We are children of the living God. Our 'threescore years and ten' may be fraught with difficulty, but eternity awaits us, secured by the Son of God. We shall see Christ face to face, and spend an eternity in the purest worship and in consummated holiness. If we fail to respond with joy and gratitude when we are reminded of these things, it is either because we have not properly grasped the depth of the abyss of our own sinful natures and of the curse from which we have been freed by Jesus, or we have not adequately glimpsed the splendour of the heights to which we have been raised.

Happy, then, the believer who can repeat David's words with renewed understanding, 'He lifted me out of the slimy pit, out of the mud and mire; he set my feet on a rock and gave me a firm place to stand. He put a new song in my mouth, a hymn of praise to our God' (Ps. 40:2–3). Happy the Christian who sees in every sin a monster that could easily snare him eternally, were it not for the grace of God. Small wonder, then, that Peter writes, 'Though you have not seen him, you love him; and even though you do not see him now, you believe in him and are filled *with an inexpressible and glorious joy*, for you are receiving the goal of your faith, the salvation of your souls' (1 Pet. 1:8–9). The kingdom of God may be entered through suffering (Acts 14:22), but it is characterized by joy: Paul insists that 'the kingdom of God is not a matter of eating and drinking', that is, of obeying rules and observing kosher food laws, 'but of righteousness, peace and joy in the Holy Spirit, because anyone who serves Christ in this way is pleasing to God and approved by men' (Rom. 14:17–18).

But note some details in the text.

First, we are exhorted to rejoice *in the Lord*. The controlling issue is not the style of rejoicing, but the ground. We are not necessarily rejoicing in the Lord because we are boisterous and loud and uninhibited in a large conference hall where the singing is swinging. Such praise may in some instances be entirely appropriate; equally, joy in the Lord may be happily expressed in solemn silence, in tears of gratitude, in sheer delight in times of prayer. But Paul's focus is not on the style; it is on the ground of the rejoicing.

That means the ultimate ground of our rejoicing can never be our circumstances, even though we recognize, as Christians, that our circumstances are providentially arranged. If our joy derives primarily from our circumstances, then when our circumstances change we will be miserable. Our delight must be in the Lord himself. That is what enables us to live with joy *above* our circumstances. As Nehemiah puts it, 'The joy of the LORD is your strength' (Ne. 8:10). Perhaps that is one of the reasons the Lord sometimes allows miserable circumstances to lash us. Perhaps that is why James, the half-brother of our Lord, wisely counsels, 'Consider it pure joy, my brothers, whenever you face trials of many kinds, because you know that the testing of your faith develops perseverance. Perseverance must finish its work so that you may be mature and complete, not lacking anything' (Jas. 1:2–3). Whatever the mysteries of evil and sorrow, they do have the salutary effect of helping believers to shift the ground of their joy from created things to the Creator, from the temporary to the eternal, from jingoism to Jesus, from consumption to God. As the song puts it, 'He washed my eyes with tears, that I might see.'

Secondly, the text implicitly answers two questions: (1) *When* are we to rejoice in the Lord? And (2) *for how long*? To both questions, the text answers with one word: always. 'Rejoice in the Lord *always*.' And this is a command, not simply good advice. Obedience to this command is possible because the ground of this rejoicing is changeless. Our circumstances may rightly call from us grief, tears, sorrow. Unless the Lord comes back first, each of us will face death – our own, and, if we live long enough, the death of loved ones and friends. And we will weep. But even in our tears, we may rejoice, we will rejoice, we must rejoice, for we rejoice in the Lord. He does not change. And that is why we shall rejoice in the Lord *always*.

God well knows that a believer who conscientiously obeys this command cannot be a backbiter or a gossip. Such a believer cannot be spiritually proud or filled with conceit, cannot be stingy or prayerless, cannot be a chronic complainer or perpetually bitter. The cure for a crushed and bitter spirit is to see Christ Jesus the Lord, and then to rejoice in him. Lurking and nourished sins are always a sign that our vision of Jesus is dim, and our joy in him has evaporated with the morning dew. By contrast, the believer who practises rejoicing in the Lord increasingly discovers balm in the midst of heartache, rest in the midst of exhausting tension, love in the midst of loneliness, and the presence of God in control of excruciating circumstances. Such a believer never gives up the Christian walk. Resolve always to rejoice in the Lord.

Resolve to be known for gentleness (4:5)

That is what Paul commands: 'Let your gentleness be evident to all. The Lord is near' (4:5).

The word rendered 'gentleness' in the NIV is not easy to translate. Some older versions offer 'forbearance', which isn't bad. It refers to the exact opposite of a spirit of contention and self-seeking, which is why the NIV opts for 'gentleness'. But this gentleness must not be confused with being a wimp, with the kind of person whose personality is akin to a wet dishcloth. What is in view is a certain kind of willed, self-effacing kindness.

That suggests that there is some irony in Paul's exhortation. We crystallize it if we over-translate: 'Be known for being self-effacing.' The pedant might urge that being self-effacing precludes the desire to be known; trying to be known for something surely rules out being known for being self-effacing. But now we are close to the point Paul is making.

What do most of us want to be known for? Do you want to be known for your extraordinary good looks? Do you want to be known for your quick wit? For your sense of humour, or your sagacity? Do you want to be known for your wealth, for your family connections? Or perhaps you are more pious, and want to be known for your prayer life, or for your excellent skills as a leader of inductive Bible studies. Many a preacher wants to be known for his preaching.

How appalling. The sad fact is that even our highest and best motives are so easily corroded by self-interest that we begin to overlook this painful reality. Paul cuts to the heart of the issue: be known for gentleness.

The self-sins are tricky things, damnably treacherous. In one of his books, A. W. Tozer writes:

> To be specific, the self-sins are these: self-righteousness, self-pity, self-confidence, self-sufficiency, self-admiration, self-love, and a host of others like them. They dwell too deep within us and are too much a part of our natures to come to our attention till the light of God is focused upon them. The grosser manifestations of these sins, egotism, exhibitionism, self-promotion, are strangely tolerated in Christian leaders, even in circles of impeccable orthodoxy . . . Promoting self under the guise of promoting Christ is currently so common as to excite little notice . . .

That was written almost half a century ago. What would Tozer say now? He goes on:

> Self can live unrebuked at the very altar. It can watch the bleeding Victim die and not be in the least affected by what it sees. It can fight for the faith of the Reformers and preach eloquently the creed of salvation by grace, and gain

strength by its efforts. To tell all the truth, it seems actually to feed upon orthodoxy and is more at home in a Bible conference than in a tavern. Our very state of longing after God may afford it an excellent condition under which to thrive and grow.[7]

It is so very easy to mistake the genuine movement of the Spirit for assorted counterfeits. Or perhaps more difficult yet is the movement where there is something genuinely of God, and not a little of the flesh. In the last century in America, there were many 'camp revivals'. These were evangelistic and holiness meetings aimed at calling people to repentance. On the American frontier, they were often very well attended. Doubtless they were a means of blessing to many. But a rather painful study has shown that nine months after many of these 'camp revivals' there was a very high illegitimacy rate. Isn't that remarkable? One can understand why. There was such a spirit of friendship and camaraderie and closeness, that intimacy in one arena spilled over into intimacy in another, until one of the fruits of 'camp revivals' was a disproportionately high illegitimacy rate. Surely that was not of God!

One of the tests that can be applied to determine whether a movement is of God – though certainly it is not the only one – is to observe to what degree those affected are making it their aim to be known for gentleness. In this, they are becoming like their Master. Is that not one of the lessons made clear in chapter 2 of this epistle? 'Your attitude should be the same as that of Christ Jesus', Paul insists – and then outlines how this Jesus, though he enjoyed equality with God, did not view such equality as something to be exploited, but made himself nothing, became a human being, and died the ignominious and shameful death of crucifixion. He became known for selflessness.

May God grant that all who read these pages will pray earnestly for this virtue, and resolve steadily to pursue it. For such believers will never be moved; they will never give up the Christian walk.

Sometimes we sing these things better than we live them:

> May the Word of God dwell richly
>   In my heart from hour to hour,
> So that all may see I triumph
>   Only through his power.
>
> May the love of Jesus fill me
>   As the waters fill the sea;

> Him exalting, self abasing,
>   This is victory.

> May his beauty rest upon me
>   As I seek the lost to win,
> And may they forget the channel,
>   Seeing only him.
>   (Kate Barclay Wilkinson)

Resolve to be known for gentleness.

Paul gives us a specific reason for obeying this injunction. 'Let your gentleness be evident to all', he writes, and then adds, 'The Lord is near' (4:5). This could mean one of two things. Both make sense; I am not quite certain which the apostle means.

Paul could mean that the Lord is near *temporally*, that is, that he is coming soon. In that case, the argument runs like this. In the light of the impending return of the Lord Jesus (to which urgent reference was made at the end of Philippians 3), there is more than a little incentive to be gentle and selfless. The Lord's return provides incentive. As the apostle John writes elsewhere, 'Everyone who has this hope [*i.e.* the hope of the Lord's return and of our transformation at that time] in him [either 'in himself', *i.e.* in the believer, or 'in Christ', referring to the object of the hope] purifies himself, just as he is pure' (1 Jn. 3:3).

What would you like to be doing when Jesus comes again?
What would you like to be saying when Jesus comes again?
What would you like to be thinking when Jesus comes again?

Each of us can readily think of what we would *not* like to be doing or saying or thinking when Jesus comes again. When I was a boy in Sunday School we sang the chorus:

> Doing good deeds, sowing good seed,
> Leaving life's follies behind me;
> Doing my best, standing each test –
> That's how I want the Lord to find me.

'Let your gentleness be evident to all. The Lord is *near*.'

That is one way of reading the second part of this verse (4:5). But because of the particular expressions that Paul uses, I suspect it is marginally more likely that Paul means that the Lord is near *spatially* or perhaps better *personally*. He is not far off; he is very near. How then can we give ourselves to self-promotion?

Suppose, for a moment, that the resurrected and exalted Lord were to walk into the room where you and your friends were seated. Suppose that there were no doubt in anyone's mind as to his identity. How would you respond? Would you immediately rush up to him and strut your excellence? As he showed you a glimpse of his glory, and turned over his nail-scarred hands, would you be quick to parade your virtues? Would self-promotion play any part in your thinking at that point?

Not a chance! But that is the point: the Lord Jesus has promised to be present, by his Spirit, where even two or three of his disciples gather in his name. Does it change the fundamental reality simply because we cannot at the moment see him?

'Let your gentleness be evident to all. The Lord is *near*.'

Resolve not to be anxious about anything, but learn instead to pray (4:6–7)

This is perhaps the most striking resolution so far, yet it is nothing but a paraphrase of Paul's own words: 'Do not be anxious about anything, but in everything, by prayer and petition, with thanksgiving, present your requests to God' (4:6).

There is a sense in which our society demands that we worry on a broader scale than any society in the history of the race. If we were to travel back, say, eight hundred years or so, we would discover that most people in Europe worried about nothing more than local matters. Of course, those local matters could be severe: medical help was not impressive, most families lost one or more children, life could be harsh, brutal, and short. But communication with other parts of the world was difficult and late. Most people gave little thought to what people were doing in the next county, let alone the next country or the next continent. Apart from extraordinary events, like the Crusades, when your local feudal lord might sweep you up and carry you off to war, you were not called upon to worry about the international scene. Even national news that could affect you was late and essentially alien. The overwhelming majority of people could scarcely visualize their monarch, for of course no pictures or photographs were printed and circulated.

Then came the printing press. It was followed by the telegraph. Alexander Bell invented the telephone; Marconi invented the radio. Not that long ago we started decorating the sky with satellites. My E-mail exchanges with a colleague in, say, Papua New Guinea, bounce off a reflector twenty-two thousand miles out in space. But the result of these greatly improved communications, of course, is that we now speak of the 'global village'. A few shots can be fired almost anywhere in the world, and if in the opinion of the news editors nothing of greater significance has happened to claim prime-time television, the entire episode will be replayed tonight on the evening news, inviting your worry.

So our advances in communications demand that we worry about peace, economics, famine in the Sahel, enormous disparities of wealth in Latin America and the Philippines, cultural decline in the West, the breakup of the Soviet empire, civil conflict in the Balkans, genocide in Rwanda, and on and on.

Of course, our worries are not limited to international affairs. Personal and cultural problems are constantly polled, demographically checked, statistically analysed, and paraded in our newspapers and on our televisions. Then the economy changes, and suddenly very few have permanent jobs, and some of us do not have any jobs at all. Then of course we can add up the regular parade of pressures: car troubles, conflict with colleagues at work, impending exams and the expectations that family and friends impose, competition at work, a degenerating family, an arid marriage, a rebellious teenager, bereavement, financial insecurity. Pressures mount and surround us and bully us, until even the Christian who hears the injunction of this passage ('Do not be anxious about anything') smiles half-bitterly and mutters, 'You don't understand; it can't be done.'

But of course, it can be. Part of our problem is that we encounter this command not to worry, perhaps in a conference or in a book, and we smile piously, grit our teeth, resolve not to worry, and promptly begin to worry about not worrying. What we overlook is that Scripture here tells us *how* to overcome our anxieties. 'Do not be anxious about anything' is not a naked prohibition; the alternative is immediately provided: '. . . but in everything, by prayer and petition, with thanksgiving, present your requests to God' (4:6).

Those of us who have been born into the family of God know about these things. But knowing about them and finding them true in our experience are two different things. When was the last time you prayed explicitly and at length over the things that worry you, trouble you, plague you? Did you take them out and recount them to God, one by one, laying your burdens on him?

Time. Time alone and still before God. That is what we need. Our lives are so rushed that we begrudge a three-minute 'quiet time', and then we wonder where God is. Yet the psalmist had it right: 'He who dwells in the shelter of the Most High will rest in the shadow of the Almighty. I will say of the LORD, "He is my refuge and my fortress, my God, in whom I trust"' (Ps. 91:1–2). Christians who come before the Father in regular prayer discover that Peter is right: 'Cast all your anxiety on him because he cares for you' (1 Pet. 5:7). They discover that Paul is right: 'And we know that in all things God works for the good of those who love him, who have been called according to his purpose' (Rom. 8:28). We are refreshed in the assurance of God's sovereign and wise goodness. According to Philippians 4, the way to be anxious about nothing is to be prayerful about everything: '*in everything*, by prayer and petition . . . present your requests to God.' Bengel was right to insist that anxiety and genuine prayer are more opposed to each other than fire and water. I have yet to meet a chronic worrier who enjoys an excellent prayer life.

> Ye fearful saints, fresh courage take;
> The clouds ye so much dread
> Are big with mercy, and shall break
> In blessings on your head.
>
> Judge not the Lord by feeble sense,
> But trust him for his grace;
> Behind a frowning providence
> He hides a smiling face.
>
> His purposes will ripen fast,
> Unfolding every hour;
> The bud may have a bitter taste,
> But sweet will be the flower.
>
> Blind unbelief is sure to err,
> And scan his work in vain;
> God is his own interpreter,
> And he will make it plain.
>   (William Cowper)

None of this should be misconstrued as a 'Pollyanna-ish' approach to life. Christians are not ostriches, heads carefully buried in the sand. None of this means that our paths will be smooth, their borders lined with the sweetest-smelling roses. There is no hint that we shall live above the pressures of other mortals because we escape them.

Far from it. It is precisely in the context of the pressures all must endure that we find our rest in God. If you worry little simply because Providence has so far blessed you with a relatively easy course through life, or if you worry little because you have a carefree personality, you know little of the truth of this passage. This passage does not deny the existence of anxieties; it tells us what to do with them. It does not tell us that if you have the right personality you can live above tension; it tells us where we find strength and grace to help in times of need.

In fact, we are to go on the offensive. Not only are we to present our prayers and petitions to God, we are to do so 'with thanksgiving'. This, surely, is what is elsewhere called 'a sacrifice of praise' (Heb. 13:15). Any twit can offer praise when things are going well. To praise when by common human reckoning everything is the pits – this is what demands the sacrifice of praise. In Philippians 4, Paul insists that this must be our constant policy: along with our petitions and cares, we offer our heavenly Father thanksgiving. For in fact, even in the most extreme sorrow and distress, there is much for which to give thanks to God – above all, the privilege of being reconciled to him by the death of his dear Son, and all the blessings that come our way, in this life and in the next, because of this great salvation.

Resolve not to be anxious about anything, but learn instead to pray.

The result, as Paul describes it, is lovely: 'And the peace of God, which transcends all understanding, will guard your hearts and your minds in Christ Jesus' (Phil. 4:7). Once gain it is clear that Paul does not expect that the answer to our prayers will most likely take us out of the problems, but that our hearts and minds will be garrisoned by the peace of God. This is not some easily analysed bit of clever psychology. At the end of the day, it 'transcends all understanding': it is part of well-known Christian experience, as many who read these pages can attest, and it must not be reduced to a bit of clever suggestion or escapist comfort. God's peace stabilizes us, guards us, suffusing us with the joy of the Lord. Christians delight in trusting him.

In the words of a Scottish preacher from the last century:

> I stand upon the mount of God
>   With sunlight in my soul;
> I hear the storms in vales beneath,
>   I hear the thunders roll.

> But I am calm with thee, my God,
>   Beneath these glorious skies;
> And to the height on which I stand
>   No storms, no clouds can rise.

> O, this is life! O this is joy,
> My God, to find thee so:
> Thy face to see, thy voice to hear,
> And all thy love to know.
>
> (Horatius Bonar)

Or again,

> Drop thy still dews of quietness,
> Till all our strivings cease;
> Take from our souls the strain and stress,
> And let our ordered lives confess
> The beauty of thy peace.
>
> Breathe through the heats of our desire
> Thy coolness and thy balm.
> Let sense be dumb, let flesh retire;
> Speak through the earthquake, wind, and fire,
> O still small voice of calm!
>
> (J. G. Whittier)

Resolve not to be anxious about anything, but learn instead to pray. Nothing will prove so effective in strengthening your spiritual stamina, in giving you grace never to give up the Christian walk.

Resolve to think holy thoughts (4:8–9)

That, surely, is what Paul means: 'Finally, brothers, whatever is true, whatever is noble, whatever is right, whatever is pure, whatever is lovely, whatever is admirable – if anything is excellent or praiseworthy – think about such things' (4:8).

It always makes me fearful to remember that God knows my thoughts. Hebrews 4 reminds us, 'Nothing in all creation is hidden from God's sight. Everything is uncovered and laid bare before the eyes of him to whom we must give account.' Small wonder that David, after his sin with Bathsheba, could write, 'Search me, O God, and know my heart. Test me and know my anxious thoughts. See if there is any offensive way in me, and lead me in the way everlasting' (Ps. 139:23–24).

Clearly, David recognized not only that God *knew* his thoughts, but that any real reform in his life must *begin with* his thoughts. That is why the Lord Jesus taught, in the Sermon on the Mount, that murder can be traced to hate, and adultery to lust (Mt. 5:43–47, 27–30). That is also why, from God's perspective, the real measure of individuals lies in what they think: not in what they own, or in how well they deploy their gifts, or even in what they do, but in what they think. If you think holy thoughts, you will be holy; if you think garbage, you will be garbage.

So it should come as no surprise that the prophets insist, 'Let the wicked forsake his way *and the evil man his thoughts*' (Is. 55:7). One of the sovereign remedies against sin is to spend much time, thoughtful time, meditative time, in the Scriptures, for it is impossible to get rid of the trash in our minds without replacing it with an entirely different way of thinking. Even kings and leaders, extraordinarily busy people, are told to make this their first priority (*e.g.* Dt. 17:18–20; Jos. 1:7–9). On the night he was betrayed, Jesus prayed for his followers in these terms: 'Sanctify them by the truth; your word is truth' (Jn. 17:17). There is no enduring sanctification apart from the truth of the gospel taking hold of our minds. The way we avoid being conformed to this world, the way we are transformed into conformity with Christ, is by the renewing of our minds (Rom. 12:2).

I know it is possible for people to gain a sort of mechanical knowledge of Scripture that is not characterized by repentance and faith, and therefore remains spiritually fruitless. But for most of us, that is not our current danger. Our current danger is that we make very little effort to think God's thoughts after him, to hide his word in our heart that we might not sin against him (Ps. 119:11). To hide God's word in our hearts, as opposed to our computers, means we ought to memorize it, read and re-read it, think about it, turn it over in our minds. Only such committed absorption of what God says will enable us in turn to confront and change the unbiblical worldviews all around us – or, as Paul puts it, to 'demolish arguments and every pretension that sets itself up against the knowledge of God' and to 'take captive every thought to make it obedient to Christ' (2 Cor. 10:5).

In the passage before us, Paul puts things in the most concrete way. Think about true things, Paul insists, not about the false. Think about noble things, not the base. Think about whatever is right; do not dwell on the wrong. (What does this say about the programmes you watch on television?) Think about whatever is pure, not the sleazy. Think about the lovely, not the disgusting. Think about the admirable, not the despicable. Whatever is excellent, think about it.

This is not some escapist demand to avoid the harsh realities of our fallen world. The sad fact is that many people dwell on dirt without grasping that it *is* dirt. The wise Christian will see plenty of dirt in the world, but will recognize it *as* dirt, precisely because everything that is clean has captured his or her mind.

The hymnwriter was right:

> Guide my thoughts, keep them from straying
> > Into paths unwise for me,
> Lest I should, thy love betraying,
> > Turn aside from Calvary.

Or again:

> May the mind of Christ my Saviour
> > Live in me from day to day,
> By his love and power controlling
> > All I do and say.
>
> (Kate Barclay Wilkinson)

Resolve to think holy thoughts.

Moreover, this verse, Philippians 4:8, is tightly tied to the next. After telling the Philippian believers to think holy thoughts, Paul goes on to say, 'Whatever you have learned or received or heard from me, or seen in me – put it into practice. And the God of peace will be with you' (4:9). In other words, Paul is returning to a theme that was very strong in the previous chapter: we are to emulate worthy Christian leaders. In this context, that theme is now applied to the discipline of the mind. In other words, we are to emulate Christian leaders who have clearly disciplined *their* minds. Of course, we have no access to a mind other than through what that mind says and does. But that is the point. Paul is saying, in effect, 'What was on my mind when I was with you? What did I talk about? What did I read? What was the burden of my conversation? What did I value? What did I do to improve my mind? Whatever you learned or received or heard from me or saw in me, put it into practice. And the God of peace will be with you.'

Resolve to think holy thoughts. This is foundational to the commitment never to give up the Christian walk.

Resolve to learn the secret of contentment (4:10–13)

Paul begins this paragraph by commenting again on the Philippians' concern to meet Paul's needs by sending support. 'I rejoice greatly in the Lord that at last you have renewed your concern for me' (4:10). The phrase 'at last' does not in this context carry derogatory overtones that blame the Philippians for being so slow, as if Paul were saying, '*At last*, you have finally got around to it.' Rather it means that now, in these last few days or weeks, after an extended hiatus caused by all sorts of things (not least Paul's constant travels), you have renewed the concern for me that you showed in the early days ten years ago. That this is what Paul means is made clear by his next sentence: 'Indeed, you have been concerned, but you had no opportunity to show it' (4:10).

But Paul very shrewdly grasps how his exuberant thanks to the Philippians could be misunderstood. Some people voice their thanks in such a way that it is hard to avoid the inference that they are hoping for another gift. Perhaps they grovel; perhaps there is nothing tangible in their thanks that you can put your finger on, but you feel slightly manipulated anyway. Once in a while missionary prayer letters sound this way; very often the thank-you letters from non-profit organizations sound this way. Perhaps. In any case, Paul takes no chances: he wants to distance himself from all of these possibilities, so he immediately explains his own motives: 'I am not saying this because I am in need, for I have learned to be content whatever the circumstances. I know what it is to be in need, and I know what it is to have plenty. I have learned the secret of being content in any and every situation, whether well fed or hungry, whether living in plenty or in want. I can do everything through him who gives me strength' (4:11–13).

This is a remarkable stance. Note especially two features of it.

First, the secret of contentment is not normally learned in posh circumstances or in deprived circumstances, but in exposure to both. Perhaps you have come from a well-to-do background, and you have never lacked anything. You have never had anything you valued taken away from you. The question arises whether you would be comfortable and content if you were suddenly forced to live in poverty. But on the other side, you may have come from a really poor background. Perhaps you learned to handle the uncertainty and the deprivation in godly ways. But now the question arises whether you could be content if you suddenly fell into wealth. Would it instantly corrupt you? Or would you feel so guilty with all these possessions that you could scarcely look at yourself in the mirror?

Paul carefully insists that his own contentment operates under both conditions: 'I have learned the secret of being content in any and every situation, whether well fed or hungry, whether living in plenty or in want.' He avoids the arrogance that is often associated with wealth; he also avoids the kind of spiritual arrogance that is often associated with poverty. The brute fact is that Paul is content in both circumstances *because his contentment is utterly independent of circumstances*. His contentment is focused on all that he enjoys of Christ Jesus. That means he has learned, by hard experience, a relaxed contentment whatever his circumstances.

Secondly, the secret of Christian contentment is quite unlike Stoic self-sufficiency. Paul is not claiming to be so strong that nothing can move him. Nor is he simply resolving to be independent of circumstances by a superlative act of will. Far from it: he immediately confesses that if he has reached this stage of contentment he owes everything to God: 'I can do everything through him who gives me strength' (Phil. 4:13).

This verse is often wrenched out of its context. Paul is not claiming to be a kind of superman because he is a Christian and God is on his side. His 'everything' is certainly not unlimited, as if Paul could be read to mean, 'I can raise the dead', or 'I can walk on water', or 'I can show you how cold fusion is a practical possibility'. By the same token, the verse should not be deployed by well-meaning but ill-informed church leaders who are trying to manipulate church members into doing something they really do not think they should do. 'But Mrs Jones, you can't say "No" to our invitation to teach ten-year-old boys just because you've never taught a Sunday School class before, or just because you feel you have no gifts or calling or interest in this area. After all, Paul teaches us that we can do all things through Christ who gives us strength.'

This is horrible. Paul's 'everything' is constrained by the context. His point is that whatever the circumstances in which he finds himself, whether with the rich and the powerful or with the poor and the powerless, whether preaching with unction to substantial crowds or incarcerated in a filthy prison, he has learned to cast himself on God *and be content*. He can do all these things, *everything* that God assigns him to do, through the one who gives him strength. Let the gospel advance; let God's will be done in me and through me, Paul is saying; I am content, for I can trust the one who invariably strengthens me to do what he assigns me.

It takes the strength and resolution and perspective that only God can provide to live above changing, difficult circumstances. But to live above circumstances, utterly content in Christ Jesus, is to ensure that you will never give up the Christian walk. Resolve to learn the secret of contentment.

Resolve to grow in the grace of Christian gratitude and courtesy (4:14–23)

These closing verses are full of wonderful pastoral touches. However much Paul is content regardless of his circumstances, he is grateful to the Philippians for what they have provided: 'Yet it was good of you to share in my troubles' (4:14), Paul writes. Indeed, they were the only Christians in their area to be quick off the mark in this regard: 'Moreover, as you Philippians know, in the early days of your acquaintance with the gospel, when I set out from Macedonia, not one church shared with me in the matter of giving and receiving, except you only; for even when I was in Thessalonica, you sent me aid again and again when I was in need' (4:15–16). It is helpful to follow Paul's course on a map. Paul left Troas in Asia Minor and crossed over to Europe, landing at the port city of Neapolis and proceeding immediately to Philippi. There he and Silas were beaten up, arrested, and eventually escorted out of town, but not before they planted this fledgling church. Leaving Philippi, Paul quickly passed through Amphipolis and Apollonia and arrived at Thessalonica, where in short order he started another church. So what Paul is saying is that even by the time he got to Thessalonica and began preaching the gospel there, before he left there to evangelize Athens and Corinth, the Philippians were already finding ways to help, and asking for information as to what part they could play in this great ministry. Apparently Paul stayed in Thessalonica only a few weeks, but during that relatively short time the Philippians came through again and again. And for his part, Paul is not slow to express his profound gratitude.

Once again Paul insists that his words do not suggest he is angling for another gift. If he wants anything, he says, 'I am looking for what may be credited to your account' (4:17). In other words, Paul is primarily pleased that the Philippians have been so generous in the work of the gospel, not because he has been the recipient of that generosity, but because by being generous they have been acting like Christians – and God, who is no-one's debtor, will reward them. He is more delighted with the blessings they will experience because they are a giving and generous church than he is with the help that has come his way.

Paul even tries, apparently, to redirect some of their future giving: 'I have received full payment and even more; I am amply supplied, now that I have received from Epaphroditus the gifts you sent' (4:18). In any case, whether the Philippians send such generous gifts to Paul or to someone else, the gifts were first and foremost offered to God: 'They are a fragrant offering, an acceptable sacrifice, pleasing to God' (4:18).

There are important lessons of Christian courtesy here. Examine how Paul thanks believers in his letters; read and re-read the opening 'thanksgiving' sections that mark all but one of his letters. His pattern is to thank *God* for what the *believers* have done or for the signs of spiritual vitality that he detects in them.

This is doubly wise. Contrast the opposed errors into which we easily fall. On the one hand, there are Christian leaders who are so unrestrained in their praise of people it is hard to avoid the conclusion that they control others by extravagant flattery. Of course, in some cases it is nothing more than a quirk of personality. I recall one particular professor who came to our home for a meal. He was famous for his fervent courtesy. In that meal we offered him lasagne or spaghetti and meat sauce – scarcely a high-class evening meal, but something we were going to have with the children that night anyway, and they certainly loved it. The venerable professor went on and on over the wonders of the lasagne: 'Mrs Carson, this is really lovely; this is an extravagantly glorious repast' – or words to that effect. But as this professor was known for his peculiar brand of hyperbolic courtesy, we took it in our stride. It was simply the way he was. But some Christian leaders, one fears, have adopted so generous a stance of praise for others, a stance that is then imitated by others around them, that their churches are no longer Godward. They are nothing but mutual admiration societies.

On the other hand, some Christian leaders, jealous for the glory of God and firmly committed to the belief that if any believer does any good in any way, it is nothing other than the product of what God is doing in them and through them, end up offering very few thanks. They are most begrudging in praise, their tight-lipped reticence their way of avoiding cheap flattery. Besides, they are so frightened of the sins of pride, their own and others', that they avoid the compliments that might turn heads. If you tell a preacher that his sermon was good, they think, he might strut like a peacock all week. If you were helped by the sermon, go home and thank God, but do not corrode the preacher with praise. Do not corrode anyone with praise – deacons, Sunday School teachers, church trustees, caretakers, organists, whatever.

But Paul has the matter right. He does not simply thank people (though he sometimes does that), he thanks God for God's grace in them – but he utters his thanks to God *before* the people. In effect, he approaches these believers and says, 'I greatly rejoice at the grace of

God displayed in your life', or 'I thank God every time I remember you', or 'Your life is a fragrant sacrifice to God, a sacrifice with which God himself is well pleased'. That is precisely what Paul does here. He does acknowledge that it was good of the Philippians to help him (4:14), but he quickly insists that he is more interested in what this says about their character, and about what this will mean in blessings on their lives, than he is about his own enrichment (4:17). In any case, he insists, the gifts were first and foremost 'an acceptable sacrifice, pleasing to God' (4:18). And all of this excites Paul's rejoicing *in the Lord* (4:10), for he recognizes that the marks of grace in the Philippian church can be traced to the Lord Jesus himself. And meanwhile, he reminds the Philippians that, precisely because God is no-one's debtor, they can rely on him to meet *their* needs: 'And my God will meet all your needs according to his glorious riches in Christ Jesus' (4:19).

Even the final verses of this chapter reflect a Christian courtesy. 'Greet all the saints in Christ Jesus. The brothers who are with me send greetings. All the saints send you greetings' (4:21–22) – as if Paul is constantly trying to establish links amongst believers in various places. Then he smiles, enjoying the irony: 'All the saints send you greetings, *especially those who belong to Caesar's household*' (4:22). Paul may be in prison at Caesar's pleasure, but the gospel has penetrated Caesar's household. It is important to remember who is finally in charge, and how he works.

Resolve to grow in the grace of Christian gratitude and courtesy. By now it should be clear that this is not exactly like the gratitude and courtesy commonly associated with good breeding or good training. The categories are different; the values are not merely formal; even the forms are a little different. Christian courtesy, besides being merely courteous, strengthens believers, invites them to turn their thoughts toward God, multiplies the cords that draw them together as the body of Christ. Precisely because it will strengthen your own discipleship and edify your brothers and sisters in Christ, you will be multiplying the resolution of the church never to give up the Christian walk.

You may have noticed that I left out one verse: 'To our God and Father be glory for ever and ever. Amen' (4:20). This is not simply a formula that Paul feels constrained to drop into his text once in a while, without giving the words much thought. Rather, the apostle wants to remind his readers that even at this stage it is possible to pursue all the excellent advice he has provided in this chapter, resolving to be obedient to the apostolic imperatives, and yet somehow prostitute them all. The deciding factor is this: do these believers see that all of Christian discipleship, all of Christian virtue, all of Christian resolution, all of Christian perseverance, must be offered to the glory of God? Or do they think that these virtues are ultimate ends in themselves?

For the sad fact is that there are some Christians who will hear the injunctions of this chapter – resolve to pursue like-mindedness with other true believers, resolve always to rejoice in the Lord, resolve to be known for selflessness, resolve not to be anxious for anything but learn instead to pray, resolve to think holy thoughts, resolve to learn the secret of contentment, resolve to grow in the grace of Christian gratitude and courtesy – and they will treasure these virtues as little gods to be coveted. But that may lead not only to a new round of legalism. Even worse, these goals are simply not worthy of that much energy and commitment *if they are ends in themselves*. But if they are cheerfully and lovingly offered up to God – that makes all the difference. We resolve to pursue these virtues not *only* because they are good, but because God demands them and gives us the grace to live them out. And the result is that he receives glory.

What is clear from this last chapter is that Paul provides more than mere information, however vitally he construes doctrine. The apostle does provide ample information and knowledge, but he also leads his converts into wisdom: teaching them how to live as disciples of the Lord Jesus Christ, teaching them not only how to walk as his followers, but how to persevere in that walk to the very end.

Never give up the Christian walk.

FOUR STUDIES IN ISAIAH
David Jackman

5

Know and trust your God

Isaiah 40

> It is one of the defining marks of our time that God is now
> weightless. I do not mean by this that he is ethereal but
> rather that he has become unimportant. He rests upon the
> world so inconsequentially as not to be noticeable . . . Those
> who assure the pollsters of their belief in God's existence
> may nonetheless consider him less interesting than tele-
> vision, his commands less authoritative than their appetites
> for affluence and influence, his judgment no more awe-
> inspiring than the evening news, and his truth less
> compelling than the advertisers' sweet fog of flattery and
> lies. That is weightlessness.[1]

David Wells's *God in the Wasteland* is one of the most challenging and
stimulating books I have read in years. He argues that we are faced
with a weightless God, not only in our secular culture but also in the
church. And it is so across the entire church spectrum – not least, in
evangelicalism.

Our doctrine of God is impeccable in its expression; we believe in
the transcendence and the sovereignty of God; we ascribe all power
and authority to him; we believe that he is the Creator, King and
Judge; we are orthodox believers. But in our personal lives, in our
families and often in our churches, God is strangely weightless. He is
all but excluded from our reality, and a great gulf has opened up
between our theology and our practice.

Is that not why so much of what passes for contemporary
Christianity is so trivial, and so much of how we express our faith is
little more than playing games? We're happy to sing about God, or to
him. We pray when we have time and our needs are sufficiently
pressing. We read the Bible – at least, our favourite bits of it – to
acquire inspiration. We go to church, if there's nothing more
important to do, and we enjoy meeting together and being stirred.

We run our church committees and we work hard at putting our plans into action. We are sincere, even committed in our way. Yet our horizons often belong to the spiritual nursery. We are content with so little, because we know so little of the real God. And as a result, we are weightless too.

One of the characteristics of young children is that they want to be the centre of their world. They demand to be entertained, they love to be picked up and cuddled, they want what they want and they want it now. That is all part of being a child. But Peter Pan is not a biblical model, and it's tragic when childhood ways persist into adult life. Yet is it not true that a great deal of our contemporary Christianity is content to remain in the nursery? When the going gets tough we pout and throw temper-tantrums with God. We complain about how let down we feel, and reconsider whether we can go on believing in him. And at the start of these studies, I want to say that if we are to grow up spiritually and be a church in our land – a church in which God is at work and through which he can move into our culture – then we need to begin to develop a hunger for God and for spiritual reality that will not be appeased by Christian candy-floss.

The Bible is right when it says that there is nothing new under the sun. Three hundred years ago Cotton Mather, a Puritan pastor in New England, wrote: 'The great design and intention of the office of a Christian preacher is to restore the throne and dominion of God in the souls of men.' That is the office of the preacher, because it is the function of the Bible. The preacher's task is to sit under the authority of God's revelation, and then explain and apply it first to himself and then to the people; not as a clever performer or entertaining personality, but as the channel of God's Word of truth. For where the Bible is taught and believed, God's voice is surely heard. And in the church we need above all else to hear that voice in our generation, telling us what we would never otherwise be able to know.

Evangelical Christianity is a body of revealed truth. It is the word of the living God: given in history, but true in all times, in all places, for all people. Evangelical Christianity is not a long quest inside to find some sort of experience and meaning to authenticate us as people. Only as we hear the word of God coming from outside ourselves to judge, challenge, direct and encourage us are we able to live lives that really count for him in the world. Only then are we judged and changed and brought to know this living God for himself.

That is why we are studying Isaiah. There is no more magnificent mountain-range in the whole Old Testament addressing the glory and grandeur of God than the second half of Isaiah's prophecy: it is life-changing material. But these majestic chapters were directed to a situation uncomfortably parallel to our own.

The people of God were at the end of an era and facing the judgment of God. They were moving inexorably towards the time when God would give Jerusalem and the whole kingdom of Judah into the hands of the Babylonians, and all the flower of the nation would be taken off into exile. The first 38 chapters lead us through many prophecies of God's righteous wrath and judgment to that great assertion in 39:5–7.

> Hear the word of the LORD Almighty: The time will surely come when everything in your palace, and all that your fathers have stored up until this day, will be carried off to Babylon. Nothing will be left, says the LORD. And some of your descendants, your own flesh and blood who will be born to you, will be taken away, and they will become eunuchs in the palace of the king of Babylon.

The northern kingdom of Israel was conquered by the Assyrians during Isaiah's ministry and its people dispersed among the nations. Isaiah's message is that a similar fate is prophesied for Judah, the southern kingdom, and for David's line.

How was it possible? They hadn't given up believing in the Lord. The sacrifices were still offered in Jerusalem. The temple was crowded with worshippers; they had marvellous celebration experiences. Orthodoxy was alive and well. But God had become weightless. Kings like Ahaz and to a lesser extent Hezekiah had decided to put their trust in political alliances with the pagan powers of the day rather than rely on the Lord to defend them. So the people were given over to materialism and self-indulgence. The rich got richer. The disadvantaged were ruthlessly exploited. And when it came to the crunch between God's word and their desires, God was weightless.

God said some very startling things to these orthodox people. You can read them in Isaiah 1:11–14. They thought that they were being orthodox, they were going through the motions. They were doing what the law required. But God said: 'It's an offence, it's an anathema to me.'

Scripture doesn't fall like a block out of heaven; it belongs to a context. The passages we shall be looking at belong to a book that is teaching a message. If we do not go back to that context and correctly understand what Isaiah's message meant to those who originally heard it, we shall have very little chance of correctly understanding what it means for us today.

Our perspectives are very distorted. We live in a world that pressurizes us all the time. The noise of the media and the values of the world around us are constantly filling our minds. We need to renew our perspective; but coming into a book like this, written in the eighth century before Christ, we need to see why it's here in order to identify properly with it. If we get the perspective wrong, every-thing will be wrong.

Do you remember the story of the Texan farmer whose great-grandfather was a crofter in Scotland? After the family emigrated they became very prosperous. One day the farmer decided to visit the place of his origins, went to Scotland and eventually found the croft in which his family had lived. He marvelled to the Scottish farmer who then lived there: 'Everything's so small here. I can drive round your little farm in a couple of minutes, but at my ranch in Texas it sometimes takes me half an hour to drive from the freeway to my ranch-house.'

The farmer nodded and replied, 'I know what you mean. I used to have a car like that, too . . .'

If your perspective is wrong you misunderstand everything. And that is true when we read Isaiah. We must understand that the book was written not because the people of God had denied him outwardly, but because they had simply accommodated him. They had the outward performance of religion but not the heart. That's why God had become weightless to them. And as we explore Isaiah 40 – 66 (twenty-seven chapters which many commentators suggest are the same in scope as the twenty-seven books of the New Testament), we shall find that God through Isaiah is calling us back to a position where we trust him, put our faith in him, start to believe his promises, believe that he will justify us by faith not by works, and concentrate on our great need of his deliverance and salvation.

We begin in chapter 40 with the voice crying in the wilderness, just as the New Testament begins with John the Baptist, the voice preparing the way for the Lord. And we shall end our studies with chapters 65 and 66, just as the New Testament ends in Revelation 21 and 22 with the vision of the new heaven and the new earth in which righteousness dwells. In between, at the mid-point of the second half of Isaiah, we shall study in chapter 53 the drama of the suffering servant – an amazingly detailed prophecy of Christ's death on the cross, centuries before crucifixion was invented.

Running through chapters 40, 49, 53 and 65 we shall find this great Isaiah theme: that encountering the real God, being in the right with him, is possible only through God's grace and by faith. But the mark of genuine faith is obedience, it is building our lives in daily, detailed discipline as we follow God's word. Knowing God has to do with trusting and obeying. By these alone do we give God the glory, the weight, that is his by right.

Introduction

Chapter 40 marks a shift of focus from judgment to salvation. The prophet has announced that the people are to be taken to Babylon, but now he looks beyond the exile and the immediate judgment of God, to the restoration and the new beginnings that are at the heart of these chapters. He has one great theological purpose. For his own generation, he wants to engender a living faith and trust in the Lord. He wants these people to know that God has plans and purposes that will come to fruition, and for future generations he wants to assure them of God's unchanging commitment to his covenant promises, so that whether they are in Judah or in Babylon, they will learn to trust and obey him. God will fulfil his promises to Abraham that through him all the nations of the earth will be blessed. He will preserve the line of David, and from the 'stump of Jesse' will come the eternal king on whose shoulders the government will rest for ever and ever.

So the prophecy is designed to encourage the reader in every generation to present obedience and to future hope. Babylon is not the last word; God is not weightless; he has eternal purposes of grace to fulfil and nothing, not even his own people's unfaithfulness, will stop him from fulfilling them.

Verses 1–11 are a resounding message of comfort – 'This is what God will do.' But they are addressed to people who are only too aware of the gap that exists between the future promises and the present reality. So the chapter is also designed to bridge that gap between where we are now and where we shall be ultimately, by cultivating an active faith in God so that we live in the 'now' in the light of the 'not yet'.

As Isaiah preaches this message about God's utter dependability, he encounters two objections, or barriers to faith, which he envisages his audience raising. He answers them in verses 12–31. Does God really have the power to do what verses 1–11 promise? And does God really have the will to do it?

They are questions we face as Christians every day. There isn't a pastor or church leader who doesn't sometimes look out at the hardness of the soil and the comparatively small inroads of the gospel even in growing churches, and sometimes find himself saying: 'If this gospel is true, why does it make so little impact? Has

God lost interest in us? Have the twentieth-century idols rendered him impotent? Does he have the power? Does he have the will?'

And there isn't a Christian struggling with the world, the flesh and the devil (a struggle which the New Testament regards as the normal Christian life) who doesn't ask sometimes: 'Why doesn't God intervene? Is he powerless? Does he not care?'

Isaiah 40 is not about theoretical academic issues. It poses questions which, if unanswered, leave us with a God who is weightless.

God's message of comfort (verses 1–11)

What do you think of when you hear the word 'comfort'? For many of us it's the name of a fabric softener; for others it evokes sitting by the fire with a nice warm cup of cocoa on a dark stormy night. Both of those connotations can be somewhat self-indulgent. But actually the word has to do with strengthening.

Literally, the word translated 'comfort' means 'to cause to breathe again', 'to breathe life back into'. ' "*Strengthen* my people," says your God.' One section of the Bayeux Tapestry shows obviously confused and frightened soldiers running from the enemy. In the next section the same soldiers are shown back in rank, being marched into the battle to take up the fight again. The reason can be seen behind them: a mitred bishop who is holding a spear with which he's prodding the rear of the last soldier in the line. The caption reads: 'The bishop comforts his soldiers.'

This is the comfort in which Isaiah is interested. It's not a matter of supplying a cup of cocoa by the fire, but of getting you back into the battle. It's a matter of strengthening, of equipping for the fight, of breathing new life into God's people.

The doubled verb, 'Comfort, comfort', indicates intensity and urgency. The prophet is called to be the agent of this strengthening through the word that he speaks, which is God's. It's a present-tense verb. We will find strength when we listen to the word of God and obey it. That's his plan to strengthen us. The strength doesn't come from anyone other than God, and it comes through the word that he's given, applied to us by the Spirit who lives within us.

Those are God's means for making you strong: word and Spirit. In a sense, the next twenty-seven chapters are the content of this comfort. The prophet sets before them the full extent of their tragic situation and calls them to hope in God alone.

Here are words to be spoken 'tenderly' (literally 'to the heart'). They're words that are true for all the people of God, even though the city of Jerusalem will lie in ruins, even though many will be away in exile. Nevertheless, says Isaiah: looking behind and beyond that, there is good news. 'Proclaim' to Jerusalem that the judgment is over ('her hard service has been completed'), and that the Babylonian exile is ending ('her sin has been paid for . . . she has received from the LORD's hand double for all her sins'). The punishment is sufficient. The word 'double' here raises problems for some people. It doesn't mean that God has unfairly given a double quantity. It is more the concept of an exact match. If you fold a rectangular sheet of paper double, one side matches the other side exactly. So when the Lord has punished Judah for her sins it is that kind of 'doubling' – the punishment has fitted the crime exactly. It is sufficient.

We shall see later on in these chapters just what that means in the ministry of the suffering servant. But the comfort is God stepping into history. Just as he is the author of judgment so only he can be the author of salvation and that's precisely what he's going to do. He tells us in the next three paragraphs that he's going to do it in three spectacular ways.

What then is the nature of the comfort that God is giving? There are three voices in the next three paragraphs, each giving a different aspect.

God will reveal his glory (verses 3–5)

Here is the first voice that speaks. It declares massive roadworks in the desert.

Imagine some of the news films that were seen during the Gulf War, of the middle eastern wilderness – rough desert terrain with no major roads. Today we have sophisticated vehicles that can travel over such terrain at great speed. But in the eighth century BC, rapid movement across the desert would have been impossible. How is God going to bring his people back from Babylon? Isaiah says that is no problem to the sovereign Lord. He is well able to construct a motorway across the desert. He will construct whatever earthworks are required (verse 4), for the God who comforts his people does so not from a distance but by coming to them.

He will send his messenger ahead of him in the desert – 'Prepare the way for the LORD' – but God doesn't send his blessing, he brings it. He is coming to his people. Nothing will stand in his way, and when he comes he reveals his glory (verse 5). What is glory? Its root meaning is 'heaviness'. It means 'weightiness' – the exact opposite of what we started with. It is the essential being and character of God, the very 'Godness' of God. And God coming to rescue his people and to bring them back to Jerusalem will be such a demonstration of his character that all the world will witness it.

The paragraph that begins with a human voice crying out in the desert ends 'the mouth of the LORD has spoken' (verse 5). The language is very reminiscent of Exodus: God is coming down to deliver his people. Clearly we are seeing here the end of the exile. That will herald a second exodus, a new work of God on an even greater scale than ever before.

So when was this prophecy fulfilled? We know that when Cyrus the Mede conquered the Babylonian Empire he issued an edict permitting the Jews to return to their land, but that was only a very partial fulfilment. The exile really ended, and the new revelation of glory really appeared, when the voice of John the Baptist was heard in the Judean wilderness preparing the way of the Lord by preaching the gospel of repentance. It was when the Lord Jesus came into Galilee preaching the kingdom, having been baptized by John in the Jordan and having had his own identity and ministry affirmed by the voice from heaven: 'This is my Son whom I love. With him I am well pleased.' It was then that John could say in his gospel, 'We saw the glory of the One and Only who came from the Father, full of grace and truth.'

We must always read the Old Testament through our New Testament spectacles, because we know that Christ is the key to all the Scriptures and that we are the recipients of Isaiah's comfort through the gospel of Christ. We see the grace and glory of God revealed in the face of Jesus Christ. God couldn't speak to us more completely and satisfyingly than he has done in the Word made flesh. That is the first great message of comfort: God will reveal his glory, and he has done it in the Lord Jesus.

God will keep his word (verses 6–8)

If you look carefully at the text you will see a link between these two sections: the phrase at the end of verse 5 and the beginning of verse 6, 'all men' or 'all mankind'.

We all need to see God's glory (verse 5) because (verse 6) we are all like grass. We have no permanent glory of our own, nothing more permanent than the flowers of the field. It is a message that our world needs to hear. George Bernard Shaw once said, 'Death is the ultimate statistic; one in one person dies.' However great it may seem, human glory is passing and is nothing alongside the glory of God. During Isaiah's ministry Jerusalem was besieged by the armies of Sennacherib, the Assyrian. But we read in Isaiah 37 that when God breathed on them, 185,000 died in a single night.

We need the message of verse 6. It's a great corrective to arrogance and triumphalism. No-one can withstand the power of God, but by contrast God's word is eternal. And verse 5, 'For the mouth of the Lord has spoken' and verse 8, the word of our God stands for ever', are our guarantee.

Characteristically, the Old Testament links the breath of the Lord which blows in judgment (verse 7) with the word of the Lord which speaks the mind of God (verse 8). Psalm 33:6 likewise links the word and the breath of God as the same reality:

> By the word of the LORD were the heavens made,
> their starry host by the breath of his mouth.

As I speak at Word Alive my words come to you on the breath of my mouth. If the breath stops the words will stop. God's word is breathed out by his Spirit, his *ruach* – a word which means breath or wind or spirit.

Scripture is the breathing out of God in his word. It reveals his mind and his will. As I speak, things are happening in my mind which my breath carries in words to your mind. Consequently things are happening in your mind too. Someone has said that a lecture is the process by which information is transferred from the lecturer's notes to the students' notes without passing through the mind of either. But sermons are not like that. Our minds are actively involved. As the word comes to us, our minds take it in.

As God speaks his mind through his Spirit on his breath, that word stands for ever – because unlike us, God is eternal; unlike us, God is never changing; and the word of God is the will of God expressed. It is the word that creates, that rescues, that rules, that judges; and it's all done by the Spirit – the Breath – who takes the word and executes the will of God.

That's why we need to give time to Scripture. It is the 'now' word of God. It is the 'for ever' word of God. It is the only fixed point of unchanging certainty in our uncertain and transitory lives. If there is a weightlessness of God in the current Christian church, it is directly related to a famine of the word of God in the pulpits. For faith comes by hearing and hearing by the word of God. Nothing can take its place, however clever and up to date it may be. Many things will try to do so. But if Sunday teaching is reduced to ten or fifteen minutes in our churches, and if the habit of daily Bible reading is gradually eroded, then there is no doubt – and no wonder! – that God will be weightless, and that the urgent word of the world around us will drown out the voice of God.

But God will keep his word. The grass withers and the flowers fall and the best-laid plans of men will come to nothing, but the word of our God stands for ever. So invest time in eternity by studying your Bible. It's a great comfort. Nothing is going to change this word. He's not going to go back on one sentence of it.

God will shepherd his flock (verses 9–11)

Verse 9 is full of excitement. What is it that the watchmen see, the news that is shouted from hilltop to hilltop?

A great procession is coming back from Babylon. The Lord is storming across the desert bringing his people home to Jerusalem. 'Lift up your voice with a shout . . . say to the towns of Judah, "Here is your God!"'

So the content of the message is God himself. But who is this God? Look at the very significant verses 10 and 11. This God is both sovereign and shepherd. Verse 10 speaks about his sovereign rule as king. It is all about ultimate power: 'The Sovereign LORD comes with power . . . his arm rules for him.' He comes with his sleeves rolled up, we might say. He means business. God is coming to rule, to exercise his sovereign will and complete his purposes in the world. He will bring his liberated people out of Babylon as the fruit of that victory. And when Jesus came to fulfil the prophecy, he too accomplished the sovereign purposes of God by bringing us out of the darkness of sin into the light of the glorious gospel. It is the power of God that remakes the people of God.

But now look at the lovely blend in verse 11. The arm that rules is at the same time gathering the lambs. He feeds his flock; he protects his people. We are shown a shepherd whose detailed care is exactly tuned to the individual needs of every member of his flock; and the limitless power of his sovereignty is exercised in the limitless love of his shepherding. That is our God! The one who powers his way through the trackless desert gently leads the pregnant or nursing ewes in his flock. For as the New Testament will show us, he is the Good Shepherd who lays down his life for the sheep. He is as committed to us as that. And that is our comfort.

These are great things to know, aren't they? And surely they should be sufficient for us. And yet there is within us something that finds it very hard to accept them. We say things like, 'It's all very well for a preacher to say that – it's all very well for the Bible to say that – but you don't know my difficulties, you don't know what I'm up against. And just *saying* these things are so doesn't necessarily *mean* that they're so, does it?'

And indeed, saying something doesn't necessarily make that thing true. In the early days of this century two boy princes, the then Prince

of Wales and Duke of York, lived in Buckingham Palace. There's a
story that one day they escaped from the palace into St James's Park
to play football. Ball games were forbidden in the Royal Parks but
they managed to find a third boy to play with them. While they were
playing, a policeman arrived and demanded their names and
addresses, warning them that their parents would have to be told.
Turning to the first little boy he said, 'And what's your name,
sonny?'

'Please sir, the Prince of Wales.'

The policeman swallowed nervously but continued. 'And where
do you live?'

'At Buckingham Palace.'

Somewhat nonplussed, the policeman wrote it all down in his
notebook and went through the same procedure for the Duke of York.

The third little boy was watching open-mouthed, thinking, 'Well!
If they can get away with it, I'll have a go myself!'

And when the policeman turned to him expectantly, notebook
poised, the little boy announced defiantly, 'Please sir, I'm the
Archbishop of Canterbury.'

Saying so doesn't make it so. We sometimes treat the Bible rather
like that. It shows how sinful we are. But Scripture is so realistic and
so down to earth! And here it begins to dialogue with us. It is as if in
verse 12 God is saying, 'I know you're going to find that hard to
believe, and you want all sorts of small-print excuses to get out of
really trusting me. But I want to deal with your problem.'

So let us as we conclude look at the two questions we have already
identified.

Does God really have the power? (verses 12–26)

Will God really deliver us? Can he really bring about this great
salvation? Am I sure that he's going to be able to take me home to
heaven?

Isaiah answers this question by picking up the theme of
sovereignty from verse 10. Just think of it in human terms, he says.

God is beyond all measure (verses 12–17)

What can you measure in the hollow of your hand? Just a few drops
of water. What can you measure with the span of your hand? Just a
few inches. What can you carry in your basket? A few things you
might buy at the supermarket. What do you weigh on the scales?
Maybe a little flour or other ingredient for cooking.

Now think about God. What's in the hollow of his hand? The
oceans of the world. What does he measure off with a span? The

heavens themselves. What will you find in God's basket? The dust of the earth. What does he weigh on his scales? The mountains and the hills. You can understand it even if you're four years old. This is our God! He's got the whole world in his hands. And so he's beyond all measure.

In verse 13 Isaiah explains that God didn't need to form a committee to invent the world. When he was creating everything he didn't say, 'Now, who can I get to help me out with this? Who is a good person to have on the committee?' Of course not. He is God, and we are grass. So don't compare God with yourself or anybody else.

Verse 15, 17: 'The nations are like a drop in a bucket . . . Before him all the nations are as nothing.' That doesn't mean that he doesn't care for the nations that he has made. It means that in comparison with him – put alongside him, as verse 17 suggests – they are actually worthless. They are a negative quantity. They are less than nothing.

That is the perspective that we must have if we are to live godly lives. We must never reckon on any human factors as conditioning God's plans or purposes. In God's equations, even the most powerful human agencies are a minus quantity. That's why verse 16 reminds us that nothing that God has made could ever be sufficient for him. Even if you took the whole of the forests of Lebanon and all the animals as one huge sacrifice, says Isaiah, they could not make atonement. The Creator is never dependent on what his people can provide. We are dependent, utterly, on him.

Do you see what that perspective does to any fears that the gods of Babylon may be stronger than the Lord? Do you see how it stops us putting our trust in twentieth-century Christian technology, and casts us back on God's power alone? So often he is weightless, and we put confidence in ourselves. I've sat around a table at committee meetings where we have said, 'A little more money . . . a little more media exposure . . . a few more training courses and know-how . . . a few more improved techniques and methods . . . Give us the technology, and Lord, we'll get the job done for you!' And God leaves us to ourselves, because our machinery has steam-rollered him out of sight. God doesn't need our enlightenment. He is beyond all measure. And that leads logically to Isaiah's next point.

God is beyond all comparison (verses 18–24)

Just as nature abhors a vacuum, so if we do not have the weight of the living God at the centre of our lives we shall have all sorts of idols taking his place.

The contrast with the preceding section is as plain as is the folly of idolatry. God has made everything, including human beings, but then humankind makes its idols in order to send the living God into exile. So for Isaiah the worship of foreign gods is one of the clearest marks of Israel's sin. But God knows that when the blow of the exile falls, it will be fatally easy for the people to give into the syncretism of Babylon. So he begins to strengthen their faith. He says, 'Why do you allow anything or anybody else to take the place of God?'

Verses 19 and 20: Isaiah knows the sort of junk mail that's going to drop through the Babylonian letterboxes. He knows that when they get into exile the people will be told that the gods of Babylon are much stronger than Yahweh, and he knows that God's people then and God's people now are going to be diverted by idolatry. They're going to wake up one morning and read a letter:

> We're so glad you've come to reside in Babylon: and of all the families in Marduk Avenue, Babylon, you have been chosen to receive this very special offer. We want you to be the envy of your neighbours and friends. We can now offer you the latest craftsman-cast idol, overlaid with gold to the finest design and equipped with silver chains to prevent theft or accidental slippage. We're sure that you will want to establish your own garden shrine in Babylon and it's therefore very important that you should take this offer to heart. If you are looking for an economy model with your growing family to consider, we can guarantee our non-rot wooden model with its unique non-topple fixtures specially designed to avoid the embarrassment of finding that your god has fallen flat on its face.

And you put *that* in the place of the living God? You get what you pay for; the value of the god depends entirely on what you, the devotee, can afford. But it's nothing but wood and metal and human artifice.

That attitude is still with us. The hushed voice on the BBC2 documentary telling us solemnly about some pagan shrine as though it were describing a reality . . . We all know how easily we drift into the idol business. There are plenty of idols, plenty of shrines in our hearts. But – do you not know? Have you not heard? He is beyond all comparison.

Verse 22: 'He sits enthroned above the circle of the earth, and its people are like grasshoppers. He stretches out the heavens like a canopy, and spreads them out like a tent to live in.' One commentator points out that grasshoppers are squeaky little creatures that jump up and down. That is rather like us, and as God looks down on the world he sees us like that. But he has stretched out the heavens. He is the one who 'brings princes to naught and reduces the rulers . . . to nothing' (verse 23). Here they are in their great glory – but they're the grass of the field. No sooner are they planted and taking root than he breathes on them, he blows on them. The breath – the wind of God – blows, and they wither and are swept away like chaff before a whirlwind.

God is beyond all rivals (verses 25–26)

God is beyond comparison – for he can have no equal. Who will you compare me with? Go out and look up at the night's skies, says Isaiah. Ask yourself, who made all these? That starry host is there for us to see every night because God has created it. In Babylon they worshipped the stars, but Isaiah says: look beyond the creation to the creator. You don't have to worship the astral deities of Babylon. You do have to recognize that your God made them all, and that they're there only because he sustains everything with his power and calls them each by name. He's the sovereign Lord who has all the stars on parade. He's the shepherd Lord who looks after them all as though they're members of his flock. Because of his great power and mighty strength not one of them is missing.

Does God have the power? Oh, yes! He has the power.

Does God really have the will? (verses 27–31)

If the Lord knows every item in his creation, how can he forget his people?

Verse 27 is a very searching verse. 'Why do you say, O Jacob, and complain, O Israel, "My way is hidden from the LORD; my cause is disregarded by my God"?' The capital letters in the English Bible always mean the covenant name of God, Yahweh or Jehovah. He's committed to unbreakable promises. So when you see the capital letters, remember that God makes and keeps his promises.

The complaint of verse 27 is wrong on two counts: theology and experience. The theology is stated in verse 28, and the experience in verses 29–31: 'He gives strength to the weary and increases the power of the weak.' So the most foolish thing we can do is judge by what we can see, which is so limited. Now we're reminded that the sovereign God is also the shepherd God, and all that his power offers is made available through his covenant grace to his needy people.

That is the goal of God's comfort. At the end of the chapter we see the reason for all that has gone before. What does God want us to take away with us as we finish this study? He wants us to go away as weary, weak people to whom he has given strength and in whom he has increased his power. He does not want to make us into self-reliant people, who somehow think that because we've been to Word Alive we've got enough on board to go on for the next three months with no need to be in daily contact with God. The only position of power and of strength is to know that we are weary and weak and utterly dependent upon him.

And he will see to it that we learn in countless ways that we are like grass, but that his word endures for ever. He will see that we learn that if we will come to him with our weariness and our weakness, our failure and our inability, he – the mighty Creator God who reveals his glory and keeps his word and brings salvation to his people – is the one who will give us strength.

Hence verse 30 contrasts human strength with God's strength. Think of the strongest human beings, young men in peak condition, the élite marine corps, if you like, from the Judah army. Or in our own day, think of the young people who are the Olympic athletes, the gold-medal prospects for their country. Well, the strength of such men and women is finite. It is impressive for a while, but it is in decline. Only God has limitless strength and he shares it – with whom? Verse 31: 'Those who hope in the LORD'. It's the weary and the weak who prevail, because their strength is not human but divine.

So don't judge by what you see or feel; judge by the word of the living God. Those who put their faith in him, who 'hope in the Lord', will soar on wings like eagles. They will run and keep on running. That's against all human considerations, but it's the divine provision. They will 'walk and not be faint'.

This is the healthy biblical realism that knows that we need never be knocked out of the battle. We need never give up. God's word is dependable and his character is behind it and his Spirit is at work through it. And all that is available, to those who 'hope in the Lord'. The verb means both to wait for him and to trust restfully in him.

That's what he is calling us to do. And if we make time to do that while we are here at Word Alive, and if we will do it throughout the rest of our lives, then we shall know this God in a fuller and richer way than we had ever imagined possible. We shall be able to say: 'Here is our God, the sovereign Lord with power, the shepherd Lord who cares. Our cause is not disregarded, our way is not hidden. He has come to us in Jesus, and through faith in him we too will soar like eagles, we too will run and not grow weary, we too will walk and not be faint, and in our generation the church and the world will begin to see the reality of the glory, the weight, of our God.'

6

The servant solution

Isaiah 49

Do you know the experience of walking along a range of hills, with two or three peaks ahead of you? As you walk along they seem quite near; you begin to think you'll reach the third one by lunchtime. But when you get to the first summit you see a wide and deep valley that you hadn't anticipated, between you and the second peak. You begin to revise your time estimate; it's going to take a bit longer than you expected. And when you find the same thing at the second peak, then of course the third peak is also going to take much longer than you thought and you're not going to make it by lunchtime.

Studying Old Testament prophecy is rather like that; you see stretching out before you hill after hill, peak after peak of fulfilment. It's comparatively easy to see what Isaiah's message meant to his eighth-century-BC hearers in Jerusalem, as he told them about the exile that was coming at the hands of the Babylonians and the new exodus that God would bring about through his agent Cyrus. Cyrus is the Medo-Persian conqueror of Babylon named at the end of Isaiah 44 and the beginning of Isaiah 45. Look back in 44:28 – Cyrus 'is my shepherd and will accomplish all that I please; he will say of Jerusalem, "Let it be rebuilt," and of the temple, "Let its foundations be laid."' Then in 45:1, 'This is what the LORD says to his anointed, to Cyrus, whose right hand I take hold of to subdue nations before him and to strip kings of their armour . . .' And again in verse 13, 'I will raise up Cyrus in my righteousness: I will make all his ways straight. He will rebuild my city and set my exiles free . . .'

So the prophecies we're looking at about restoration are fulfilled at the first level through Cyrus. He comes and conquers the Babylonians, he liberates the Jewish people to return to their homeland. And as those exiles came back across the desert to Jerusalem in 538 BC, you can imagine how high their expectations were. This was to be the new beginning that Isaiah had prophesied and that Jeremiah and Ezekiel had also spoken of. This was the fulfilment of Isaiah's vision of a glorious new Jerusalem, to which the Gentile nations would come flocking to learn the law of the Lord.

But it didn't quite work out that way. Only a comparatively small remnant returned from Babylon, and they took a hundred years to finish rebuilding the temple and the city walls, eventually under Nehemiah: three generations, before the city was really secure. And through those generations and afterwards they faced one round of invaders and conquerors after another. Could this have been what Isaiah prophesied? In a small part, yes. But it's only like the first hill of fulfilment. There was a very wide valley between that first hill and the second level of fulfilment when the exile really ended, as we saw in yesterday's study; when Jesus came into Galilee proclaiming: 'The time has come, the kingdom of God is at hand, repent and believe the good news; the fulfilment is here' (*cf.* Mk. 1:15). That is level 2, and that's where the greater fulfilment begins.

But beyond the second hill, as Christian believers looking back at all that the Lord Jesus has done in order to gather a new-covenant people to himself, we realize that wonderful though the blessings of the gospel are, there is a third peak that is still ahead of us, an even more glorious future fulfilment that is not yet ours, but which awaits us in the heavenly city.

We must always keep these three different horizons before us when we study a chapter like Isaiah 49. The first level: what it meant to his generation and the generations immediately following. The second level: its fulfilment in Christ. And for us, the third and ultimate level of its fulfilment in the everlasting kingdom, when Jesus is revealed as sovereign King of kings.

It's important to keep them in mind, because the servant at whom we're going to look in this study is not a political figure. We might expect that if God is going to restore his people to the land, the servant's work would deal with the returned community with its needs, hopes and fears. But clearly, although it's described to us in terms of going back to Jerusalem and repopulating the land and rebuilding its cities, the servant's ministry is not a geographical, or a political, or a spiritual one – which suggests that what Isaiah 49 and the other great prophecies are talking about is not primarily release from Babylon, but release from all that Babylon stands for in terms of opposition to God, into the freedom of living under God's truth. The pilgrimage that God is calling his people to follow is not just a pilgrimage of the feet from Babylon to Jerusalem, but a pilgrimage of the mind and heart as the church of Jesus Christ moves through this world to the ultimate realities of heaven.

Background

The chapters between Isaiah 40 and Isaiah 49 are full of questions and problems which we do not have time to explore in depth here.

Let me try to sum matters up by taking you to two representative verses which both come at the end of chapters.

First, 41:29. In this chapter the whole world has been called before the bar of God's justice on a charge of idolatry. In our first study we saw Isaiah making fun of idols that couldn't stand up for themselves. Now God calls out to the idolatrous world and to his idolatrous people, Judah, that there is no hope in these idols and the world is left trembling before God's righteous judgment. The last verse of chapter 41 sums it all up: 'See, they [both the idols and the idol-worshippers] are all false! Their deeds amount to nothing; their images [idols] are but wind and confusion.' The whole world is guilty before God's throne.

What is God going to do with that world? 42:1: 'Here is my servant, whom I uphold . . .' The answer to a guilty world is the Lord's servant, and this servant (chapter 42 tells us, in the first of four poems about him) is a servant who will bring justice to the nations. 'He will bring justice to the nations' (42:1); 'In faithfulness he will bring forth justice; he will not falter or be discouraged till he establishes justice on earth' (verses 3–4).

'Justice' is not here so much a legal word as one suggesting the king calling out his mind, expressing his decisions. The nearest equivalent we have is probably the idea of the referee or the umpire, who says what is a foul and what must be punished. He shows the yellow card or the red card, he calls out the decisions. That is the way in which the servant is going to reveal God's will and show God's ways to the Gentiles.

The title 'servant' has been used of God's covenant people Israel elsewhere in the Old Testament, but Israel is now disqualified from this role, for she has given herself over to idolatry and is blind and deaf: 'Who is blind but my servant, and deaf like the messenger I send? Who is blind like the one committed to me, blind like the servant of the LORD?' (42:19). So the situation is that Israel is disqualified by her spiritual blindness and deafness, but God is going to raise up a servant who will declare his mind to the nations, a servant who will bring justice to the earth.

At the end of chapter 48 the same thought is echoed, because in that chapter God has pronounced his verdict on Babylon. He has called on his people to get ready to leave (48:20), because – again, God's verdict – '"There is no peace," says the LORD, "for the wicked"' (48:22). That is God's verdict on wicked Babylon and on unfaithful Judah.

What is the answer? It is this: 'You are my servant, Israel, in whom I will display my splendour' (49:3). The answer to the problems of the world, a world out of touch with God and consequently out of joint, is the ministry of this servant whom God calls Israel, whom he will equip, defend and use to bring about this new work of salvation, the establishment of the new covenant and the fulfilment of all his promises.

The identity of the servant

But the question that occupies our mind is: who can this servant be? If Israel is blind and deaf, who is going to be God's agent to touch a guilty world with love?

Our passage begins with the second introduction of this character called 'my servant'. There are four poems about the servant in Isaiah, and here we look at the second.

Written in the first person singular, the poem imagines the servant addressing the whole world: 'Listen to me, you islands; hear this, you distant nations' (49:1). Hebrew thinking takes one extreme end of a spectrum and the other extreme, and implies that between the two is included everything else. So when the Bible says, 'as far as the east is from the west . . . [God] has removed our transgressions from us' (Ps. 103:12), it means there is nowhere in between where our transgressions can be found. It takes either extreme to express totality. As far as the heavens are above the earth, so far are his thoughts above our thoughts (cf. Is. 55:9). Everything in between is included when you've mentioned either end of the spectrum. If you call on the islands and the distant nations, the Hebrew mind thinks of the totality of the world. Thus 49:1 summons the remotest parts of the earth to listen to what the servant is going to say.

Much of what Isaiah says must have been very dark and mysterious to his contemporaries. But as we stand beyond that second hill, looking back at the fulfilment of all this in the Lord Jesus, we can see it in the perspective of the universal spread of the gospel. Wearing our New Testament spectacles we know that Jesus is the servant, because that is the title he is given repeatedly in the New Testament, and the New Testament always controls our interpretation of the Old Testament.

Turn to Acts 3 and 4, where we find the early church continually referring to Jesus as the servant. 'The God of Abraham, Isaac and Jacob, the God of our fathers, has glorified his servant Jesus. You handed him over to be killed, and you disowned him before Pilate . . . You disowned the Holy and Righteous One . . .' (Acts 3:13). Yes, but he is God's servant. And because Peter is speaking to Jews in the temple, they know that the theme of the servant is a dominant note of expectation as they look forward to what God is going to do in the future. Peter says the servant is Jesus: 'When God raised up his servant, he sent him first to you to bless you by turning each of you from your wicked ways' (Acts 3:26).

Turn the page to chapter 4. On their release Peter and John go back to their people and they're praying to the Lord. 'Indeed Herod and Pontius Pilate met together with the Gentiles and the people of Israel in this city to conspire against your holy servant Jesus, whom you anointed' (4:27). And verse 30, 'Stretch out your hand to heal and perform miraculous signs and wonders through the name of your holy servant Jesus.' So the apostles, inspired by the Spirit, have no doubt who the servant is. We are looking in Isaiah at prophecies about the Lord Jesus. One further reference in Acts makes it abundantly plain. In Acts 13 Paul is preaching the gospel in the Gentile city of Pisidian Antioch, and he makes exactly the same declaration: 'We tell you the good news: What God promised our fathers he has fulfilled for us, their children, by raising up Jesus' (13:32), and verse 38–39, 'Therefore, my brothers, I want you to know that through Jesus the forgiveness of sins is proclaimed to you. Through him everyone who believes is justified from everything you could not be justified from by the law of Moses.' Then in verse 47 he says: 'This is what the Lord has commanded us: "I have made you a light for the Gentiles, that you may bring salvation to the ends of the earth."' And this is a quotation from our passage: Isaiah 49:6.

So Paul and Barnabas have no doubt that chapter 49 of Isaiah refers to the Lord Jesus. And as we take that apostolic key, we're able to unlock its meaning for us as twentieth-century Christians.

Thus what we have in Isaiah 49 is a unique prophetic insight into the mind and purpose of God, centuries before Christ came into the world. You might ask yourself, as many have asked: why would God provide that? What's the point of prophecy?

The purpose of prophecy

The answer, all through Isaiah, is to show that he is the one living and true God. No-one else can predict and perform as God does. He alone is able to make and keep his promises. All the gods of the nations, all the idols of unfaithful Judah, are but wind and confusion; but God speaks, and what God says he does.

Why is that important for us? There are two reasons.

First, *to assure us that the gospel is not 'Plan B'*. God is not saying, 'Well – I really wanted to have my people the Jews, but because they failed me I'll go to the Gentiles as a second resort.' Prophecy assures us that running as a great and glorious purpose, like a golden thread through all the centuries of human history, is the purpose of God to

117

gather a people for himself from every tribe and kindred and nation. We need to know that. That is the great desire in God's heart, it's the great motivation for mission.

But secondly, prophecy is given to us, as we look forward to the third hill of fulfilment and the heavenly fulfilment to what is not yet ours, *so that our faith will be strong because we believe that he is going to complete the work that he's begun, and we take encouragement from seeing what he's already done.* So we can say, 'Well then; he is going to fulfil that purpose too, and we shall be with him in glory.'

So when Paul wrote that 'everything that was written in the past was written to teach us, so that through endurance and the encouragement of Scripture we might have hope' (Rom. 15:4), he was talking about the Old Testament. Do you want to be an enduring, strengthened Christian? Do you want to be a hopeful Christian? Read the Old Testament. Study it. See God at work and say, this God is our God and he is going to bring all his purposes to a marvellous conclusion.

Now although we must be careful not to constrain Scripture to our preconceived patterns, it does seem to me that our passage divides into three clear sections.

The servant's song (verses 1–6)

The song begins with the calling of God on the servant's life.

His calling (verses 1–3)

It's a very unusual opening. No Old Testament prophet ever says, 'Listen to me.' They always say, 'Listen to God.' So we know that this isn't just Isaiah speaking: it is the servant speaking, and it tells us right at the beginning something about the servant's identity.

'Listen to me' is used only in Isaiah and then only when it introduces a direct word from the Lord. So here we have a figure who at the very outset is shown to possess divine authority. But he is clearly a human figure. Look at the second part of verse 1: 'Before I was born the LORD called me; from my birth he has made mention of my name.' So he's chosen by God before his birth, and ever since his birth his whole life has been governed by that call.

What is he being called to do? The key is in the opening words of verse 2: 'He made my mouth . . .' He is called to a work of words, words given penetrating power by God himself, words that are like a sharpened sword or a polished arrow. I was fascinated to discover that comparing words with arrows is a well-known Hebrew metaphor. They fly swiftly; they penetrate targets. So the Lord trains his servant for a penetrating ministry of the word. Verse 2 speaks of

God preparing him, concealing him, protecting him like a sword in its sheath or an arrow in a quiver, until the moment of revelation arrives. When that moment arrives, God's mission is put into action.

At that point, the servant is suddenly named for the first time. 'He said to me, "You are my servant, Israel"' (verse 3). What can it mean? Is he talking about the nation of Israel? Certainly the birth of the nation was by God's direct choice; and hadn't they been given his words at Sinai for their national life and as a witness to the world – those which we call 'the Ten Commandments' (literally 'the Ten Words')? Is he then talking about Israel the nation?

No. For as Isaiah spoke, the northern kingdom had been decimated by the Assyrians, and the capital, Samaria, had fallen. The people were exiled or scattered. Isaiah can't mean Israel the nation, for in verse 5 you'll see that the servant is going to gather Israel to himself. How could Israel gather Israel?

No; something much more profound is happening here. What we are witnessing in this chapter is the transfer of the name of Israel from the nation to the servant.

Remember, Israel was the name given originally to Jacob when 'the Twister', as his name implied, became a prince with God. It was the family name that was carried down the generations in Egypt, when God announced to Pharaoh through Moses in Exodus, 'Israel is my first-born son, and I told you, "Let my son go, so he may worship me." But you have refused to let him go; so I will kill your first-born son' (Ex. 4:22–23). Now in Isaiah 49:3, 'He said to me, "You are my servant [my son] . . . in whom I will display my splendour."' The servant is the one through whom the glory of the Lord is going to be revealed.

It is quite clear in the Old Testament that it was God's purpose to reveal his glory to the world through the nation of Israel. But what a sad failure they had been! So as God begins his new work after the exile, he nominates and equips a new servant to be all that the old Israel had failed to be; a servant who will declare his powerful word to the nations and who will be the living manifestation of his glory. God will display his splendour in the new Israel. And so when the only-begotten Son of God, the real Israel, came into our world, our Lord Jesus Christ began a word ministry which gathered a new people of Israel to himself when he came as the servant. 'The word was made flesh and pitched his tent among us and we've seen his glory, glory as of the only begotten Son of the Father, full of grace and truth' (cf. Jn. 1:14). So the living word was committed to a revelatory ministry of words. The living Son is sent in order that on his mouth the word of God may be heard, and in his life and death and rising again, God might display his splendour. That is the calling of the servant.

His crisis (verse 4)

But at verse 4 the mood changes. It's as though the servant takes a step back from his task and reviews what he's done (of course, all this prophetically looks forward). He says that it all seems to be a failure. This new beginning appears to be doomed. The servant seems to have carried out his work to no lasting purpose.

It certainly looked like that to the watching world on Good Friday. The Palm Sunday crowds had turned against the King. One of his inner circle had betrayed him; the rest had run away in fear. And where now were the thousands who'd been fed? Where were the supporters who'd mobbed him in Galilee and so frightened the religious leaders? It looked as though the whole enterprise had miscarried. John says that 'even after Jesus had done all these miraculous signs in their presence, they still would not believe in him' (Jn. 12:37).

Verse 4, one of the great evidences of the divine inspiration of the whole of Scripture, gives us a unique insight into the heart and mind of the Lord Jesus Christ. Here is the mind of the Son of God, in his incarnation, revealed through the Spirit of God to Isaiah, centuries before it would seem that his ministry was a failure. Jesus wept over Jerusalem because of its hardness of heart. And we must not be surprised if, as we try to follow the servant's footsteps, we often feel discouraged by the apparent lack of success. Gospel word ministry is hard work. We can all be tempted to wonder whether it's really worth it. But you see, the verse goes on, 'Yet what is due to me is in the LORD's hand, and my reward is with my God.'

I may be speaking to some Christian servant who has been labouring for the Lord, perhaps abroad as a missionary, perhaps in a very difficult part of this country. You have come to Word Alive and you're thinking, 'I've laboured to no purpose, I've spent my strength in vain and for nothing.' People look around and say, 'What on earth are you doing it for?' My friend, it is the way the Master went. Should not the servant tread it still? God has not called us to be sparklingly successful by this world's assessment, but he *has* called us to be faithful labourers who get on with the business of proclaiming the Lord Jesus. And he has never allowed any of his servants to spend their strength in vain.

There is a reward for faithfulness. What is due to you is in the Lord's hand. He is no man's debtor, and if you will remain faithful to him – whether or not you see great fruit – then what is due to you, your reward, will be given to you from God just as he rewarded his own Son. Just as we are incorporated into Christ by faith, so it is true for us that God will always reward faithful service.

His confidence (verses 5–6)

And so the song ends with great confidence. The Lord is in control of it all. It moves through the calling to the crisis and from the crisis to the confidence, because God can be relied upon to be faithful. 'And now the LORD says . . .' begins verse 5, and goes on to remind us of who the Lord is. He's the one who formed the servant, he's the one who commissioned him, he's the one who honours him and gives him strength. This great sovereign Lord says, 'It is too small a thing for you to be my servant to restore the tribes of Jacob . . . I will also make you a light for the Gentiles, that you may bring my salvation to the ends of the earth.'

That's why the islands and the distant nations are summoned in verse 1. The ministry of the servant is a world-wide ministry, and the light of the gospel is going to go out from him to the very ends of the earth to the Gentile nations sunk in their idolatry. And the servant's ministry will be to bring a new Israel, a new covenant community from every tribe, kindred and nation, to acknowledge God as Lord and to worship around his throne for ever.

That is the third hill of fulfilment which we are pressing on towards, and which he gives us a part in ministering to and serving. 'I will . . . make you a light for the Gentiles . . .' So as the servant comes, he says to those who follow him, 'You are the light of the world' . . . 'You are the salt of the earth' . . . 'You are the city set on a hill that cannot be hidden' . . . 'I will make you a light for the Gentiles'. And if you're in Christ, you're part of that light 'that you may bring my salvation to the ends of the earth'. For what Jesus has done, he incorporates us in; and he enables us to reflect his light throughout the world wherever he has placed us, in all the people-groups that we move in; and he is gathering his eternal people out of every human society into his everlasting kingdom.

This passage is saying to us: 'Never underestimate God's ability to turn the game around.' We are familiar with sports stories in which players have been facing certain defeat, with match point against them; and then they come back from the dead to win. Suddenly they find new energy and strength, and the whole match turns round and they win.

That is a trivial comparison, because God is always totally in control. But our passage tells us: 'Don't be persuaded that the final outcome will be anything other than the servant's victory and vindication. Our Lord Jesus is going to be seen to be King of kings and Lord of lords. Every knee will bow to him, and the sign of that is that the light of the gospel is even now reaching out to the ends of the earth.'

The Lord's confirmation (verses 7–13)

The second section is really a commentary on the first. All of the servant songs are followed by comments in which God explains more fully what he's going to do. And this one is no exception.

Commitment to the servant (verse 7)

The signature 'This is what the LORD says' at the beginning of verse 7 is enormously important. It gives strength to the promise that follows. In our contemporary world we are so used to promises being made and broken that we consider them scarcely worth the paper they're written on. We see it every day in the newspapers; one side in politics discredits the other and tries to claim that all its promises are useless and empty. Recently the Chancellor of the Exchequer, in a memorable phrase, described the Leader of the Opposition and his promises as 'vacuous flannel'. That's typical politicians' rhetoric, and all political parties use it. And we're used to the currency being devalued, because human beings can rarely deliver what they promise.

But here the signature comes before the promise. This is what Yahweh, the sovereign Lord, the covenant-faithful God Jehovah, says. He is the one who redeems. He is the Holy One of Israel, standing in sharp contrast to his unholy disobedient people. What this utterly righteous, morally pure God says – this one in whom there is no darkness at all – is to be relied on totally. Although the nation will abhor the servant, although God's people will reject him (John says that he came to his own and his own did not receive him), and although he will seem to be totally under the control of the world's rulers, yet the outcome is certain. Herod and Pontius Pilate met together with the Gentiles and the people of Israel in Jerusalem to conspire against God's holy servant Jesus, but they could do only what God's power and will had decided beforehand should happen. And what is that? That the very highest individuals in human society should acknowledge the servant and submit to him. 'Kings will see you and rise up, princes will see and bow down.'

So there is no doubt that God will answer his cries for help and rescue him. He will not let his holy one see corruption. The reason is given in verse 8. 'This is what the LORD says: "In the time of my favour I will answer you, and in the day of salvation I will help you."' Why? '"I will keep you and will make you to be a covenant for the people."'

We have here a development of the thought. The servant is himself to be a covenant, a new covenant for the people.

We should pause for a moment to think about this great idea of 'covenant', because the word lies at the heart of all God's dealings with his people in the Old and the New Testaments. Biblically, a covenant is an arrangement by which one party determines to be a blessing to another party, irrespective of return, because they're motivated by concern and love. The nearest equivalent is when you make a covenant with your church to give a certain amount monthly so that the church can reclaim the tax from the Inland Revenue. It's not a *quid pro quo* arrangement. Out of your heart of love for the Lord and for his work you give voluntarily. You place yourself on oath as you sign the covenant. You say 'I will do this', and you do it entirely out of your grace. In the same way, God determines to have a people for himself more than any man can number. He begins with one man, Abraham, and he promises him descendants and a land. They will be living in God's place in fellowship with him as God's people. He covenants – he signs his name to this agreement.

As the family grew and became a nation at the exodus, God took them to Mount Sinai, where he came down and revealed himself in his law and covenanted with the people. Having redeemed them, he taught them how they could live in fellowship with him, the Holy One. 'Be holy as I am holy' (Lv. 11:45). So he promised them covenant blessings when they obeyed him, but covenant curses if they sinned and rebelled against him (*cf.* Dt. 30:11–20).

The Old Testament is the story of how they broke that covenant again and again, until God had to remove them from the land and take away their national identity and send them into exile. But you will know that he had covenanted with King David and with his son Solomon, 'I will be his Father and he will be my son. I will never take away my love from him. I will set him over my house and my kingdom for ever. His throne will be established for ever.' And God keeps his promises.

So instead of the shattered tablets of the broken law and the unbelief of national Israel, he plans a new covenant written not on tablets of stone, but on the tablets of the heart. He will create a new covenant people through the servant, those who believe his word from all the nations of the earth. That new covenant is to be achieved through the servant's life and ministry, through his word and through his death and rising, through his work. The servant is the new-covenant man who brings covenant blessings to all of God's people. In our passage those blessings are defined as *being restored to the land* (verse 8) and *having freedom renewed* (verse 9).

In New Testament terminology, Jesus is the covenant. Through him the covenant blessings become available to us through faith, and in relationship with him God's people are able to enter into the enjoyment of all that the Lord has for them. Having assured the servant of his commitment to this great work of the new covenant, the Lord spells out the benefits. He will bring us to his land (obviously a picture of heaven in the New Testament), and he will call us out of the darkness into his marvellous light, and out of the bondage of sin and Satan into the freedom of the children of God. He is committed to do it. That's the first great blessing that comes as a result of the servant's work as the maker of the new covenant. And here's the Lord's confirmation: he's committed to his servant.

Restoration for the nation (verses 9b-12)

The second great blessing is that he will restore the nation (verses 9b-12). Because of this great Old Testament prophecy, we think of the blessings in terms of Old Testament terminology: about people coming back to the land from exile. The image is that of a flock. It links up with what we saw in our first study, about the sovereign shepherd leading his people home. The Palestinian shepherds always lead their flocks; and here the idea is of God leading his people through the barren wilderness, protecting them, granting them food and water, turning his mountains into roads so that they come home under his protecting hand to Jerusalem.

Some friends of mine were on a trip to Israel. They had just been told by their guide that Israeli shepherds always lead their flocks, when they saw a man walking behind his flock, driving it forward. They asked their guide why this was so, and he went to check. Returning, he informed them: 'That wasn't the shepherd. It was the butcher . . .' But the Good Shepherd leads his flock, he nurtures and cares for his sheep.

That, of course, translates into us, the church. God is committed to bringing us home to heaven; because the Lord is our Shepherd we have everything that we need. They are his mountains, they are his highways, they are his people, it is his land. And God is committed to restore us.

Hope for the whole world (verse 13)

Do you see the widening circles as the second section ends? Commitment to the servant who is the covenant; restoration for the nation, which becomes the new Israel, the church; and then hope for the whole world. Verse 13, 'Shout for joy, O heavens; rejoice, O earth; burst into song, O mountains! For the LORD comforts his people and will have compassion on his afflicted ones.' It's not just the mountains of Israel that are singing, but the whole earth, because we know the light will stretch to the Gentiles. So the whole world is involved in this celebration.

Here is the comfort that we saw in chapter 40. Here is the new life he puts into his people. He's going to gather them from all across the world and he will bring into his eternal kingdom the inexhaustible riches of his mercy as he brings his people home to heaven. Can you imagine a greater privilege than that? That is the Lord's commitment to the servant's ministry.

Zion's objections (verses 14–26)

Verse 14 hits us like a bolt from the blue. Let us look at the main points.

Alec Motyer comments, 'While the world sings, Zion groans.' I know a few Christians like that, don't you? Zion is, strictly speaking, the temple mountain; but it comes to mean in Isaiah the whole city of Jerusalem, and then the whole people of Judah, the people of God.

There are three objections that Zion makes, three basic expressions of unbelief with which they react to God's marvellous word about the servant's ministry. Each of them is wrong, each of them may be in our hearts and each of them needs to be corrected by the Spirit of God.

Zion says, 'I am forsaken and forgotten' (verse 14)

It's not a new complaint. We saw it yesterday in chapter 40: 'My way is hidden from the LORD, my cause is disregarded by my God.' He doesn't know, he doesn't care. They're still saying it here in verse 14; and God in his mercy and love turns to them and says, 'Stop and think about this. You are my people. Can a mother forget the baby at her breast and have no compassion on the child she has borne? Well, yes, that might even happen. But though she may forget, yet I will not forget you!'

He says to them graciously, 'Look, the relationship that I have with you is so rich, so wonderful and so real. I am a Father to you whose love is more dependable even than a mother's love to a baby. Don't tell me that I've forsaken and forgotten you!' Yet how often we find ourselves as Christians doing just that.

We need to be realistic. There was an elderly preacher, a confirmed bachelor until he married late in life. His wife was rather dragged round the world with him. He changed few of his bachelor habits; he preached all around the world and she was there carrying his bags. On one trip he found her weeping in their cabin and gruffly asked her what the matter was. She replied, 'I'm feeling sick and I'm cold and I'm worn out. And nobody loves me.'

To which he replied, 'Don't be silly, woman. God loves you. And put another cardigan on.'

Low marks for empathy, I think! But it is true; sometimes we do have to put another cardigan on and say, 'I know it's true that I'm not forsaken and forgotten. My *feelings* may be saying all sorts of things, but I *know* that this God will never desert me. He will never let me go, because he says to me as he said to those old covenant people, 'I have engraved you on the palms of my hands; your walls are ever before me and I'm going to bring your people back' (verses 17–18).

'"As surely as I live," declares the LORD, "you will wear [your returning children] as ornaments; you will put them on, like a bride"' (verse 18).

Don't fear for the future of God's church. He is building it, not we ourselves. He's going to bring every one of his children home to glory. Don't fear for the future of the gospel. Get on proclaiming it, get on trusting God. Put another cardigan on and know that he loves you.

Zion says, 'I am bereaved and barren' (verse 21)

Verses 19–21 present a lovely picture. In the Old Testament, having many descendants is always a mark of God's blessing. 'Like arrows in the hands of a warrior are sons born in one's youth. Blessed is the man whose quiver is full of them' (Ps. 127:4–5). That's the blessing that the servant is going to bring about, the multiplication of the people of God as the new covenant is established.

So don't say, 'I'm bereaved and barren.' God is gathering his family, he's bringing new children to birth all the time. Verse 21 is almost humorous: can a mother forget her baby? But Israel, the mother of a multitude, seems to have no idea of the multiplication miracles that the Lord is producing. These seem to be totally unexpected children to God's people. It will be like that in heaven! But God is multiplying his people. He is building his church. He is at work fulfilling the servant's ministry.

And from the Gentile nations the people of God come into the kingdom (verses 22, 23). These verses probably mean, 'Cyrus the Gentile king is going to allow you to come back to the land; he's going to facilitate that under the hand of God.' But they could also mean that as the Gentile people come to Jerusalem carrying their own sons and their own daughters, they are the people of Israel. That would certainly be the New Testament view. And from every nation they will come to know that he is the Lord and those who hope in him will not be disappointed.

Christian friend, every time you say, 'I'm forsaken and forgotten' – you're wrong. And every time you say, 'The church of God is bereaved and barren' – you're wrong. God is committed to his purposes; nothing will stop him. We're caught up in those glorious purposes. Let's trust him! Let's rejoice in all that God is doing, and let's pray on to see yet more of those purposes fulfilled.

Zion says, 'I am plundered and captive' (verse 24)

Verse 24 is a flat denial. What Zion is objecting to is the promises of God. Zion is saying they can't happen.

It's not hard to understand historically, is it? How can a tiny, weak, subject people like Judah overthrow the might of Babylon? Ah, but read what the Lord says (verse 25). The impossible will happen, says God. Why? Because God is not governed by opinion polls or by the law of averages. Someone is stronger than the warrior, someone is mightier than the fierce. The Lord will contend, and when God steps into the ring, the contest ends. It means rescue for his people and it means total defeat and shame for his enemies. That's why to oppose God is the short route to self-destruction; it is the craziest possible way to live.

But the emphasis at the end is on his purpose. 'All the world will know that I am the Lord.' And what does it mean to be the Lord? Look at verse 26. It means to be Saviour, it means to be Redeemer, the one who pays the price to buy back his people, the Rescuer, the Redeemer, the Mighty One of Jacob. His sovereign power will judge and overthrow his enemies. His shepherd care will save and redeem his people. He is the Mighty One. He can do it, he is doing it, and he will do it, and the servant's work is the guarantee of it all.

7

The good news about Jesus

Isaiah 52:13 – 53:12

It was a desolate road the Ethiopian was travelling: south-west out of
Jerusalem, down to Gaza on the Mediterranean coast and on into
Egypt and ultimately to Cush (Cush is the name Isaiah gives to the
country that we call Ethiopia). Through the Judean desert, winding
up and down the hills and down to the coastal plain, it was a long
haul, even if you were the Chancellor of the Exchequer, travelling in
the best-sprung and upholstered chariot currently on the market.
There'd be plenty of time to get to grips with the scrolls that you'd
bought in Jerusalem, especially the text of the Hebrew prophet Isaiah
who centuries earlier had prophesied a servant of God who would be
a light to the Gentiles, and through whom all the nations would
come to know Israel's Lord.

But it was difficult stuff; Isaiah isn't an easy book to understand.
When Philip ran up to him and asked that wonderful evangelistic
question, 'Do you understand what you are reading?', he replied –
you remember the story in Acts 8 – 'How can I, unless someone
explains it to me?'

He was, Luke tells us, reading Isaiah 53:12. He'd reached verses 7
and 8. 'He was oppressed and afflicted, yet he did not open his
mouth; he was led like a lamb to the slaughter, and as a sheep before
her shearers is silent, so he did not open his mouth.' So, Luke says,
Philip began with that very passage of Scripture and told him the
good news about Jesus. That's how the gospel spread to Africa.

Philip had no doubt who the servant of Isaiah 53 really was. None
of the early Christians had. Peter, Paul, Matthew and John all quote
this final servant song in their New Testament writings, and they
unanimously refer it all to the Lord Jesus. As John expresses it: 'Isaiah
. . . saw Jesus' glory and spoke about him' (Jn. 12:41). In that they
had, of course, the authority of the Master himself. Jesus clearly
embraced the mission of the suffering servant and he explicitly
applied this very chapter to himself. Luke records it: 'It is written:
"And he was numbered with the transgressors"; and I tell you that
this must be fulfilled in me. Yes, what is written about me is reaching
its fulfilment' (Lk. 22:37).

We need to keep that very clearly in mind as we come to this holy

128

ground of Isaiah 53. Its detailed fulfilment in the Lord Jesus should give us great confidence in God's ability to make and keep his promises, to prophesy and to perform. And one of the major purposes of prophecy like this, which is so stunningly accurate centuries before its fulfilment, is to stimulate God's people in every generation to a truly biblical faith. One of the most important questions we can ever ask is, 'What is the word of the Lord?' For if we can identify that, we know that we have identified absolute truth and that that word will infallibly, in every detail, be performed.

It is such a joy to know that the word of the Lord is bound up for us in this book we call the Bible, the sixty-six books of Scripture; to know that every word is given by him, every word is infallible, every word will be fulfilled. We don't need the fantasy of imagining words of God in our heads, when we have the fact of his revelation on the pages of Scripture. That is the guarantee that he will accomplish everything that he's promised, and that's why we give our minds, our hearts and our wills to Scripture; because this is the word of the Lord, and the word of our God stands for ever.

The final poem of the servant

Our text is a very well-known chapter, but I am sure we will see some things in it freshly. Every time we come to Scripture there's something new. And the first thing to notice is that the chapter division is really an odd one. Clearly, the poem or song about the servant begins in 52:13: 'See, my servant will act wisely . . .' But nobody's quite sure where the chapter divisions came from or why. Ignore them!

The use of parallelism

This very carefully crafted poem begins at 52:13 and runs through to the end of chapter 53. It is a poem of five stanzas or verses, of regularly increasing length. Each of these stanzas represents three verses in our version of Isaiah's text. So we're going to look at it under the five sections into which the poem very clearly divides itself.

Hebrew poets love symmetry. They love to balance one idea against another. One of the basic units of Hebrew poetry is the way in which one half of a verse balances the second half of the verse; but they also employ balance through the poem as a whole. So the first and the last sections balance each other by repeating the same theme. It's a very common device in Hebrew poetry.

Here the theme is the great one of the servant's victory. 'See, my servant . . . will be raised and lifted up and highly exalted' (52:13): 'I will give him a portion among the great . . . he will divide the spoils with the strong.' The exaltation of the servant is the theme of both stanza 1 and stanza 5. When it's first introduced, it seems an impossible outcome because the servant has apparently been bruised and beaten and battered. How can he possibly be the victorious one? But the song shows us how it happens, and then gloriously reaffirms it at the end.

Now the poem itself. Stanzas 2, 3 and 4 correspond to verses 1–9 in our Bibles. Stanzas 2 and 4 balance each other – they explore the facts about what the servant has done; verses 1–3, the facts about his humiliation; verses 7–9, the facts about his eventual death and burial. They are statements about the servant's work that explain how this great new initiative of God comes to its fulfilment.

Then stanza 3 (verses 4–6). In Hebrew thinking the meaning is often in the middle. In the Old Testament narratives the meaning of stories is often put in a little comment right in the middle of the story itself. And in Old Testament poems the heart of the poem is at the structural centre. We are not used to that in our culture; sermons often suffer from what Jim Packer used to call 'muddle in the middle'. But Hebrew poems have focus and clarity in the middle. So in verses 4–6 you find the heart of the matter.

Go further, to verse 5 at the precise mid-point of the stanza: 'He was pierced for our transgressions, he was crushed for our iniquities; the punishment that brought us peace was upon him, and by his wounds we are healed.' That is the heart of the poem's meaning. We shall allow it to control our interpretation of this magnificent chapter. It is the good news about Jesus.

The use of the past tense

But why is it all in the past tense? Isaiah is prophesying something that is going to happen centuries later. So why does he say, 'He *was* pierced, he *was* crushed?

He uses the past tense to indicate certainty. People sometimes talk about the 'prophetic perfect', referring to the fact that the prophets often used the past tense to speak about something that was yet to happen, because they knew that in the mind of God it was already decreed and therefore it had as good as happened. When God says something, he determines that it will be done.

Paul was 'a Hebrew of the Hebrews' (Phil. 3:5). It's not surprising he uses this device in the New Testament. He does so in those lovely words in Romans 8, where he talks about all things working together for the good of those who love God: and he says that those whom God called (past tense) he justified (past tense); and those he justified, he glorified (past tense) (Rom. 8:30).

If you're a Christian, you are a justified sinner; but Paul goes on to say that those he justified he glorified. We are not yet glorified – but Paul says it's just as certain as the fact that you're sitting here justified today, that you *are* glorified in God's eyes. It will come about when you see him face to face and he transforms you into his likeness; so, says Paul, I can use the Old Testament device of the past tense because it's absolutely certain.

Stanza 1 (52:13–15): the mysterious identity

In our previous studies we have become used to the introductory formula 'See, my servant'. It introduced the first servant song in chapter 42: 'Look, here is my servant, the answer to the world's need.'

The context here is that God is calling his people to get ready to leave Babylon. 'Depart, depart, go out from there! Touch no unclean thing! Come out from it and be pure . . .' (52:11). The new exodus is about to happen. And God says: 'Now, look, it's because of the work of my servant that all this is going to be put into effect.' Clearly we have at 52:13 the culmination of the sequence that has run from chapter 42 onwards all the way through those long chapters. We've learnt that the servant of God is in fact the answer to Israel's persistent failure and to the world's great need. Only the servant will be able to cure Israel of her idolatry and its resulting defeat and despair.

But God's salvation plan now extends far beyond Israel, to the Gentiles. And it is through the servant's ministry of word and action that the islands, the farthest distant parts, will put their hope in the Lord. So the person and work of the servant are the divinely appointed remedy to the very deepest needs of rebellious, sinful humanity, whether we are Jews or Gentiles. And now in this last great song, God is about to reveal the methodology. He's going to show us how it will happen, because when you know how something works, you have much greater confidence in it.

That's why the Bible is a book of teaching. The very word *Torah* – the Law of God, the first five books of the Bible – means 'instruction'. The whole Bible is God teaching us. Now, in any teaching you appeal to the mind, the heart, and the will. In a memorable phrase in his book *Preaching and Preachers*, Dr Martyn Lloyd-Jones talks about the truth of the Bible going through the mind, to the heart, to activate the will. That's what the Bible is always doing. Every time you open it, pray that it will happen! First the mind; there is no bypassing the mind. Second the heart; truth is not just intellectual, it affects the whole being. Third the will; because the only evidence that we have

131

really understood and received God's truth is when we put it into action.

Here God is giving us truth for our minds so that we understand the cross. He is pouring his grace and love into our hearts so that we are motivated to feel what Jesus has done for us; not in any superficial way but in a way that actually moves us into action, to live lives that reflect our gratitude. As somebody tellingly observed, 'If theology is grace, then ethics is gratitude.'

But as the song begins it is dark and mysterious. Three verbs in verse 13 seem to bring about a very strange contrast with verse 14. Verse 13 is all about triumph: 'My servant will act wisely; he will be raised and lifted up and highly exalted.' He will be risen, ascended and glorified. The first half of the verse tells us that it is to be the result of the servant's wise action. That is an English version of Martin Luther's translation. The verb that is translated 'act wisely' means 'to know exactly what to do in order to achieve a result'. So it comes to mean 'to be successful' or 'to prosper', as some of the translations put it. We'll find same the verb again in 53:10 – 'the will of the LORD will prosper in his hand'. And Joshua was told that if he meditated on God's law day and night and obeyed it, 'then you will be prosperous and successful' (Jos. 1:8). That is the idea expressed here. The servant knows how to do God's will and therefore he prospers; the will of God is successfully completed and as a result he is raised, lifted up and highly exalted.

But the contrast with verse 14 is stark. This successful, exalted, glorified servant is disfigured and marred in the most appalling way. How can this possibly be the same person? But it is, because verse 15 swings back to the exaltation theme: 'Kings will shut their mouths because of him.' He is going to have a profound effect on the far-distant places. He will sprinkle many nations, and the most exalted people in those nations will submit to his authority.

So the song's introduction shows us that we're witnessing an unprecedented event in the history of the world. No-one has seen or heard anything like it before. What they were not told they will see; what they have not heard they will understand. This is going to be something that will turn the world upside down. It is a fresh revelation from God himself. But, as the song begins, what a mystery it all is!

In our matter-of-fact age we must never lose that quality of our faith. We must never lose the mystery of the cross, as Charles Wesley expressed it:

> 'Tis mystery all! The Immortal dies:
> Who can explore his strange design?

The clarity of our understanding will only increase our sense of wonder and awe at the fact that God should do it. Robert Murray McCheyne, the old Scottish preacher, was asked, 'What is the greatest miracle in the world?' He thought for a while, then replied, 'Well, the miracle of creation is a very great miracle, and the miracle of redemption is a greater one. But I think for me the greatest miracle in all the world is that God goes on bothering with a man like me.' There is someone who bows before the mystery of the cross!

And we need the strong assertions of verse 13 because of the depth of horror in verse 14. This servant suffers so much that he is hardly recognizable as a human being any longer, but the victory is accomplished not in spite of the suffering but through it; and the effect of the victory (verse 15) is that 'he will sprinkle many nations'.

Some translators (notably of the RSV) have felt that this cannot be the right verb and have substituted a closely related Hebrew verb which is translated, 'He will startle many nations.' It seems to them to fit better with the next phrase, which shows the kings shutting their mouths in sheer astonishment at him. But there is no good reason to change 'sprinkle'. It's a technical Old Testament term for performing a purification rite. The priest would sprinkle the altar with the blood of sacrifice. And its use here tells us that the suffering servant will bring purification and cleansing to the nations.

Under the Old Testament law the Gentiles were excluded from that. The priest could sprinkle the blood on the altar, but it would only atone for the sins of the sons of Abraham. But as the servant's work is revealed and as his blood is shed, he will atone and he will sprinkle the nations. The mystery became clear on that Friday afternoon outside Jerusalem when a young man was crucified. He'd been buffeted and beaten, he'd been hit on the head again and again, his face had been lacerated by a crown of thorns forced into his flesh, he'd been scourged and whipped to within an inch of his life, and there – a broken, battered figure, almost unrecognizable as a human being – he had died on a cross.

That is God's way of cleansing the nations. And like the kings of verse 15, our mouths need to be shut. There's nothing to be said. But our ears and our eyes need to be opened to learn and to understand that he did it for me. ''Tis mystery all! The Immortal dies.' But do you remember how the hymn goes on? ''Tis mercy all, immense and free; For O my God, it found out me!'

Stanza 2 (53:1–3): an incredible strategy

At verse 1 we pick up the idea at the end of the preceding chapter, and once again the note is one of astonishment. 'Would you ever believe it? Who would ever have thought to see the arm of the Lord revealed in this way?' When Paul in Romans 10:16 quotes Isaiah 53:1 he says that 'not all the Israelites accepted the good news'. That is what this verse is saying. There will be many people for whom this method of sprinkling the nations is unacceptable. It's only by hearing the message of the cross that faith can come, but notice how the text picks up the idea, which the New Testament later expands, that the message of a man of sorrows dying on a cross seems so weak as to be unbelievable. It is Paul's theme in 1 Corinthians 1 of the cross being a stumbling-block to Jews and foolishness to Gentiles; it is Peter's observation (1 Pet. 2) that those who do not believe see the crucified Messiah as a stone that causes people to stumble, a rock that makes them fall.

When the unbelieving world looks at the cross, it's all incredible. See how verses 2 and 3 depict the person and ministry of the servant. His whole life-span has one predominant characteristic: suffering. The tender shoot of verse 2 is a sapling that grows out of a trunk or the roots of the tree. It's weak and vulnerable, very easily cut off with secateurs. A root out of parched soil – it has to struggle to preserve its very existence.

The New Testament genealogies tell us that Christ's human ancestry could be traced to the royal line of David, back to the stump of Jesse. But when Jesus was born in Bethlehem of Judea the occupant of David's throne was Herod the Great. Half-Jew, half-Arab, he was a puppet of the occupying Roman army; a paranoid tyrant, who did his best to cut the tender shoot off at birth with his massacre of baby boys in Bethlehem.

Born in obscurity and poverty, cradled in a manger, fleeing as a refugee to Egypt, reared in a despised Galilean village where (according to archaeology) it seems just a few families lived in homes that were basically extended caves. Is this how the Lord reveals his powerful arm? Are these few kilos of human vulnerability really God? It's an incredible strategy.

Verse 2 adds that as he grew up there was nothing especially striking or attractive about his outward appearance. Some Bible heroes were impressive to look at – Joseph, David for example – but not Jesus. Nobody took a second look. There was no personal charisma that wowed people from the moment he became known. There were no film-star looks. There were none of the trappings of majesty. Those who were drawn to him came because of what he taught and did.

Verse 3 takes it further. Twice we're told that he was despised. How often that echoes through the gospels! 'Isn't this the son of

Joseph, the carpenter? Why do you bother to listen to him? Can any good thing come out of Nazareth? Does anyone who really matters believe in him? Have any of the Pharisees or priests put their faith in him?' He was continually beset by contempt and rejection. It culminated in his false arrest, in the mockery of his trial, in the torture he endured and the ignominious shame of a public, appallingly painful death on the cross.

'He was despised.' People threw the Lord Jesus on the garbage heap of rejected humanity, and they still do. He was a man of sorrows and acquainted with grief. The verb means 'to know someone as a close friend'. The NIV's 'familiar with suffering' doesn't quite capture the thrust of it. His close friend was grief; that was the story of his life. 'Like one from whom men hide their faces he was despised.' Even his disciples didn't esteem him. One betrayed him, the others forsook him and fled, and Isaiah says, 'Is this the arm of the Lord?'

But before we leave this second stanza, I want you to look at that incriminating pronoun at the end of verse 3: 'He was despised, and *we* esteemed him not.' That takes it from Isaiah to the present day, and to everyone in between. It says: 'That is the verdict of our humanity on the Son of God.' We are included in those who have not esteemed him. Oh, we patronize him, we praise his teaching, we give the nod of agreement to his ethics, we're very happy with him as a good man and a fine teacher and a splendid example. But when we see him on the cross rescuing us from our sins, that's the test of whether or not we're going to say that he is the Lord.

In our culture it is acceptable to consider Jesus as one holy man among a number of others. But if I say that he is the Son of God, dying on a cross to rescue me from hell, then the reaction of most of my contemporaries is to look away and pour another cup of coffee. 'Surely you don't believe in the religion of the slaughter-house, old chap? How could a Son of God die on a cross like a common criminal?

It's always been like that. On a wall in the Roman catacombs is a small drawing. A man is kneeling before a cross, and on the cross is a donkey. The caption scratched into the rock reads, 'El Alaxemenos worships his God.' Nothing has changed. He was despised.

But if nothing has changed, the great danger for us Christians is that *we* will change, that we will lose our nerve and our faith about this incredible strategy of the cross; that we contemporary evangelicals will deny the crucified Saviour by watering down our presentation of the gospel to make it more market-friendly. All that the world sees when it sees Jesus Christ on the cross is one big zero.

The message that you and I must take into the market-place is the gospel of Jesus Christ and him crucified. We preach it in a world that worships self, the feel-good factor, and the goals of success, image, influence, wealth and power. How do you feel about preaching that message into the secular world? It's going to be very tempting to move from his work to our experience. It's going to be very tempting to want to preach a message that asks people to sign up for all the blessings of the kingdom without any true repentance or humbling of ourselves before the cross of Christ. We may do all in our power to persuade people to accept Jesus (whatever that may mean), but the real question, according to the Bible, is this: is there any way that God will be willing to accept us?

If you move away from the cross of Christ, there is no other way. You are left with a man-made, man-centred religion of the feelings, for which no-one will sacrifice and no-one will suffer. That's why you meet so many people around today who've 'tried Christianity' when they were in their teens or as students, and now say, 'I've left it all behind me.' And as you explore what's happened you find that they were offered a free meal-ticket version of the gospel which bypassed conviction of sin, bypassed repentance and sidelined the cross. They were given the sort of gospel that said, 'Vote for Jesus because he is the one who will meet all your needs.' And when the going gets tough they are the first to get going.

All because we Christian communicators don't really believe in God's incredible strategy. All because we Christians are so worldly in our outlook that we want an attractive, worldly hero-Jesus, a superstar who'll take us into his orbit so that we hide our face from the man of sorrows and preach a message with no offence of the cross in it and therefore no gospel at all. This is God's incredible strategy, and if we are not prepared to work with that and to move with that, then we are not gospel people and our words will have no power.

Stanza 3 (53:4–6): the exact remedy

Now we come to the very heart of this wonderful song. The dramatic change, for which the last words of verse 3 prepared us – 'we esteemed him not' – is that we who were observing all this from the outside as a historical event, suddenly become intensely involved in it.

See how it changes. 'Surely he took up our infirmities and carried our sorrows, yet we considered him stricken by God, smitten by him, and afflicted. But he was pierced for our transgressions . . .' So the servant's suffering becomes very personal for us as we are taught its

136

true meaning. Here is the revelation of the mind and arm of God that could never have been guessed at or known in any other way.

What is being said here is that as the watching world sees the servant suffer, it is at least partially right in its assessment of what is happening. Verse 4: 'We considered him stricken by God, smitten by him, and afflicted.' People say there's no smoke without fire: if he's suffering so appallingly he must be a very great sinner. And the religious leaders at the cross saw this as God's punishment for his blasphemy. They taunted him as he hung there, and they said he richly deserved it.

It was indeed a divine punishment. But at verse 4, it suddenly all becomes blindingly clear. Yes, he is being stricken by God, smitten and afflicted. But it is our punishment that he is suffering.

Look at the detail in verse 4 with me. He (literally) lifted up our infirmities and he (literally) carried away our sorrows. So this servant is dealing with all that blights and spoils our lives. We're right to see him as one smitten by God, for he's carrying the curse as he dies on the cross. But what is shocking and undreamed of is that it is all for us.

Verse 5 carries us to the very heart of the matter as it moves beyond the sorrows and the grief to the sin which is their root cause. For this verse tells us that the greatest problem faced by any human being is the problem of 'our transgressions' and 'our iniquities'. No other issue has such eternal consequences.

Transgressions speaks about conscious, wilful acts of rebellion against God through disobedience. Whenever I cross the line and break God's commandment, I transgress. And because those commandments are an expression of the character of God, every transgression is an insult to God's person.

It's not just that we violate an objective standard that we call the law, but that we have shattered a relationship. We will not let God be God in our lives. That's transgression. The Ten Commandments are not like a pile of ten bricks, of which you can remove one or two and still have a pile. They are not like an examination paper that requires candidates to attempt any five of the ten questions. No; the law of God is like a car windscreen. One stone shatters it. And we are all great transgressors, we have broken his law again and again, and our iniquities are the inevitable outcome of our transgression.

Iniquities means the ineradicable stain, the dye that's in our character, the stain we can't remove. It's the expression of our fallen nature, the hidden man or woman of the heart that has no real desire to go God's way, and no real desire to let God have his way in our lives. That's what we're like. We're all iniquitous people.

137

And verse 5 says it was for your transgressions and iniquities and for mine that our Lord Jesus Christ was – what? Well, the verbs are very strong: pierced through, trampled, and crushed to death, because of our sins and our rebellion.

The second half of verse 5 explains how exact the remedy is. He has met the death penalty that our sins rightly deserve. And because he has carried our punishment we can know peace; peace with God, and on that basis, peace with one another. Our spiritual healing depends on his being wounded, and in this context the healing probably has the meaning of forgiveness. It's the healing of the great gulf that has opened up between us and God, the great offence that exists in our lives when God looks at them. It's not just the removal of the suffering, it's the forgiveness that God pours in as he binds up our wounds. The punishment lies on him, in order that we may have peace.

It is an exact remedy. And it is the heart of the good news, in the doctrine that has come to be known as 'substitutionary atonement'. There is no biblical gospel without it. It's as clearly taught in the vocabulary of verse 5 as in its thought-forms.

The little word 'for' in 'pierced for our transgressions, crushed for our iniquities' means 'on account, on behalf of'. The servant carried the righteous sentence of God's wrath against sin in our place as our substitute. Only the Lord Jesus could do that, because only he was without sin. And so it is a penal substitution, because he bears sin's penalty instead of me.

God is not at peace with us. The greatest problem we face is not even our sin, so much as the wrath of God which we must ultimately meet beyond this life. It is already 'being revealed against all the ungodliness and wickedness of men', Paul says in Romans 1:18, but it will be revealed in all its horror on the Last Day when men and women will appeal to the rocks to hide them from the righteous wrath of their offended Creator and Judge. And on that day we will know what a great Saviour we have. For those who trust the servant's work, he has assumed the sentence. He has paid the price so that peace and pardon and wholeness come to us through his wounds.

In a very helpful magazine called *The Briefing*,[2] Mark Thompson writes:

> Penal substitution is not one amongst many models of the atonement as some assert, neither can it be described as a theory arising out of the biblical text. Evangelical theology insists that while penal substitution doesn't exhaust all that

can be said about the cross and resurrection of Jesus, it is the basic biblical understanding without which other perspectives are devoid of any real meaning. At the heart of the atonement is Jesus' death in our place, a death which involves bearing the penalty for our sin. Here is God's most profound answer to the human dilemma. This is what makes the gospel such good news.

Never be moved from the penal substitutionary death of Christ on the cross. That is the heart of evangelical theology. And verse 6 summarizes it beautifully. It begins with 'We all . . .' and ends with '. . . us all'.

A sheep that has gone astray has no provision for food, no defence from danger, no company, no comfort. It's a solitary, lost, miserable animal vulnerable to death, and that's all of us by nature. We are separated from the Lord by our sin: 'We all, like sheep, have gone astray, each of us has turned to his own way.' That's the human condition we were born in, and we confirm it by a hundred daily choices. But look, the straying sheep are rescued by the sacrificial lamb; for the Lord, the covenant God of grace and faithfulness, is active in all this.

The Lord has (literally) caused to mete on him the iniquity of us all. It's a lovely picture of God taking your iniquity and mine and the iniquity of millions of our fellow believers, and bringing all that iniquity together and meting it on the head of Jesus, the Lamb of God. So that the grace that brings our pardon is greater than our deepest need, and God himself has carried the guilt that belongs to us, in the person of his beloved Son, the servant. By that one sacrifice for sin once for all, for ever, our whole lives and our whole future have been eternally changed. Hallelujah! What a Saviour!

Stanza 4 (53:7–9): his unparalleled humility

We have passed the midway point, and we're moving back from explanation to description. Here are more of the stark facts as to what price the servant paid to make us whole. We have seen that his suffering is *vicarious* suffering, it's on our behalf; but in the fourth stanza the emphasis is on the fact that it's *voluntary* suffering. We may think that the picture of the lamb about to be slaughtered in verse 7 implies powerlessness in the hands of others, and indeed it does to some extent: 'He was led like a lamb to the slaughter.'

Recently a Briton convicted of murder was sent to the electric chair in America. Interestingly, his lawyer stated, 'They are treating him like a sheep to be slaughtered.' Whether or not he was aware of the biblical imagery, his words bring it all suddenly into the present. It's one thing to wear a cross round your neck, but would you wear an image of an electric chair? That's what the cross means. You must not get romantic about the cross. The idea of suffering was meted out to him. He was oppressed – but the determined submission comes out in the verb used in verse 7: 'He was afflicted.' In the original it's a reflexive verb, 'he humbled himself', or perhaps better 'he allowed himself to be afflicted'.

Of course the primary meaning of the Old Testament image of the lamb is sacrifice. In verse 6 we are the straying lost sheep, in verse 7 the servant is the sacrificial lamb, refusing to defend himself by word or action. So he humbles himself, he allows himself to be afflicted.

Last week I was on the Mount of Olives, near to the site of the Garden of Gethsemane where the Lord Jesus agonized over the prospect of the cross. And what was brought home to me very forcefully was that at that point in the garden he only had to climb the Mount of Olives another ten minutes or so and he would have reached the beginning of the Judean wilderness. He could so easily have slipped away while the disciples were asleep. But he didn't run, he didn't resist. Patiently the Lord Jesus endured it all, the beating, the spitting, the mockery – because he was offering up a will that was 100% obedient to the Father in the place of our rebellious wills, and that was why his work was sufficient for the redemption of the whole world.

We need the New Testament to explain it to us more fully. Turn to the letter to the Hebrews, which picks up all the sacrificial image of the Old Testament and explains it in terms of Jesus. Chapter 10 helps us to understand much more fully what Isaiah is explaining:

> The law [that is, the Old Testament revelation, both in the instruction and in the sacrificial system] is only a shadow of the good things that are coming – not the realities themselves. For this reason it can never, by the same sacrifices repeated endlessly year after year, make perfect those who draw near to worship. If it could, would they not have stopped being offered? For the worshippers would have been cleansed once for all, and would no longer have felt guilty for their sins. But those sacrifices are an annual reminder of sins, because it is impossible for the blood of bulls and goats to take away sins. (Heb. 10:1–3)

So every time you went to the temple for the Passover, the Day of

Atonement, the Feast of Tabernacles or any other sacrifice, you were reminding yourself: 'I am a sinner, I've got to present another sacrifice.' And the reason was that the most perfect, unblemished animal was deficient at the point of consent. The animal had no will, it was literally a dumb animal.

Now the Lord Jesus, just as submissive as the lamb led to the slaughter, was consciously and voluntarily fulfilling the Father's will. Hebrews 10:5 – 'Therefore, when Christ came into the world, he said [quoting Psalm 40]: "Sacrifice and offering you did not desire, but a body you prepared for me; with burnt offerings and sin offerings you were not pleased."' God had decreed that they should happen, but they were not his major purpose. 'Then I said, "Here I am – it is written about me in the scroll – I have come to do your will, O God"' (verse 7).

So Jesus comes to live a perfect life in the body prepared for him in order to be the perfect offering (verse 8). Look now at the comment: 'He sets aside the first [that is, the Old Testament sacrificial system] to establish the second [that is, the offering of his perfect will]. And by that will, we have been made holy through the sacrifice of the body of Jesus Christ once for all' (verses 9–10).

Thus the sacrifice of the body of Jesus is the presentation of his perfectly obedient will to the Father; and that once-for-all sacrifice is sufficient to make us holy, not only because human blood has flowed for human sin, but because a perfect will has been sacrificed in the place of my rebellious will and it is a complete and totally sufficient sacrifice and offering for the sins of the whole world. That's what Jesus is doing on the cross.

Now, back to Isaiah 53. Verse 8 speaks of the miscarriage of justice, the fact that his trial was a mockery: 'By oppression and judgment he was taken away.' His judges confessed they could find no fault in him, yet they still condemned him. It speaks prophetically about the fact that he was assigned a grave with the wicked: that is, he died between thieves, and the grave that he was assigned was the rubbish dump outside Jerusalem. He would have been thrown on to Gehenna where the rotting bodies of crucifixion victims were always thrown. But in the mercy and grace of God he was with the rich in his death, for Joseph of Arimathea claimed the body to give it decent burial – and, of course, so that the resurrection could be documented and proved by the empty tomb.

That's what he went through. He offered his perfect will as a voluntary sacrifice, like a lamb; not retaliating, not reviling, in spite of the miscarriage of justice and the appalling shame of his death, in spite of the fact that he was cut off in the very midst of his life without any sort of descendants. 'For the transgression of my people he was stricken' (verse 8).

Stanza 5 (53:10–12): his total victory

But now the song comes full circle. Look at the beginning of verse 10, a tremendously important statement: 'Yet it was the LORD's will to crush him and cause him to suffer . . .' The verb 'to crush' is a very strong one. It means 'to grind down'. The death of Jesus is not ultimately in the hands of wicked men, but in the hands of the faithful covenant God. That was why he came. All that Christ suffered in being put to grief was in God's purposes. Not because God is a vengeful deity, venting his anger on a innocent third party, but because God is Jesus in human flesh, bearing our sin and our suffering.

Verse 10 says his life was made 'a guilt offering'. An offering is that which you have to present in order to draw near to God. Jesus presents his life in order that we may draw near to God and find our forgiveness. This too is the will of the Lord. In the beginning of the verse it's his will to crush him, but as the verse proceeds, after he has offered his life up, it is the Lord's will that he shall prosper and that God's purposes will find their fruition in him. For verse 11, 'After the suffering of his soul, he will see the light of life.' That's an amazing thing. Here he is, facing death itself, but beyond death, after he has poured out his spirit, after he has given his very self for us, 'He will see the light of life and be satisfied.'

He will be raised. That's why verse 10 can talk about 'offspring' and 'prolonging his days'. This is not the end, it is only the beginning. For beyond the guilt offering there is the new life, there is the resurrection, there are the millions upon millions who become the offspring of his death, the beneficiaries of his sacrifice. And 'by his knowledge' (or, 'by knowledge of him') 'my righteous servant will justify many, and he will bear their iniquities.'

So we come to our last verse, which celebrates the limitless victory the suffering of Jesus has achieved. He has a portion among the great, he divides the spoils with the strong. It's the image of the conqueror. He's won the battle. 'Finished!' he cried. 'The work is complete, the door to heaven is open, the veil in the temple is torn down!' Everyone can come into God's presence now, because he poured out his life unto death and was numbered with the transgressors.

So to the last sentence. 'For he bore the sin of many, and made intercession for the transgressors.' If you've trusted him, you're one of the many. He's carried your sin. His death is your intercession, he pleads at the Father's right hand as our risen, ascended high priest, but it is his death that he pleads. That is the ground on which we transgressors can enter the presence of God as forgiven sinners. What a glorious work he's done! And it means for us, practically, that we must have done with sin. It means that we cannot go on tolerating things in our lives that we know are fundamentally displeasing to God. If our Shepherd has demonstrated his sovereign power in going all the way to the cross for us, if we are of such incalculable value to him that he laid down his life for the sheep, then how can we go on refusing to bear one another's burdens, refusing to forgive and forget one another's misdemeanours, falling out with people in our churches and not talking to them, bearing grudges in our hearts, being envious and proud and bitter, having all sorts of ambitions that are unworthy of him, trying all the time to be one up on other people – how can we live like that if the Lord Jesus went all the way to Calvary for our sins?

Beginning at this Scripture, Philip preached the good news about Jesus. And we have the same privilege, to give ourselves to the work of gossiping the gospel, but also to the work of living the crucified life. He went through suffering to glory, and we shall follow in his footsteps because he is a faithful God. He does what he has promised, and when we join the heavenly song, 'Worthy is the Lamb who was slain to receive power and wealth and wisdom and might and honour and glory and blessing' – then we shall know, as we cannot know here, what a wonderful Saviour the Lord Jesus is. And we shall spend eternity praising him for such mercy and such grace.

8
Jerusalem, the Lord's delight
Isaiah 65

There is a Bible study book on Isaiah entitled *A Tale of Two Cities*. I think it is a very apt title for this prophecy. At the beginning of Isaiah's masterpiece, we saw introduced the earthly Jerusalem of the eighth century BC as a city that was a great disappointment to God. The faithful city has become a harlot (1:21). God says she was once full of justice; righteousness used to dwell in her, but now murderers do, and chapter 1 of this great book explains how the Lord's hand is against Jerusalem, to purge and to purify but also to restore: 'You will be called the City of Righteousness, the Faithful City.' In one sense all sixty-six chapters of the book of Isaiah are the story of how that transformation is going to happen, how the faithless city is going to become the faithful city. And by the time we reach the last two chapters which are the climax and the epilogue to this prophecy, we are at the place of fulfilment. '. . . I will create Jerusalem to be a delight and its people a joy. I will rejoice over Jerusalem' (65:18). 'Rejoice with Jerusalem and be glad for her, all you who love her; rejoice greatly with her, all you who mourn over her. For you will nurse and be satisfied at her comforting breasts; you will drink deeply and delight in her overflowing abundance' (66:10–11).

It is a tale of two cities, both called Jerusalem. By the end of the book, the city of Jerusalem is a totally different entity from the eighth-century-BC capital of Judah. Indeed, one of the most important strands of Isaiah's prophecy is to redefine both the people of God, whom he increasingly calls Zion, and the city of his dwelling, Jerusalem. We have already seen that the Gentiles have now been brought in to this new covenant community, which has been brought about by the servant's work; and the city is no longer the geographical entity in the state of Israel, but has become the heavenly and eternal Jerusalem.

The structure and development of this idea through the book of Isaiah are quite complex. Obviously we can only touch on them here. But the great movement of the book is from the earthly Jerusalem with all its failure, to the heavenly Jerusalem with all its fulfilment. Sadly, Christians have often allowed the details of interpretation to become a breeding-ground for dogmatism, and it has unnecessarily divided evangelical Christians. An elderly minister, accused of being an extremist for his faith in biblical inerrancy, retorted to his accuser: 'That may be so, but it's because I'm extremely right and you're extremely wrong.' Sometimes people adopt that position over their view of prophecy. Perhaps a better one is that described by a certain theological-college principal as the 'AFL position' – Awaiting Further Light. But whatever position we hold we need to be humble about it. Our priority must be to find the clear main line through Scripture.

Most students of Isaiah agree that the book falls into three sections. Chapters 1 – 39 deal with the historical situation of Judah in Isaiah's day: the faithlessness of King Ahaz leads the people to put their trust in political alliances rather than the promises of the Lord, and as a result Jerusalem, the city, is eventually surrounded by the armies of Assyria and seems certain to fall. That brings us to the climax of the first 39 chapters, when Hezekiah, who is Ahaz's successor, takes the whole situation to the God of Israel in prayer and pleads for his deliverance, which comes miraculously by divine intervention. But Isaiah is called by God to say to Hezekiah, 'This is only a temporary respite.' After his death the city of Jerusalem will fall to Babylon. All its brightest and best, all its treasures and people will be carried off to exile.

When the second section opens, at chapter 40, the prophet envisages what will happen after the fall of Jerusalem and the exile, proclaiming the new beginning of God's new purposes, a new covenant. Jerusalem's warfare is ended. God's people are going to return from Babylon, the Lord is going to re-inhabit a rebuilt temple in a renewed Jerusalem. But what we must realize is that in the second half of Isaiah there is no turning back the clock. The fall of Jerusalem in 587 BC and the exile had an irreversible effect. The old order had finished. The kingdom, north and south, had been exiled; the twelve tribes had been broken up. The new work that God is going to do through the servant is going to bring the Gentiles into the community of God's people. So gradually the image of Jerusalem moves from being the geographical city (which was rebuilt, but on no great scale), to become also the name for the people of the new community, the Zion people; those who are going to be gathered to God from all the nations of the world. Chapter 55 verse 3 talks about the covenant mercies promised to King David being offered to everyone who accepts the message of deliverance from sin through the work of the servant.

So this new Zion community will be faithful to the Lord, and will emulate the servant of the Lord by living a life of obedience to God.

This morning we are in the last section of the book, chapters 56 – 66. This section increasingly pushes the ultimate fulfilment forward along the time-line of history. The restored community in the physical city will demonstrate the same characteristic as the community before the exile. Even the restored earthly Jerusalem is a place of failure and frustration and sin. Gordon McConville observes that the righteous and the poor suffer at other people's hands, that's chapters 57 and 58; there's division and alienation in the community, that's chapter 63; and in chapter 64 Zion is again a wilderness and the ideal of servanthood is embodied only in a minority.

So as we come to this last section what we're learning is that though the servant's work has changed everything, the fulfilment and the completion of that are not yet being experienced either in the physical Jerusalem of the eighth century and afterwards, following the exile – the sixth, fifth, fourth century up to the coming of Christ – or fully in the church, the new community, the new covenant people. We have the seeds of the fulfilment through the work of the servant and through the great grace of God that brings us into his family, but we do not yet possess the fulfilment. So the book is always pushing us forward to the great end-point of human history, where God creates new heavens and a new earth of which the glory is the new Jerusalem. And that idea becomes the Old Testament's seedbed for the great vision of the end of the book of Revelation, the end of the whole Bible, where heaven is unveiled for us.

So by the end of Isaiah, Jerusalem, or Zion, is to be understood as God's glorified people in the new creation which will mark the end of this world's history and the inauguration of the eternal kingdom. The second city is much bigger, much broader, much more wonderful; because it is the eternal city of God.

If we understand that, we are brought into the time-line. We are awaiting the ultimate fulfilment, the perfection of God's people in the heavenly city, just as Isaiah's hearers awaited the immediate fulfilment of the restoration of the earthly city after the exile. In terms of the illustration with which we began this series, we have not yet reached the summit of the third hill.

We can look back on the foothills of the first hill, when Israel returned to the land to rebuild the temple and the city under Ezra and Nehemiah, but those hopes were never fulfilled. When the destroying armies of Rome invaded and demolished the city in AD 70, that was another great disappointment and turning-point.

But we can see the second hill, where the Lord Jesus creates through his substitutionary death and the resulting spread of the gospel a new-covenant community that includes us, the Gentiles, grafted into Christ. We are part of that covenant community, Jews and Gentiles who believe in the Lord Jesus.

We are the living church, but we are not yet in the new Jerusalem. That's the far horizon, to which we press forward. We look back, and our faith is immensely strengthened as we see how many of God's promises he has already wonderfully fulfilled in Christ and in the church. And we look forward to their ultimate completion with renewed hope, knowing that it's equally certain that all that yet remains to be completed will be completed, because the word of our God stands for ever. So we live in this world as citizens of heaven. We live in the 'now', as those who understand, at least in part, what the 'not yet' will bring us.

With those important principles in mind we can see that the message of chapter 65 operates at all three levels. It is a word to the faithless people of Isaiah's Jerusalem and to exiled successors: much of the detail of the first seven verses is taken up with that. But it is a word to us too, as new-covenant people, since the same God is our God and he deals with us on the same unchanging principles of his character and of his grace. As fallen sinners, albeit forgiven and redeemed, we exhibit the same faithless, sin-prone natures as they did. Our great advantage is that because of the servant's work, because he is highly exalted in heaven, he has shed forth the gracious Holy Spirit. He has given his Spirit to live in us so that he writes the law of God on our hearts and increasingly empowers us to live in obedience to that law.

That's the great difference between being an Old Testament and a New Testament saint. But the line from eighth-century Israel is to the twentieth-century church, the covenant people of God, and there are important lessons for us to learn here, as we make our pilgrimage from earth to heaven through suffering to glory.

The hermeneutical principle that the apostles always follow is to interpret the Old Testament as referring to the new-covenant people, the church of Jesus Christ. You can see the principle at work in 1 Corinthians, where Paul picks up an obscure Old Testament quotation from Deuteronomy 25 and says: 'It is written in the Law of Moses: "Do not muzzle an ox while it is treading out the grain"' (1 Cor. 9:9). Now, what would you do with a text like that? Look at what Paul does with it. 'Is it about oxen that God is concerned?' Well, yes, initially – but that isn't the whole significance. He continues, 'Surely he says this for us, doesn't he? Yes, this was written for us, because when the ploughman ploughs and the thresher threshes, they ought to do so in the hope of sharing in the harvest.' So he says, 'God has given that Old Testament land-based principle which I now, as an inspired apostle, see relates to the way in which gospel ministry should be supported financially by those who receive it and benefit from it. He wrote it for us.'

Look at 1 Corinthians 10, which opens with the story of Israel's failure in the desert after the exodus from Egypt. Paul comments, 'Now these things occurred as examples to keep us from setting our hearts on evil things as they did' (1 Cor. 10:6). And verse 11: 'These things happened to them as examples and were written down as warnings for us, on whom the fulfilment of the ages has come.' The fulfilment of all the old-covenant promises in Jesus, into which we enter as new-covenant people, means that all that was written in the Old Testament is written for our learning so that we through endurance and encouragement of the Scriptures might have hope.

So it's not just for the Jews, it's not just Old Testament. It's for us. And the principles on which God operated with them, he operates with us. The warnings that he gave to them, he gives to us. The promises he gave to them, he will fulfil in and through us. That's the basic hermeneutical key, the interpretative principle by which the Old Testament comes alive to us today.

Let us now return to our text. We will divide it into three sections.

The old problem (verses 1–7)

Chapter 64 is a great prayer for God to come down in revival on his people. Confessing the people's unfaithfulness, Isaiah pleads for God to reveal himself in mercy, to put away his anger, to restore the land and rebuild the temple. You see that in verses 10 and 11 at the end of chapter 64. 'Lord,' he pleads, 'come and do this new thing you've promised to do.'

And chapter 65 begins with God's answer. The first two verses demonstrate that there has been no hesitation or reluctance on God's part to meet with his people and bless them. Indeed, he's been making countless efforts to win a nation that hasn't called on his name back into a close faithful relationship with him. All day long he has held out his hand, saying, 'Here am I, here am I.'

In the first three verses we see the three areas of their failure. They did not ask; they did not seek; they did not call on him. Their religion was at best perfunctory, but all the time God was offering himself to them, revealing himself in the words of the prophets, holding out his hand to this obstinate, disobedient people. And when they should be pleading with God, God is pleading with them. That's how good and gracious the Lord really is. But their reaction is the reason they haven't experienced revival. They are 'an

148

obstinate people . . . pursuing their own imaginations' (verse 2).

So Isaiah cries out, 'Lord, do this new thing, revive us, come among us in power!' And God says, 'But how can I come among you in power when you're an obstinate, disobedient people and you will not obey my will?'

He catalogues the contention that he has with his people in verses 2–5. It's the same old problem, the problem of the human heart. And in verses 3–5 especially we have revealed to us the pathology of the hardened, rebellious heart as God diagnoses it. There is a wilfulness about it. He says, 'You are obstinate people.' It's not an accident, it is a deliberate refusal to accept God's authority while all the time pretending to be terribly religious.

The outward sign is behaviour: verse 2, they 'walk in ways not good'. Jesus said, 'By their fruits you will recognise them . . . A good tree cannot bear bad fruit, and a bad tree cannot bear good fruit' (Mt. 7:20, 18). The evil behaviour indicates an internal disease. The Master Physician's diagnosis is there in verse 2.

What is wrong? They are pursuing their own imagination. More literally, they are following their own thoughts. That is exactly the daily problem that you and I grapple with in living the Christian life, isn't it?

Isaiah 55 makes it abundantly clear. God says, 'My thoughts are not your thoughts, neither are your ways my ways' (55:8). That is the problem we always face. It's as old as the Garden of Eden. The battle to live holy lives in the world, to be citizens of the new Jerusalem here on earth, is a battle in the mind. It's about our imaginations and our thoughts. Our sinful human nature would much rather go the way of our imagination than submit to God's revelation in Scripture. It is the battle we face on the threshold of becoming Christians and it's a battle that never leaves us when we do become Christians. Am I going to go God's way or am I going to go the way of my own imagination, my own thoughts? We face that struggle corporately as the church. We face it individually as Christians.

Let me bring it very much up to date. Is the church going to accept the clear prohibition of homosexual practice and lifestyle in Scripture, or is it going to pursue its own imagination, fired by the pressure of contemporary culture? Is the church going to stand for the sanctity of marriage and family life, or is it going to lean to its own thoughts and drift with the disintegrating culture? Are Christian young people going to determine to maintain their virginity before marriage as Scripture clearly teaches they should, or are they going to pursue their own imagination fuelled by the world? 'Everybody does it nowadays, it doesn't really matter, so long as we're in a stable relationship.'

149

There are a hundred and one issues of that sort facing new-covenant people every day. This is not something that just belongs to eighth-century Jerusalem. We are going to be tempted to pursue our own imagination, and we need verse 3 to encourage us to understand the devastating consequences of that. We are, says God, 'people who continually provoke me to my very face . . .' It's a continual process, this obstinate refusal to accept God's truth, and it provokes him to anger.

The phrase 'to my very face' means much more than just being flagrant or impudent. It is the phrase used in Exodus 20:3 at the beginning of the Ten Commandments, the commandment to have 'no other gods before me' – 'no other gods to my face'. In the new covenant, God calls us into face-to-face communion with him. That is the greatest privilege of new-covenant people.

And it is as if in that context we snap our fingers in the face of God and say, 'No, I would rather follow my own imagination.' That is why God cannot come to bless his people.

It is important to explore the nature of this provocation, because the detail of Isaiah is written for our instruction. Although it's written in eighth-century-BC terms, there are distinct principles communicated that you and I need to take into our own lives and into our churches. And we must humbly and honestly, before God, pray that he will preserve us from drifting into our own thinking, which provokes him and angers him. Notice four things they were doing.

Unauthorized sacrifice (verse 3b)

What was it that provoked God? 'Offering sacrifices in gardens and burning incense on altars of brick'. That's very eighth-century; what does it actually mean? It means that it was more convenient to have a do-it-yourself altar in the back garden than to have to go to Jerusalem and the temple and get involved with the priests. It was an expensive business; surely God would understand if they provided an alternative, more user-friendly method in their own back yard.

But the garden is the wrong place; God has said they must sacrifice only in the temple at Jerusalem. And bricks are the wrong material for an altar. And though it didn't seem to matter very much, what they were really doing was despising the temple, the priesthood, the law and God himself.

Do-it-yourself religion, on your own terms, always indicates that things are going wrong in the church. It is particularly so when people begin to think they can make themselves acceptable to God by their own alternatives: good works, Christian service, religious ritual, and years of church membership.

There is no other altar than the cross. There is no other lamb than the Lord Jesus. There is no alternative sacrifice. We must stand for that and fight it, in a day when the church is leaning to its own imagination.

Alternative revelation (verse 4a)

They 'sit among the graves and spend their nights keeping secret vigil' (verse 4). This is a reference to occult practices. 'Sitting among the tombs' is an attempt to communicate with the dead. The 'secret' vigil (literally, in guarded places) means that they were hidden away safe from interruption, unseen, they thought, except by God. Isaiah has already clearly condemned this in 8:19, where in a famous verse he says: 'When men tell you to consult mediums and spiritists, who whisper and mutter, should not a people enquire of their God? Why consult the dead on behalf of the living? To the law and to the testimony!'

The prohibition goes right back to Deuteronomy 18. Alternative means of revelation provoke God. If there is any sort of occult involvement in your life – astrology, New Age channelling, meditation techniques, *etc.* – it is a provocation to God. And if you're expecting to understand more about God and the ultimate from that channel than you are from his word, you need to repent of it and put it behind you, for his word says we must have nothing to do with it. The danger is that we want to know what God has not revealed, and we reject what he has revealed.

That's always a sign of disease among God's people. As soon as we start to write off God's written revelation in Scripture as culturally conditioned – 'Oh, that was only Paul! Even Jesus was a man of his times' – we provoke God. When we start to look to contemporary scholars to help us wriggle out of the plain meaning of Scripture because it challenges our worldliness and our own cultural conditioning, we provoke God to his face. When we allow the word of today's pundit, scholar or teacher to sideline God's clear revelation in Scripture, and we say, 'The Bible is a book God wrote to his people yesterday', we demand a direct revelation to us today; we turn our backs on the sufficiency of Scripture, we provoke God to his face, we become a church under his judgment.

Flagrant disobedience (verse 4b)

'[They] eat the flesh of pigs, and [their] pots hold broth of unclean meat.' That follows alternative revelation as surely as the night follows the day. When God's authoritative word is ignored, anything goes and the most flagrant rebellion will flourish.

The point here is that the distinction between the clean and the unclean is being disregarded. Pigs' flesh was forbidden to the Israelites (*cf*. Lv. 11), and the unclean meat in their stew is rotting meat that's been kept beyond the time the law allowed. It may be that there's some pagan ritual involved, but the law which was given to draw the dividing line between what is acceptable to God and what is not, on the basis of his holy character, is being systematically flouted.

It's a mark of sickness in the church when God's standards of holiness are gradually eroded and the people of God become virtually indistinguishable from the world around them. Jesus said, 'If you love me, keep my commandments.'

A false spirituality (verse 5a)

The culmination is a false spirituality that says, 'Keep away, don't come near me. I'm too sacred for you.'

The people who were seeking other channels of revelation, who were worshipping in their own way, who were flagrantly disobeying what God had said, actually believed that they had a superior spirituality that set them apart from ordinary mortals, because of these detestable practices. 'They developed their own notions of holiness. In particular a holiness of élitism, that stood aloof from fellowship and created divisions of first-class and second-class citizenship based on special experiences or claims such as find no place in the Bible' (Alec Motyer).

Does that ring any bells? When a contemporary evangelist claims that he has an end-time vision from the Lord which is not in the Bible, but can be yours if you send in a monetary gift; or that two of your relatives will be converted through his prayers if you send so much money for each of them – do you not think that is a provocation to God? Is it not smoke in his nostrils? Isn't it a constant irritant of fire that keeps burning all day? And when we're told that real spirituality lies in wordless prayer or the mindless repetition of Christian mantras, or the contemplation of icons, or the latest in group nostrums, don't we have to realize that all we're being offered is membership of an élite club, a mutual admiration society?

The Bible shows us that these are signs of the old problem, the disease of man-centred substitutes for the living God. Twenty-five years ago John Stott wrote, 'It is the contention of evangelicals that they are plain Bible Christians, and that in order to be a biblical Christian it is necessary to be an evangelical Christian.' How much we need to hear that today! Biblical, evangelical Christianity is not just one alternative among many equally acceptable strands of

Christian belief and practice. We believe in one way to God and only one way, through the substitutionary death of Jesus Christ, the incarnate Son of God on the cross. We believe that the Scriptures stand as the unique and totally sufficient revelation of the character and mind of God, that they are the living and enduring active word of God, and that what Scripture says, God is saying today. We believe that the life of holiness and the life of obedience to God's revealed word must be lived in the power of his Spirit and expressed in faith, hope and love. And we believe that as we respond in obedience to the Word of God, through that indwelling Spirit, we're united together – 'all one in Christ Jesus' (Gal. 3:28) – and are progressively being changed into his likeness.

My friends, if we stray from those great convictions we bring ourselves under God's chastening hand. There is a great battle being fought today in the church for those convictions. I urge you, if you believe that truth, to stand for and contend for that truth. For God says in verse 6, 'It stands written before me; I will not keep silent but will pay back in full . . . both your sins and the sins of your fathers . . .' It's the old problem. We shouldn't be surprised about it, and we shouldn't be daunted by it, but we must be realistic about it. We must be prepared to have backbone and stand for what is true and right in our generation. But the God with whom the chapter began is not the helpless victim of his people's sin.

And so we come to the second, quite short section.

The remnant remedy (verses 8–12)

God is coming to do something about it. He is going to answer even though they don't call properly upon him. He is a God committed to working out his purposes. And whenever God comes to rescue he comes both to judge and to divide. He's going to save his people from a situation on which his wrath is poured.

Verse 8 is the salvation aspect of the judgment in verses 6 and 7. The picture is of the grape harvest. A cluster is discovered in which there's still some juice, so it is preserved rather than destroyed. There's still some 'blessing' in it – the literal meaning. 'So,' God says, 'I will select a remnant of faithful people.' He describes them in verse 9 as 'my chosen' and 'my servants'. They will be the descendants and possessors of the land. That takes us right back to the ancient promises to Abraham, which become the agenda for the whole of the Bible. The echoes of covenant language are a certain indication of this.

Those who are chosen become the Lord's servants. The true sign of living faith is always obedience. The mark that God has chosen me to be his child is that I obey him as my heavenly Father. What happens when the remnant is obedient to God is described in verse 10. In Old Testament vocabulary, 'Sharon' is a name for the far west of the Holy Land, and 'Achor' for the far east. Thus he takes the land of Israel from west to east and symbolizes the whole breadth of the country from Sharon to Achor. From the extremities and including everything in between, the land is going to be secure and prosperous. It's going to be a pasture for flocks and a resting-place for herds. To what end? 'For my people who seek me.' It is a direct contrast with verse 1, where his people do not seek him.

A righteous remnant of people will seek God. The rebellious are the focus of verses 11 and 12 again; rather than seeking the Lord, they forsake him and forget to worship him. They are busy devoting their time to the false idols of fate and destiny. But in a play on words, God says that the only destiny they're securing is God's wrath in death and destruction. Just like the remnant, they were called, they were spoken to. But they didn't answer and they wouldn't listen. They pursued their own ways and their own imaginations.

So you see, everything depends on the authenticity and reality of our relationship with God. 'Seek the Lord while he may be found; call on him while he is near' (Is. 55:6).

Just as there was a remnant of faithful Jews within the larger body of national Israel, so in the covenant era there will always be a true remnant of the godly among a visible church which may sometimes seem largely apostate. Our task is to recognize that reality, to search our own hearts and seek humbly and in dependence on God to live according to his revelation in the power of his Spirit; to instruct ourselves according to the mind of God in Scripture; to teach ourselves and our families and our local congregations to be faithful to the Lord.

And if this week at Word Alive means anything at all in the long-term future of your life or of your church, it must mean that we go back, from all we have learned together this week, with a new confidence and commitment to the centrality of the living word of God as it speaks to us of the living Lord. And that as we submit to Jesus and ask him to fill us afresh day by day with his Spirit, he guides us into the ways that he wants us to live through his revelation, so that we are – people of the book? Yes, but people of the *living word* that changes our minds, our hearts and our actions.

It was said of John Bunyan, author of *Pilgrim's Progress*, that his blood was 'bibline' – if you cut his veins the Bible would flow out of them. Oh for some John Bunyans in our generation! God is looking for people who will take him seriously. He has spoken sixty-six books of his truth to us; what are you doing to get into it? How will you respond when Obadiah asks you in heaven, 'Did you enjoy my book?'

God's solution is a remnant of people who take him seriously. It's always been the way, and we need to keep encouraging one another to persevere in that demanding task.

The new order (verses 13–25)

The last section is introduced by the formula, 'Therefore this is what the Sovereign LORD says . . .', and the rest of the chapter forms one long unit exploring the glorious future God has for those who seek him.

Remember, it starts here. Remember those hills again. It starts in the 'now' of the gospel, but here in this world it is always going to be partial and imperfect because we are not yet sinless. We're pressing on to know him better; we're longing to see his victory in our lives more and more. His Spirit is given to us to experience that, but we know that it isn't until we see him that we shall be really like him, when we see him as he is. So we always have the tension of what we have now (the down-payment, the first instalment), and what is not yet ours but will be one day in heaven.

That's why the notion of perfection on earth is an illusion. That is what heaven is for! We are not promised that we'll be infinitely healthy, wealthy and wise in this world. But we are promised that in the world to come we will be made into the likeness of Jesus Christ. We mustn't try to pull the 'then' into the 'now', because if we do we'll live in a fantasy land. But we must live in the now in the light of the then; and we must let the then – the future, the 'not yet' – activate us as we live in this world as citizens of heaven.

We've already noted the division between 'my servants' and those who follow the ways of false religion, but in verses 13–15 it is spelt out very clearly in a number of contrasts. The 'you' to whom he speaks are of course the people he's been addressing in the first half of the chapter: outwardly religious, but their hearts far from God; compromising, following their own imaginations, forsaking and forgetting the Lord.

Notice what he says the new order will first produce.

A new lifestyle (verses 13–16)

A clear contrast runs all the way through the Old Testament, between salvation and judgment, clean and unclean, blessing and curse. Just as Israel, at the end of the Torah in Deuteronomy, is presented with the contrast between the blessings that accompany obedience and the curses which inevitably accompany rebellion; so here at the end

155

of Isaiah, the same black-and-white issues are focused. This is how the promises and threats of the previous paragraph work out.

How is the new order characterized for the faithful remnant?

'My servants will eat . . . drink . . . rejoice . . . sing out of the joy . . .' (verses 13–14). So for those who follow God's way, the new lifestyle – here in this world in a measure but supremely in that world in fullness – is characterized by satisfaction and fulfilment. God's external provision of food and drink is matched by the internal rejoicing.

But for those who forsake the Lord, the exact opposite is the case. Hunger and thirst are matched by shame and wailing, anguished hearts and broken spirits. 'You will go hungry . . . go thirsty . . . be put to shame . . . you will cry out from anguish of heart.' They're pictures of heaven and hell. Jesus taught that one of the greatest torments of hell will be the gnashing of teeth, the knowledge of what might have been. If only, if only! There are ultimately only two ways to live; two gates, two roads, two destinations. And while many things in this life may be grey and unspecific, that is not true of the paths that lead to two utterly different eternal destinies.

The end points are very clear. Verse 15, 'You will leave your name to my chosen ones as a curse; the Sovereign LORD will put you to death, but to his servants he will give another name.' To be put to death by the Sovereign Lord is to prove to be under his curse. Significantly, 'you' in verse 15 is singular, bringing home to every individual the message of our personal responsibility before God.

'But to his servants he will give another name.' Just as Abram was called Abraham, and Simon was called Peter, so, as we become the focus of this great plan of God, he gives us a new name. He calls us by his name. We are Israel, the new people of God. The new name speaks of a new nature, destination and prospects. They're linked by it to the God of truth. He is, as verse 16 tells us, the God of the Amen. So under the new name, living the new lifestyle in the new land of heaven, whoever invokes a blessing will do so by the God of truth, the God of the Amen, who can always be relied upon to keep his promises. That's why the blessing is so certain and why the oaths are so powerful.

Thus the new land will have new standards and new characteristics; and even God himself (verse 16) will forget the past with all its troubles; and if it's no longer valid before God, it no longer exists.

We have the measure of that now. He has 'hurled all our iniquities into the depths of the sea' (Mi. 7:19). As the old preacher said, he's erected a sign: 'No fishing.' God has finished with our sins. He's removed them as far as the east is from the west. And yet, we still know that we are sinners. We are daily reminded of our fallen nature. But when we're in his presence we won't even remember that. It will be no longer a part of reality. Our new lifestyle begun here will be fulfilled in heaven.

A new city (verses 17–20)

These are wonderful words of promise for us as we seek to live according to the new lifestyle and as we wait for its ultimate fulfilment in heaven. Everything is going to be made new (verse 17). The new city is going to be God's special delight and ours too. Verse 17 takes us right back to Genesis 1:1. 'In the beginning God created the heavens and the earth.' That's the totality of creation. Genesis 1:1 is saying that everything that is, exists because of God; and here in verse 17 is the totality of a new creation. At the end of what we call time, God's final work of new creation will parallel his first creation as it was at the very beginning. It takes us to Revelation, the new heaven and the new earth, with the holy city, the new Jerusalem, coming down out of heaven from God.

Much of the detailed reality of that is, of course, hidden from us. But there is enough in Scripture to fill our hearts and to whet our appetites. One of the most glorious of heaven's realities is the newness of it all. As God blots out the past, so shall we. 'The former things will not be remembered, nor will they come to mind.'

'The former things' is a very comprehensive phrase. Not just the troubles of the past, but all of the old order will be forgotten; the failure and the sin will not be remembered. Look at that lovely word at the end of verse 17; it's not simply that God will not remember them, they won't even come to *our* minds to accuse us.

For a long time now I've realized that one of my spiritual gifts is the gift of amnesia. I think it's a great spiritual gift! So often I can't remember details of what happened, and that can be an enormous spiritual blessing. Amnesia about this old order will be one of the supreme blessings of heaven. Our minds will be taken up instead with the great new works of God's creative power. 'Be glad and rejoice for ever in what I will create,' says the Lord. For at the centre of the new world stands the new Jerusalem, entirely and solely God's work, a delight to him, its people a joy. 'I will rejoice over Jerusalem and take delight in my people.'

So the book of Isaiah has moved from the false, hypocritical worship of the physical Jerusalem which was under God's judgment, to the true worship of the Lord in the new Jerusalem. And it's not just the space or the location that God delights in, but its inhabitants; 'its people' (verse 18) are 'my people' (verse 19). The holy city is

157

inhabited by sanctified people, and that's the guarantee of perpetual joy and happiness about which verse 19 speaks: 'the sound of weeping and of crying will be heard . . . no more'. It's the Lord's presence among his people that makes heaven heaven. Do you remember what Jesus promised us? 'I will come back and take you to be with me, that you also may be where I am' (Jn. 14:3).

That's what heaven is. The same note is sounded in Revelation, in those great verses which are the fulfilment of Isaiah's vision: 'And I heard a loud voice from the throne saying, "Now [at last] the dwelling of God is with men, and he will live with them. They will be his people, and God himself will be with them and be their God"' (Rev. 21:3).

When? When the holy city, the new Jerusalem, comes down from God to be the dwelling-place of his people: 'He will wipe every tear from their eyes. There will be no more death or mourning or crying or pain, for the old order of things has passed away. He who was seated on the throne said, "I am making everything new!"' (Rev. 21:4). And towards the end of the chapter, in verse 22: 'I did not see a temple in the city, because the Lord God Almighty and the Lamb are its temple.'

The temple is no longer required. We need God in Jesus, the Lamb; that's where our sacrifice is, that's where our altar is. 'The city does not need the sun or the moon to shine on it, for the glory of God gives it light, and the Lamb is its lamp. The nations will walk by its light, and kings of the earth will bring their splendour into it.'

Look on to 22:3: 'No longer will there be any curse. The throne of God and of the Lamb will be in the city, and his servants will serve him.' We're not going to have to sit on a cloud all the time twiddling our thumbs! There's going to be plenty to do. 'They will see his face, and his name will be on their foreheads. There will be no more night. They will not need the light of a lamp or the light of the sun, for the Lord God will give them light. And they will reign for ever and ever.'

That's the New Testament fulfilment, in eternal and spiritual terms, of the blessings of the covenant which God delights to lavish on his chosen ones.

Back in Isaiah 65, those blessings are expressed in concrete, Old Testament terms. So verse 20 speaks about people living beyond a hundred, about no infants dying. Those are pictures of the Old Testament covenant blessings of long life, which is a symbol in the Old Testament of eternal life in the new order. But the last thing that this passage gives us in verses 21–25 is not only the new city and the new lifestyle, but the new security.

A new security (verses 21–25)

'They will build houses and dwell in them' (verse 21). The long history of Israel was beset by frustration and fruitlessness. So often they built houses and planted vineyards, both investments for the future, only to see the land overrun by marauders, and what they treasured, plundered and destroyed. Of course it was the judgment of God on their disobedience that brought it about. But the new Jerusalem has none of these frustrations, for now God's people are wholly at one with him; they're fully justified, so the tree in the second part of verse 22 is a picture of long life and stability. Heaven will be the eternal enjoyment and fulfilment of all that we are and have in Christ. No-one will deny us the fruit of our labour. No invading armies will spoil or destroy our families. Instead, God's people from every generation will share the blessings of the Lord.

The last two verses relate the security of heaven to the unity of those who dwell there. Verse 24 is a great verse: 'Before they call I will answer; while they are still speaking I will hear.' We often take it out of context, but it has here a limited meaning: here in this world we do live in fellowship with the Lord, although it's marred and spoiled so often. He is a God who often answers us before we pray. While we're still speaking to him we know he hears and that he is moving in his grace toward us. But that will be even more our experience in heaven. There he anticipates every need of his people, providing even before they call. There's such a closeness of relationship that every word is heard and responded to by God.

This deep heart unity between God and his chosen ones is reflected throughout the new creation. The new heavens and the new earth are going to have wolves and lambs and lions in them, but the wolf and the lamb will feed together and the lion will eat straw like an ox. The old hostilities will disappear; the whole new order is an order at peace. But again, to quote Alec Motyer, the only point in the whole of the new creation where there is no change is in the curse pronounced on the serpent and on sin, which still stands. That's the other side of the new creation. It is the eternal judgment of God on those who rebel against him. But for those who are his people, the whole created order is now God's holy mountain. That's what rules out danger and destruction, because the Lord dwells in holiness with his people there, and that is eternal security.

And that, friends, is the hope that gives focus to our discipleship in this world. That's what keeps us living in the now, in the light of eternity. That's the context in which we go out to live gospel lives back in the world. We are citizens of the new Jerusalem, the meeting-place between heaven and earth. All our enemies have been defeated by the Lord who reigns in Zion. We his chosen ones from all the nations will come to his holy city, to discover the promise of his total salvation and to live in unhindered harmony with our Creator-redeemer, our sovereign shepherd.

All the effects of the fall and sin are reversed. Everything that spoils is removed and forgotten. All things have become new, and all these blessings are based on the relationship of love and trust with Yahweh, our sovereign Lord – begun in this world, completed and experienced in full in heaven, when we see him face to face, and are made like him and are with him for ever. This is the word of our God and it stands for ever. And he will do it.

THE SINS OF HALF-HEARTEDNESS
Studies in Malachi
Roy Clements

9
Doubt

Malachi 1:1–5

We knocked on the door and went in. The mother burst into tears almost immediately, and pointed to the little cot in the corner. We knew already that it was her first baby, for whom she and her husband had been praying for many months. The child had been born handicapped. Between sobs, the mother blurted out the question: 'Does God care?'

It is the question we always ask when any kind of tragedy strikes. It was the question that Jews had been asking for a couple of centuries, long before Malachi had arrived on the scene. They had had so long to grieve that now they no longer expressed their doubt about God's care through tears, but with a sarcastic curl of the lips and a wearied shrug of the shoulders.

'"I have loved you," says the LORD. "But you ask, 'How have you loved us?'"'(Mal. 1:2).

Almost everybody who has ever tried their hand at open-air preaching has encountered the heckler; the person who shouts from the audience in an attempt to throw you off your stroke or embarrass you. Martin Luther probably delivered the best response to such an interruption. A trouble-maker demanded loudly, 'Well, what was God doing before he made the world then?' Luther, quoting his theological mentor Augustine, is reputed to have replied: 'Making hell for people who ask stupid questions like that!'

If you have ever faced that kind of hostile questioning, you will have plenty of sympathy for Malachi, for it seems that there were plenty of hecklers disturbing his attempt at public speaking too. Every time he makes a statement throughout the course of these four chapters, some sarcastic or dismissive retort is thrown back at him from his audience. Here is the first example. 'I have loved you,' says the Lord. 'But you ask, "How? You don't expect us to believe that!"'

Another example: 'You have despised God's name,' says Malachi. 'Prove it!' shouts back the wise-cracker (cf. 1:6).

Again in chapter 2: 'You have wearied the Lord,' he says. 'Pull the other leg, Malachi,' comes the riposte (cf. 2:17).

'You are robbing God,' he asserts. 'Stuff and nonsense,' they reply (cf. 3:8).

Some commentators regard this heckling dialogue merely as a literary device to express the unresponsiveness of Malachi's contemporaries. But to me it sounds far more like authentic, live reporting.

Imagine, then, Malachi preaching his open-air sermon in the Jerusalem market-place. But his hearers are giving him a rough ride. It is quite clear that the Jews to whom he is speaking do not feel they deserve his prophetic rebukes and comment. 'What right has this fellow to criticize us?' they say. 'We are not irreligious – why, if anyone deserves to be put into the dock, it is God. Considering all we have done for him, he has done very little for us. He just does not care.' And superficially perhaps they had grounds for their indignation.

For Malachi's hearers are not faithless apostates. There *had* been a time a few centuries earlier when prophets like Elijah, Isaiah and Jeremiah had had very good grounds for their pulpit invective. For Baal worship was corrupting the people then.

But now all that was past history. These Jews to whom Malachi speaks are not like that any more. God punished the Jews for all their previous idolatry. He sent them into Babylonian exile for seventy years, and that chastening experience has, to a considerable extent, had the desired effect. They have learned the folly of their idolatrous ways, they have come to appreciate their national heritage and want to preserve it. Indeed, so committed are they to their Jewish culture and their Jewish religion now that this particular group of Jews had actually sacrificed what for many of them would have been quite a comfortable and prosperous existence in Babylon. They had returned to Judah to rebuild the temple in Jerusalem and to reoccupy the city and reconstruct its ruined walls. You can read the whole story in the books of Ezra and Nehemiah.

Of course, it did not all happen in a few days. Malachi is preaching his sermon some ninety or one hundred years after the first group of Jews had returned to Jerusalem from their exile. By now the rebuilding of the city is complete. In fact we are told in Nehemiah 8 – 10 (which is useful background material to Malachi) that when the reconstruction of the walls, the temple and everything was complete, Ezra the scribe read the law of God (probably to these very Jews, or at least to their parents). And they were brought to tears by the reading of God's word. They collectively confessed their earlier sins and made a solemn promise in writing, signed by all their leaders, that in future they would be true to the covenant which God had made with Israel. There would be no more compromise with paganism; no more disobeying the Ten Commandments; no more neglect of God's temple. From now on they were going to do right what their forefathers had so conspicuously failed to do right.

Their promise had not been without effect; there were indeed no more altars to Baal among them, no more cult prostitutes to Ashtaroth, no more child sacrifices to Moloch. All those abominations were past. The temple of Jehovah was once again the religious centre of the Jewish community. No-one would have dreamed of abandoning that temple now. They had built it with their own bare hands.

And yet, in spite of all their piety, Malachi is not satisfied. With the insight of a prophet, he can detect a new form of spiritual failure in the people. Not the gross and obvious sort of apostasy that characterized the pre-exilic period, but a subtle invasive weed growing up in the midst of God's vineyard nevertheless; a weed that could grow and blossom, even in the midst of their apparent orthodoxy.

In these four morning studies we are going to identify some of the symptoms of that malaise. Tomorrow in 1:6 – 2:9 we shall hear Malachi bemoaning the *apathy* the people displayed in regard to public worship: they attended the temple, but they made sure their religion did not cost them too much. One gets the distinct impression that for many of them, public worship had become a tedious and mechanical routine. And to make matters worse, the clergy were encouraging them in this lukewarm, lackadaisical attitude.

Next, in 2:10–16, we shall find Malachi addressing the *infidelity* of the people in their domestic lives. Not necessarily the sort of infidelity that issues in adulterous relationships, though there may have been some instances of that. No, these Jews simply did not demonstrate any spiritual commitment to God in their family life. They went to the temple, but that was where it ended. So, for example, they were not bothered about the religious affiliation of their marital partners. 'My wife is a pagan – so what? Everyone will get to heaven in the end. You've got to live and let live. It doesn't matter what you believe so long as you are sincere.'

Doubly disturbing for Malachi was the fact that the divorce rate was also escalating. People were dumping their marital partners in the way you might dump an old car to make way for a newer, more attractive model. In neither of these areas – choosing a pagan partner or abandoning an existing partner – were the people of God showing the least sensitivity to what God thought about their behaviour.

Then finally in 2:17 – 4:6 we shall see Malachi putting his finger on the prevailing *cynicism* of their general moral behaviour. They were becoming sceptical about the whole business of right and wrong.

'Look,' they were saying, 'people get away with murder in this world. It's all very well for old-fashioned preachers like Malachi to waffle all that theology about God's justice – but let's face it, God has created a thoroughly unjust world. There's no profit-margin in goodness. Look at us: we have left our homes in Babylon, cashed in our life savings, come back here to Jerusalem to work on a building site, and why? Because prophets like Malachi told us God was going to renew the old kingdom of David in all its glory, that's why.

'And what have we got for all our pain? We've got a third-rate temple that would make us a laughing stock if we'd built it in Babylon; we've got a jerry-built city wall that would have a hard job keeping out a troop of Boy Scouts, and we've got empty stomachs half the time. The economy is not picking up. The dream just hasn't materialized. The kingdom of David hasn't arrived. We are still political pawns of the Persian Empire. We have no real freedom; the wealth and the power lie in the hands of our enemies – pagan enemies, who couldn't care less about Jehovah, the God of Israel. Yet they're the ones with money in their pockets! A God of justice? Don't make me laugh! "Do others before they do you," that's the moral philosophy that works.'

Let me repeat: these are not blatant unbelievers with whom Malachi is dealing. They are church-goers, people who pride themselves on their religion. This is the seed-bed from which the Judaism we meet 400 years later in the time of Jesus was to sprout. These are not idolaters. If anything, they are incipient scribes and Pharisees. Yet there is apathy in their public worship, infidelity in their domestic relationships, and cynicism in their moral attitudes.

Such attitudes, I suggest, are far from uncommon among the people of God. In fact they are typical second-generation temptations. In the early days of any movement of spiritual renewal among God's people the danger is always fanaticism: zeal can all too easily be perverted into error as people go over the top in their new-found spiritual enthusiasm; and heresies, cults and sectarian divisions are often the result. But once the first flush of that early excitement dies away and the battle for theological orthodoxy has been won, then a new danger starts to emerge: the 'second-generation' temptation to complacency, to compromise, to worldliness, to indifference.

You can see that story repeated over and over again. Every new denomination that has ever emerged in church history was, in its infancy, an attempt – often a laudable and necessary one – to rediscover the enthusiasm, purity and commitment of the apostolic age. They read the book of Acts, they looked at the church around, and said, 'It is not like that any longer: we must make it like that.' And every denomination, in the wake of that early pristine devotion, has discovered the perils of second-generation half-heartedness. Disillusionment sets in, our fond dreams do not materialize, our triumphalism is drowned by the icy water of realism. And, just like Malachi's audience, we start to doubt as a result.

That was the root of their spiritual malaise: doubt. Not the sort of doubt that questions the existence of God, but the sort of doubt that questions whether it is really worth the effort to worship him; that questions what profit there is in being a Christian, with all the effort it involves; that questions whether the Bible really does bring blessing to those who obey it; that questions whether God cares in the least for those whom he calls his people. And there are many among evangelical Christians today who walk the same dangerous path.

In the earlier part of this century it was the battle for truth that was critical. The inspiration of Scripture, the atoning significance of the cross, the deity of Jesus – those were the cardinal issues. But for most evangelicals those battles are now fought and won. We are committed to an orthodox confession of faith. Most of us are embedded in a theological tradition that in its biblicism cannot be faulted. And yet, just like these post-exilic Jews, we can still make the cardinal mistake of resting on our laurels.

For some of us, I suspect, the passion of our spiritual youth has decayed into mid-life spiritual inertia. It shows perhaps in our attitude to worship, as it did among these Israelites. We go to church, but once a week on a Sunday morning is quite enough with a schedule like ours. We sometimes take a look at our Bibles, but habits of personal prayer and Bible study have become undisciplined – when was the last time we spent much time with God on our own? And though we still manage to show a certain amount of emotional engagement in our choruses and our songs while we are worshipping together in public, maybe the words 'What a burden it all is!' sometimes hover, if not on our lips, then at the back of our minds.

It shows too in our attitude to family life. 'What does it matter if I go out with a non-Christian?' says the Christian Union member. 'So my wife and I are getting divorced – what does it matter? It's not the unforgivable sin, is it?' says the church member.

It shows, perhaps most of all, in our attitude to moral action generally. Evangelical preachers of an earlier generation used to talk a great deal about 'holiness', about the need for a thorough moral repentance in our lives. They preached the law as well as the gospel. They preached the need for church discipline as well as church growth. They wanted to see people sanctified as well as justified, discipled as well as converted.

But today I detect a cosier and less disturbing spirit abroad in our evangelical churches, one more at ease with the values of the secular world. It is a spirit that wants to identify with evangelical Christianity, but lacks the whole-hearted commitment that authentic biblical faith demands of those who would profess it. In short, I detect doubt.

It's not the kind of doubt that denies the creed – we can be vitriolic about bishops who question Christ's bodily resurrection when we want to be – but the sort of doubt that is unwilling to give one hundred per cent. It is not the doubt of the atheist, but that of the nominal Christian; that questions not whether it is true, but whether it is important; not whether God exists, but whether he is really worth the effort – whether, at the end of the day, faith makes a difference.

What then is the answer to this insidious, second-generation half-heartedness? How do you restore enthusiasm and motivation in spiritual things to people who have grown weary and disillusioned in their profession of faith?

The temptation, I suppose, is to address the symptoms. You can counter the apathy by whipping up more emotion in public worship, by putting a stronger beat in the choruses perhaps. You can counter the infidelity in domestic life by getting someone to publish a good book on sex and marriage. You can counter the rise in divorce rates by getting some Christian pressure group organized to campaign for stricter divorce laws and so forth. You can counter the moral cynicism of the church by carting everybody off to Keswick, or to Spring Harvest, for some good holiness teaching. Best of all, of course, organize a mission! If you cannot have true piety, you can at least have plenty of evangelistic activity in the church.

Malachi certainly does deal with a number of specific symptoms, as we shall be seeing in subsequent studies. But what I want you to notice very carefully, is this: *that is not where he begins*. His response to the compromise and the complacency of God's people is far more radical than merely to address the outward symptoms of failure. In these opening verses he goes to the root of the problem, the root of the doubt that was feeding their lack of commitment.

God's special love

'"I have loved you," says the LORD.'

I want you to notice that Malachi is not talking here about God's general love for all people. He is speaking about God's special love for his own people: 'I have loved *you*, my chosen people.' For the root of their complacency, their indifference, infidelity, cynicism and apathy, lay in the fact that they did not really believe that God did love them or even care about them. Their adversities had destroyed their assurance of God's personal commitment to them. So Malachi sees his first task as a prophet to be that of reassuring them of the indestructible covenant love of God.

'"I have loved you," says the LORD. "But you ask, 'How have you loved us?'"'

'"Was not Esau Jacob's brother?" the LORD says. "Yet I have loved Jacob, but Esau I have hated, and I have turned his mountains into a wasteland and left his inheritance to the desert jackals"'(1:2–3).

We have already observed that the recent history of the Jews had been traumatic. Their homeland had been devastated by the Babylonian invasion. The temple had been destroyed. Most of the population had been exiled. It had been a crippling blow to their national pride.

Their sense of humiliation had not been eased by the fact that their neighbour Edom had not suffered the same fate. In fact, as the little book of Obadiah tells us, the Edomites had derived great personal satisfaction from Israel's catastrophe, and had exploited her military weakness to settle some old scores. The Edomites were the descendants of Esau, Jacob's brother, and there had been bad blood between these two tribes ever since the very early days when Jacob had cheated his older brother out of their father Isaac's blessing. So as far as the Edomites were concerned, when the Babylonian army stormed Jerusalem the Israelites were finally getting what they deserved. They were elated at the prospect of the Israelites' economic and political misery and they did everything they could to rub salt into the wound.

For the Jews, of course, that simply added insult to injury. How could God – their God, the God of Jacob – stand idly by and let the sons of Esau gloat over the misfortunes of Jacob's sons? It was a cruel and treacherous stab in the back! How could they go on believing that the covenant God was faithful to them?

And yet Malachi insists that God *is* faithful, and that they can and they must believe in his faithfulness. If only they would open their eyes to the working of his providence, they would realize how much he loved them. After all, just look at what has happened to Edom now!

'Esau I have hated. I have turned his mountains into a wasteland and left his inheritance to the desert jackals,' God said.

This is a reference to what happened in the century following the Babylonian conquest. Though Edom escaped the punitive treatment by the Babylonians, another very aggressive people had in due course overrun Edomite territory; and now Edom was in a far worse condition than Israel. The Israelites had been invited by the Persian emperor to return to their homeland and reoccupy it; but no such decree had been made for the Edomites. On the contrary, their land was a ruin. No national resurrection was scheduled for them, said the Lord.

> Edom may say, 'Though we have been crushed, we will rebuild the ruins.'
> But this is what the LORD Almighty says, 'They may build, but I will demolish. They will be called the Wicked Land, a people always under the wrath of the LORD. You will see it with your own eyes and say, "Great is the LORD – even beyond the borders of Israel!"' (1:4–5)

Malachi, then, insists that the Jews were doubting God's special love for them only because they were looking at events in the short term. If they wanted to understand what was happening to them they must remove the myopic distorting lenses from their eyes and see God's purpose through long-distance glasses. They must cultivate a broader perspective on events. Yes, God had punished Israel for her sins: but he had not consigned Israel to permanent destruction. Yes, he had disciplined them, but he had not abandoned them. As Malachi will record later on in his prophecy, 'I the LORD do not change. So you, O descendants of Jacob, are not destroyed' (3:6).

This then is the central thrust of Malachi's prophecy, the context for everything else he is going to teach us over these four days. '"I have loved you," says the LORD.' Do not doubt it. Certainly you can point to plenty of unbelievers who seem to be having a much easier time than you are having right now. 'So what?' asks Malachi. 'It's all purely temporary.' For to be outside the covenant people of God is to be under God's judgment. It is to stand in danger, not only of his chastening hand, but of his everlasting judicial anger. What could be worse than that? Any blessing the world may think it now enjoys,

Malachi tells us, is going to be proved in the final analysis to be very ephemeral and shallow. This universe will witness the vindication of God's people. Believe in it! How can you doubt it, when God has said, 'I have loved you'?

If you are a Christian, God says the same to you. No matter how much pain you may have had to endure, no matter how much humiliation you may feel you have suffered, God says to you and to me just as he said to his prophet Malachi and the Israelites, 'I have loved you.'

What does Paul say in his letter to the Ephesians? 'He chose us in [Christ] before the creation of the world . . . In love he predestined us to be adopted as his sons . . . in accordance with his pleasure and will' (Eph. 1:4–5).

Make no mistake about it, our conscious awareness of that special, electing, eternal love is the root of all true Christian commitment. It is the fuel that stokes all true Christian enthusiasm. Christianity is not a legalistic duty, a tedious routine in which we are driven by guilt or habit or mere tradition. Christianity is a joyous celebration of an unshakeable divine affection for us. '"I have loved you," says the LORD.' Do you believe that?

A young couple were to be married. A few days before the wedding the young man was becoming a little nervous about the huge promises he was expected to make. So he went for some fatherly advice to one of the older church members who had been married for many years. 'Tell me,' he asked, 'in all those years you have been married, have you never contemplated divorce?'

The old man thought for a few moments, then replied, 'Divorce, never. Murder – often!'

Perhaps that comes close to what God feels about us. Yes, he is rough with us sometimes; but that is precisely because he loves us. Whatever happens, he will not be separated from us; he is determined to take us to glory.

The implications of love

Consider with me then a few implications of this remarkable opening statement. 'I have loved you.' What does it mean?

First let me say what it does *not* mean.

No élitism

It does not mean that there is any excuse for elitism among the people of God.

That danger has always existed, of course. The Jews have fallen into it at times. The Christian church in South Africa has done so too in certain respects. All Christians are vulnerable to the danger of treating God's covenant as the ground for some kind of racist arrogance. Put that idea out of your head; it is quite illegitimate. For the fact is, as Paul affirms on this very issue in Romans 2, God does not show favouritism.

In that connection it is important not to misunderstand the phrase, 'Esau I have hated.' The Hebrew language often exaggerates to make a point. Technically it is called 'hyperbole'. Jesus used it once in Luke 14:26, when he said that anyone who comes to him must 'hate' his father and his mother. Can you imagine Jesus encouraging hate? But he was a Hebrew and he was used to using Hebrew hyperbole. He did not mean, of course, that Christians should literally detest their parents, as his own attitude to Mary so conspicuously proves. But it was a vivid, idiomatic way of saying, 'There must be absolutely no condition or hesitation about your devotion to me. You must love me above everything else.'

A boy might very easily say something similar to his girlfriend.

'You have been making eyes at that Julia Jones,' she might say to him accusingly.

'Rubbish,' he replies. 'I can't stand the sight of Julia Jones.'

The truth is that Julia Jones might be a very attractive young lady, but he says, 'I cannot stand the sight of her', because he wants to reinforce his affirmation of devotion to his own true love.

In the same way, the Bible insists God loves the world. The psalmist says God is good to all, loving to all he has made. But he has a special love, a unique covenant love for his own people; a love which he does not share with the world at large.

A special responsibility

With the privilege of that special love comes also a special responsibility; a responsibility to be holy in the world, and to be a witness to the world. Israel had that privilege and that responsibility. When she failed in it God judged her harshly. As the prophet Amos records, 'You only have I chosen out of all the families of the earth, and that is why I am going to punish you for all your sins' (cf. Am. 3:2). In other words, precisely because you are special to me, I am going to be specially careful to punish you when you go wrong.'

Anyone who thinks that God showed partiality to the Jews should re-read those tortured passages from the book of Lamentations describing the Babylonian siege of Jerusalem. Indeed, anyone who thinks that God shows partiality toward the Jews ought to look again at the photos of Belsen and Auschwitz. Israel was never God's pampered pet. If she interpreted the covenant that way, history has disillusioned her and rightly so. Israel was not God's favourite, and neither, in that sense, is the church. In every age, the people of God are his chosen vehicle to carry forward his purpose to the world at large. Yes, they have his word, but their responsibility is to obey it. Yes, they have a special covenant relationship with him, but their responsibility is to welcome others into that relationship.

As someone has put it, the church is the only organization that exists for the sake of its non-members. The people of God exist for the sake of the world. The promise to Abraham was that through his seed all nations would be blessed. And Peter in the New Testament confers that role upon Christians: 'You are a chosen people, you are a holy nation, you are a people belonging to God' – why? 'that you may declare the praises of him who called you out of darkness into his wonderful light' (cf. 1 Pet. 2:9).

When God says, 'I love you', then, it is not to feed any élitist arrogance in us but to feed our missionary calling. Esau was outside the covenant, but there would be sons of Esau gathered around the throne on that last day, just as there will be people drawn out of every other tribe and nation and kindred. And how will they be there? Because the people of God have shown them the holiness of God and preached to them the love of God.

No spiritual pride

Again, it is all too easy to interpret the special love of God as grounds for spiritual pride. Perhaps your reaction when you hear God saying, 'I love you, but Esau I have hated' is to think how arbitrary it seems. There are the sons of Esau being allowed to plunge on their reckless route to hell, but God has arrested me. He has allowed me to discover spiritual life, he has opened my eyes, by some miracle he has awakened faith in my heart. Why me?

Every child of God asks that question. It is inevitable that they should; every child of God is *meant* to ask it. But the vital thing we have to realize is that there is no answer to it. God told Israel what his reasons for choosing them were *not*. 'I did not choose you because you were a bigger nation than any other, in fact you are one of the littlest. And I did not choose you because you were a better nation than any other, because you are one of the worst' (cf. Dt. 7:7). But never, never did he tell them why he had chosen them.

In fact immediately we start to speculate about the answer to the question 'Why me?' we create a heresy. To answer it is invariably to generate a false anti-Christian religion of good works and spiritual pride. To answer it is to destroy grace. Why did he love me? 'Well, he loved me because I am a good person . . . because I go to church . . .

171

because I have been baptized.' Or, of course, for the evangelical, 'He loved me because I put my hand up at an evangelistic meeting. I went forward and made my decision. I signed my name on a little card. I prayed the prayer with the counsellor.'

No, no, *no!* God's love is not a response to any merit found or foreseen in us. It is a unilateral act of his own grace. It is unconditional, free and generous. The correct answer to the question 'Why me?' is not any sentence that begins 'Because I . . . .' There is only one correct response, and it is, 'Thank you. I did not deserve your love, I had no claim upon it, I could not earn it, I cannot repay it. But you, Lord, out of your sovereign choice, have bestowed it upon me; and I am moved to the depths of humble gratitude by your generosity in doing so.' Do any of us understand why someone should love us? Do we understand why our husband or wife loves us? The whole point about love is that we do not know why.

Beware of spiritual pride, then. A halo only has to slip a few inches to become a noose. What does the apostle Paul say? 'God chose the foolish things of the world to shame the wise' (1 Cor. 1:27). Lowly and despised things, mere nothings, to bring to nothing those who think they are something. Why? So that there may be no boasting in his presence. That is the key. There will be no boasting in glory, nobody sticking their thumbs in their golden waistcoats saying, 'Didn't I do well?'

No. We will be there because he loved us, and God knows why. We are not required to understand this love, to rationalize or justify it; but to accept it, believe it, trust it.

The difference love makes

What difference should it make to the Jews to whom Malachi speaks, what difference to us, that we trust God's word when he says, 'I have loved you'? I am almost embarrassed by the number of avenues of application that suggest themselves. Let me give you just a couple.

Self-esteem

If we really believe that we have been loved by God in this way, it will mean we can have great dignity even in the midst of trouble and adversity. These Jews were cringing, complaining, and whining, because they thought Edom had had a better deal than themselves. But in fact, says Malachi, it is Edom who deserves their pity.

The same is true of us. There are an awful lot of people in the church who suffer from what psychologists call 'low self-esteem'. They wallow in self-pity, just as these Jews were doing. They tell you they are worth nothing. You can never pay them a compliment, because they invariably assume you do not really mean it. On the other hand, they leap at any opportunity to construe any comment as a possible criticism. Haven't you met people like that? The church is full of them. Perhaps, if you are honest, you recognize yourself as one. There is at least a strand of vulnerability to low self-esteem in most of us. But it is unnecessary.

For if you are a Christian, God loves you. That is no trite platitude to be stuck in a car windscreen. It is the truth of our existence. God loves us. The trouble with our world is that we have trivialized the words, 'I love you.' Love has become a romantic vapour of the emotions, a sentimental measles which people catch and then recover from. We fall in and out of love. And that is sad, for it means love is not something people can rely on any more. 'Till death us do part' – more likely, 'Till the judge us do part.' Love in the twentieth century has become a fair-weather friend: love for better, but not for worse. Consequently our world is full of people disillusioned about love.

But that is not how God uses the vocabulary of love. For him, love is no casual affair, no wild adventure. For him, love is promise and covenant. For him, love is a moral commitment to a quality of relationship which he is determined will last for ever. That is what he means by love: 'I have loved you with an everlasting love,' he says.

Now, how can you know that you are loved like that, and then run yourself down in a self-pitying inferiority complex?

I read once of a college student in the days of the Black Power movement in the United States. This young negro had found his own way of handling the problem of racial discrimination. He had a banner on his wall that said: 'I'm black, and I'm OK, 'cause God don't make junk.'

God does not love junk, either. Is that not a reason then for every believer to hold his or her head up high?

I am reminded of the story of the little boy who was being jeered at in the playground by his peers, because they had discovered he was adopted. Eventually he rounded on them. 'All right,' he said, 'so I am adopted. All I know is, my parents chose me, but yours couldn't help having you.'

Every Christian can say the same: 'God chose me.' In the mists of eternity past he saw me, loved me and determined to save me. Of course, he may sometimes discipline me. What good parent does not? But he will never abandon me.

Perhaps, as for the heartbroken parents in the illustration with which we began, there is something in your life which is a root of bitterness between you and God. You have suffered a grievous disappointment, a broken engagement, a failed marriage, a bereavement. Maybe you have been made redundant, maybe you have failed a vital exam. Well, it is not for the Christian to wallow in demoralized self-pity. You are loved by God. You have dignity, you had better believe it. And if you do not feel that dignity, it is no wonder that your enthusiasm for spiritual things is on the wane.

Holiness

If we know we are loved by God in this special way, we will also have a hunger for holiness. 'I have loved you, you are special to me' – and therefore, you must be different.

That is the repeated logic of the Bible. There is an invisible line separating God's people from the world. It is the line defined by his love, his special relationship with his people. Anything that blurs that line will bring the world into the church and the church into the world. If the people of God are compromising with the world it is ultimately because they have forgotten who they are; they have lost the consciousness of their distinctive call. They have forgotten that the king of the universe has loved them with a special love. If the world is in your heart, it is because you need to hear again that God has loved you. You – in particular! How can we treat his worship half-heartedly, if we know he has loved us? How can we treat his covenant law so loosely when it matters so much to him? How can we speak such blasphemy as to suggest that he will let the wicked escape without punishment?

A strong sense of the special love of God for his people is the root of all gospel holiness. Walk worthy of your calling; Paul says it again and again. If we knew who we were, the world would be no threat to us. We would not be afraid to behave differently from other people. We would not fear to be called old-fashioned or narrow. We would know ourselves to be God's people, and the assurance of his love would nerve us against all those secular pressures that would seek to conform us to the ways of the world. Here is the source of that hunger for holiness, which so many in this second generation of our evangelical movement seem to lack: God says, 'I have loved you.'

God has loved you; how much do you love him?

If you have done any pastoral counselling you will know all too well that marriages break down in one of two fundamentally different ways. Sometimes it is through unfaithfulness. An adulterous relationship is involved.

Often, however, marriages do not shatter under the attack of external sexual attraction in that way. They die slowly from within.

Imperceptibly, by degrees, husband and wife drift apart, affection cools, communication dries up, until suddenly to their horror they discover they have become strangers living in the same house. No third party is necessarily implicated at all. The couple have been utterly faithful (in the technical sense) to each other, but sadly – in the latter years of their marriage at any rate – a chill has descended on their relationship. It was a case of faithful, yes, but frigid.

And what is true of marriages is lamentably also sometimes true of Christians. The church is not called the bride of Christ for nothing. He expects of her not simply a dutiful fidelity but a loving attachment. Sometimes with the passing of the years, the fidelity remains preserved in our doctrinal formulae and our denominational traditions. But the warmth ebbs away; and so churches lose the spark of devotion. They die slowly from within. Not for lack of doctrine, but for lack of love. That is exactly what was happening in Ephesus, of whom Christ complained at the very end of the New Testament: 'You have forsaken your first love' (Rev. 2:4). Would he say the same of us?

Christianity is not about loving the creed, it is not even about loving the Bible. Christianity is about loving Christ. We love the Bible because it tells us about him, but he is the object of our faith. We embrace the truth by embracing him, because he is the truth. Once any Christian – perhaps even out of a commendable concern to define the truth – separates love of truth from the love of Christ, then no matter how excellent their theology, no matter how explicit their creed, they have lost the truth. For the truth is in Jesus, and once that truth is detached from a committment to him personally it becomes academic and desiccated and therefore erroneous, no matter how propositionally accurate it may be.

It is so important that we understand this. Christianity is not just a matter of how we think, it is a matter of how we feel toward God and he toward us. We are precious to him, he is committed to us as a husband to a wife; and when we backslide in our enthusiasm and our devotion cools, it disappoints and hurts him. He will not put up with it. He sent Israel into exile because her love had cooled. He may do the same for us, for he wants our love and he is not satisfied with anything less. He will turn our lives upside down if he thinks it will re-awaken that love in us. He will put his finger on many issues as we study Malachi, but God's intention in this book is not to harangue us and make us feel guilty about all the things we have not done.

Fundamentally, his intention is to woo us to a new devotion to him. 'I care,' he says. 'I care about you. How could you possibly suggest I do not? I have loved you. Where is your love for me?'

10
Apathy
Malachi 1:6 – 2:9

I want to read to you from a letter written about thirty years ago, from a young Latin American student to his fiancée, to explain to her why he was breaking off their engagement.

> We have a high casualty rate. We get shot, lynched, jailed, slandered, fired from our jobs. We live in virtual poverty. We give away every penny we make above what is absolutely necessary to keep us alive. We do not have time for movies or concerts. We are described as fanatics; perhaps we are, for our lives are dominated by one great over-shadowing cause. This is the one thing about which I am in dead earnest. It is my life, my business, my hobby, my sweetheart. I work for it in the daytime and dream of it at night. I cannot carry on any friendship, or love affair, or even conversation, without relating it to this force which drives and guides my life.

That young man had been converted to Marxism.

People sometimes ask me what it is about left-wing politics that is so attractive, especially to students in the developing world; for intellectually, they point out, Marxist philosophy has more holes than a garden sieve. Its economic theories have conspicuously failed, its political predictions have invariably proved false, its violent revolutions have indisputably misfired. How can any intelligent person still believe in it?

The answer, of course, is that Marxism has never appealed primarily to the mind but to the heart. 'Nothing great in this world', wrote Emerson, 'is ever achieved without enthusiasm.' Too true; the hallmark of every great revolutionary movement in the world has been that it is able to awaken passion in people. Merely capturing academic interest is never enough, because the strongest springs of our human motivation are wound on the wheel of our emotional, rather than our intellectual, life.

You may want to argue that it ought not to be so; if so, you have a case. Emotion detached from reason is fanaticism, as that young

176

Latin American almost recognized, perhaps, in his letter. Yet anybody who wants to change the world, especially if by harnessing the energies of the young, must reckon with this basic fact of human nature. It is the emotional dimension that drives people and gives them enthusiasm for the task. And our problem, at least in the western world, is that in large measure we have lost that passion. Back in the 1950s John Osborne, the original angry young man, wrote a play, *Look Back in Anger*. Some of the lines from it are interesting:

'How I long for a little ordinary human enthusiasm. Just enthusiasm – that's all. I want to hear a warm thrilling voice cry out, "Hallelujah! Hallelujah! I'm alive!"'
'Oh brother, it's such a long time since I was with anybody who got enthusiastic about anything.'

Osborne is identifying a sense of disillusionment, particularly among young people in the second half of our century. Modern men and women are in the grip of a mental inertia so severe it is in danger of anaesthetizing their drive. The prevalent attitude is 'I couldn't care less'; that is the motto of the late twentieth century, and I fear it may prove to be our epitaph. We are a tired, apathetic culture.

'Apathy' is a word originally coined by the Stoic philosophers of Greece. For them it expressed their grim determination not to allow their feelings to jeopardize their inner tranquillity. The Stoic said, 'By an effort of my will, I am determined not to be bothered.' There was something courageous, almost noble about that Stoic apathy, even if it did tend to make them rather cold people. But for us today apathy is not a virtue cultivated by such disciplined mental effort. For us, apathy is a state of lassitude born of disillusionment and bored indifference: not 'I won't be bothered', but 'I can't be bothered.'

Thirty years ago, left-wing politics provided at least the illusion for some that there might be something worth bothering about. 'Maybe the enthusiasm of my youth', said that young Latin American student, 'can be channelled into something.' Marxism, for all its crazy theories, at least had the power to excite and inflame. It had a self-assurance that demanded sacrifice. It had a dream which, no matter how spurious, could give young lives purpose and hope. Little wonder that a Latin American student of the 1960s was willing to sacrifice his marriage to his Marxism. But the tragedy is that thirty years on, even Marxism has become a broken reed. Not even a fanatic can continue to believe in it.

Even as early as the end of the 1960s, graffiti were appearing in students' toilets around Europe expressing disillusionment with left-wing philosophy. One of the most famous read:

> 'To do is to be' – Sartre
> 'To be is to do' – Camus
> 'Do-be-do-be-do' – Frank Sinatra

When I was at university many of my friends were very radical left-wingers. Many of them are now bank managers and such like. One of my great heroes when I was a sixth-former was a particularly left-wing revolutionary thinker. Now (as I discovered about ten years ago to my chagrin) he runs a Paris boutique.

Apathy – a church's crisis

Yet sadly the greatest tragedy in the wake of this collapse of credibility in Marxist revolutionary politics has been that so few of these disillusioned young men and women from the sixties and early seventies have found a new focus for their enthusiasm in the church of Jesus Christ. Why is that? Because, all too often, the church of Jesus Christ has sold out to apathy too. The church of the twentieth century, at least in the West, has lost its zeal.

Some years ago, attending a conference on church growth, I was rather amused to find that one of the major questions being addressed was, 'Why are the mainstream denominations in Britain all declining numerically?' One of the preliminary pre-conference exercises had been a survey of church attendance, to determine whether statistics and graphs could shed any light on this situation. I was amused at the irony, for I suspect that the survey was symptomatic of the disease they were trying to identify.

Once any group or movement starts analysing its failures with statistics and graphs, it is a sure sign that it is on its death-bed. It has lost its vigour and confidence. It is like a hypochondriac, who pores over medical charts but never recognizes that the real cause of his malaise is in that negative and morbid attitude which moved him to look at those charts in the first place.

So the church in the late twentieth century has called in the sociologists, when the rot lies in the grassroots of the Christian movement. We have lost our passion. People used to talk about the church 'militant', but we have abdicated that word to the left-wing politicians. The average church member today is more emotionally involved in his football team than in the kingdom of God. He or she is more moved by the latest soap opera than by the gospel of Christ. Like those Laodiceans of old, we are neither hot nor cold.

We are just tepid, lukewarm, half-hearted Christians. In a word –
apathetic.

The apathy of God's people

In that respect we are remarkably similar to the people of God in the
days of Malachi, for they had become apathetic. A 'couldn't care less'
casualness infected every aspect of their spirituality, nowhere more
obviously than in their attitude to public worship.

See how God speaks to them here.

'You have shown contempt for my name.' How? 'You placed
defiled food on my altar.' How have we defiled it? 'By saying that the
Lord's table is contemptible. When you bring blind animals for
sacrifice, is that not wrong? When you sacrifice crippled or diseased
animals, is that not wrong? Try offering them to your governor!
Would he be pleased with you? Would he accept you?' (cf. 1:6–8).

The law of Moses laid down strict guidelines on the quality of
animals to be used in the ritual sacrifices of the Old Testament
religion. They had to be the best; you were not allowed to bring
anything inferior. The animal had to be young, healthy, unblemished
and perfect. But Malachi's compatriots were ignoring those rules. If
they could get away with presenting a second-rate or even a third-
rate animal to the priests, they did. And Malachi is outraged by it: it
is the brazen impertinence of it that gets to him. Do they really think
that they can deceive God with their cheap sacrifices? 'Try offering
them to your governor,' he says.

Some years ago Her Majesty the Queen visited Cambridge where I
live. As part of her visit, local traders clubbed together to provide a
floral tribute. Can you imagine her reaction if the Guild of Commerce
had presented her with a bouquet of withered dandelions? Such a
gift would have been an outrageous insult to her elevated person and
office. Well, says Malachi, it is the same sort of outrage you
perpetrate when you come to church. How dare you present these
tatty offerings to God! Do you really expect him to be impressed by
such off-hand expressions of your devotion? Do you anticipate that
his mercy or his blessing is going to flow into your life, when you
have so little concern to win his approval? This is not worship. This is
insufferable insolence!

'"Oh, that one of you would shut the temple doors, so that you
would not light useless fires on my altar! I am not pleased with you,"
says the Lord Almighty' (1:10).

What an appalling thing for God to have to say! Yet, says Malachi,
that is how God feels about it. You would be better off going down to
the pub on Sunday mornings than going to church in that frame of

mind. Why, if all you are going to do is to engage in such half-hearted empty rituals, you would be better off staying in bed! Do you not realize who it is you are dealing with?

'Universalism' in Malachi

'My name will be great among the nations, from the rising to the setting of the sun. In every place incense and pure offerings will be brought to my name, because my name will be great among the nations,' says the LORD Almighty (1:11).

We need to pause here. Those of you who have read any commentaries on Malachi will probably be aware that this verse has provoked quite a considerable amount of debate among the scholars. Many liberal interpreters of the Bible have hailed it as a thrilling affirmation of universal salvation. 'Look,' they say, 'Malachi here sees pagan worship as worship of the true God.'

Such a multi-faith pluralism, of course, is very congenial to our modern mood. The Roman Catholic theologian Karl Rahner has often insisted that other faiths are really already worshipping Christ, unwittingly, under different names. We should no longer talk about 'non-Christians', he suggests, but 'anonymous Christians', for everyone is a Christian really. John Hick, a Protestant theologian, has gone so far as to recommend that competitive proselytizing – the different world religions seeking to win converts – should be abandoned. He urges instead a combined mission on the part of all the great world religions together, in the name of some kind of common amorphous spiritual consciousness.

It comes as no surprise, when that ethos prevails in the theological establishments, that multi-faith services in our cathedrals are becoming so fashionable. Indeed, one has to wonder: if and when Prince Charles is crowned, who will be standing alongside the Archbishop of Canterbury in Westminster Abbey? – always assuming that the ceremony is held in Westminster Abbey, and not in some temple dedicated to New Age mysticism.

I shall have more to say about this subject tomorrow, because it is an issue that was of great significance to Malachi in his day as well. Suffice it to say here that verse 11 provides absolutely no grounds for that kind of universalism, though it has often been cited in support of it. It is quite unthinkable that Malachi is endorsing pagan idolatry, as if it were an acceptable expression of human spiritual awareness of the true God.

Three things at least count against such an interpretation. First of all, if you read his words carefully in verse 11, you will see that *the worship he is talking about is quite explicitly directed to the unique God of the Bible*. 'My name will be great among the nations . . . Pure offerings will be brought to my name, because my name will be great.' What name is that? Certainly not Baal, or Zeus, or Allah, or Krishna. The name Malachi is speaking of is Jehovah, the LORD. He is speaking here of worship offered to the true God.

Secondly, if Malachi were endorsing a universalist theology as these modern theologians suggest, *it would fly straight in the face of the very tough line he takes later, on mixed marriages between Jews and pagans* (*cf.* 2:11). As we shall see tomorrow, he is definitely not in favour of such things. But he could hardly object to them, if he were the universalist some paint him.

But the third reason such an interpretation fails is that *it does not recognize the ambiguity of the tenses used in this verse*. The time reference of a Hebrew verse is often much more flexible than in English. The tense used in verse 11 can have a future rather than a present sense. Thus the NIV translates it, 'My name *will be* great among the nations . . . In every place offerings *will be* brought.' I am quite certain the NIV is right to do so. Malachi is not saying that worshippers of Baal and Zeus are unwittingly worshipping Jehovah under another name. He is saying that one day soon, worshippers of Baal and Zeus – indeed worshippers of every false deity this fallen world has ever invented for itself – will acknowledge the true God.

This is in fact the first hint of a very strong emphasis in Malachi on the prophetic future, the last days. Malachi *is* anticipating a universalism, but it is not the universalism of multi-faith services in Westminster Abbey, where Hindus and Muslims address Brahma and Allah in spiritual fellowship with bishops of the Christian church. No: Malachi is anticipating here the universalism of heaven, a time when the whole human race will bow the knee to one name. 'The LORD, he is God,' they will say.

Already, in exile, Malachi and other faithful Jews (such as Daniel) had proved that the God of the Bible could be acknowledged, even by pagan emperors like Nebuchadnezzar. There was even increasing evidence of proselytes coming to the Jewish faith from a Gentile background. Already books such as Ruth and Jonah warned them of the dangers of xenophobic prejudice. Their traditional enemies, the Moabites, the Assyrians and the Philistines, would one day respond to God's word. They *could* respond to God's word even now. God's purpose was wide enough to embrace them; it was not just for the Jews. And in the oracles of many of the prophets, a day when there would be a huge harvest from the Gentile nations was regularly anticipated. (If you want an extraordinary example of that, look at Isaiah 19:19-25.)

This then is Malachi's universalism. It is not the universalism of liberal theologians. It is the universalism of the gospel of John, where we find the Master saying, 'A time is coming when you will worship the Father neither on this mountain nor in Jerusalem . . . a time is coming and has now come when the true worshippers will worship the Father in spirit and truth' (Jn. 4:21, 23). It is the universalism of the book of Acts: 'So then, God has granted even the Gentiles repentance unto life' (Acts 11:18). It is the universalism of the book of Revelation. There are no dissidents among that crowd gathered around the throne; no-one shouting, 'Let's hear it for Muhammad!', 'Three cheers for Buddha!' The whole of heaven is united around the praise of a single name: 'Jesus is Lord.'

' "My name will be great among the nations, from the rising to the setting of the sun. In every place incense and pure offerings will be brought to my name, because my name will be great among the nations," says the LORD Almighty.' It will happen, says Malachi: and yet you Jews, who of all people should be giving God the glory for his unique, incomparable, sovereign lordship over the entire world – you dare to treat his public worship with indifference, with apathy! You are not doing God any favours by worshipping him, you know. He does not need your pathetic gifts. He is the Lord of the cosmos, the great king who one day will be revered by everyone.

'But you profane [his name] by saying of the Lord's table, "It is defiled", and of its food, "It is contemptible." And you say, "What a burden!" and you sniff at it contemptuously,' says the LORD Almighty' (1:12–13).

Many commentators suggest that the picture Malachi is portraying for us in the phrase 'sniff at it' is of these Jews turning up their noses disdainfully at the sacrificial offerings they were having to bring. But the Hebrew verb actually means to exhale rather than to inhale. So I wonder if the picture is not rather that of a heavy, weary sigh rather than a sniff: a weary 'Ugh, what a fag! What a burden!'

You can just see them, can't you, looking at their watches to see how long it is all going on; fidgeting with their chorus books, counting the tassels on the high priest's robe to pass the time, wishing this tedious, boring business would all be over so that they could get their Sunday lunch. Apathy is almost too weak a word to describe the appalling lack of emotional engagement with the public worship they were performing.

The reasons for apathy

Now, what were the reasons for it? If we can identify them, maybe we will identify some of the reasons for apathy in the Christian church of the twentieth century too.

A lack of reverence for God's person

'A son honours his father, and a servant his master. If I am a father, where is the honour due to me? If I am a master, where is the respect due to me?' (1:6).

Yesterday we saw that one of the primary reasons for this half-heartedness and apathetic spirit in the people of God was that they had lost their assurance of God's love. They did not really believe in that love any longer. And that, as we saw, contributed in a major way to their spiritual half-heartedness.

But here in verse 6 Malachi sets against that their fear of God. He wants to guard against any sentimentalizing of the divine love, which might lead to a diminished respect for God's authority. 'He may love Israel, indeed he does; but you must not forget he is your sovereign master, he deserves honour' (literally, weight, gravity), 'he deserves respect' (literally, fear, or even terror or dread). So to treat God with honour and respect is the very opposite of treating him as somebody insignificant or not intimidating.

We must never let our view of the love of God distort our thinking so that we can treat him like some kind of heavenly buddy. He is a great king, to be feared among the nations; but they did not fear him. They did not treat coming into his presence with the seriousness it deserved. Instead they seem to have breezed into the temple, offering their sacrifices as if they were tipping some waiter in a cheap restaurant.

Am I not speaking the truth when I say that we too need to heed this word about the fear of God? There is a great deal said about the love of God today. It is rightly and necessarily said, but it can lead us into a sentimental view of God and we can lose our reverence. In trying to make our public services of worship user-friendly, welcoming, suitable for all the family and informal, there is the danger too that we no longer communicate to one another and to ourselves the awsomeness of God. Partly, I suppose, it is cultural. We are not used to showing ordinary human beings honour and respect any longer, are we?

A group of American tourists were being shown round the Houses of Parliament. As they were being taken along one of the corridors, Lord Hailsham, who was then Lord Chancellor, appeared on his way to some civic occasion; he was dressed in his Chancellor's robes and regalia, with heavy gold chains and all the rest, and made a very impressive figure. As he approached he saw, beyond the party of tourists, the Leader of the Opposition, Mr Kinnock. Wanting to speak to him, he raised his hand and called out, 'Neil!' Whereupon all the tourists dropped to one knee.

We smile at the story because it is somehow incongruous in our modern democratic western world, to imagine people spontaneously kneeling like that to someone of higher rank. Even bowing to our sovereign the Queen has become a perfunctory nod of the head, these days, has it not? If we do not kneel to our earthly masters, it's no wonder that we do not kneel any longer to pray. I wonder if I am alone in thinking that something has been lost in the abandonment of that traditional body-language of prayer – something that would have gone some way, perhaps, to protect us from apathy. '"If I am a father, where is the honour due to me? If I am a master, where is the respect due to me? . . . I am a great king," says the LORD Almighty, "and my name is to be feared among the nations"' (1:6, 14).

A hypocritical spirit among the people

'Cursed is the cheat who has an acceptable male in his flock and vows to give it, but then sacrifices a blemished animal to the Lord' (verse 14). That is revealing; it shows that there is an element of pretence in what these people were doing. Like Ananias and Sapphira in the book of Acts, these Jews wanted the kudos of being known as pious people but were not prepared to pay the price such a reputation required. So they cheated and lied; they substituted knackered mutton for the prime lamb they had promised to bring to the temple.

Hypocrisy is often the partner of apathy, implying as it does a lack of genuine feeling. Do you remember those famous lines from Shakespeare's *Hamlet*?

> This above all: to thine own self be true,
> And it must follow, as the night the day,
> Thou canst not then be false to any man. (I.iii)

As a playwright, Shakespeare was more familiar than most with the business of acting a part. And as he studied human behaviour, he clearly observed that such theatricals were not confined to the stage; all too often the image we try to project of ourselves is an artificial one, one we play for the benefit of others.

Some years ago a young undergraduate in Cambridge confessed

this to me very candidly. She said, 'I come from a Christian home. When I go home in the vacation I am the decent, respectable, virgin Christian daughter my parents want me to be. But when I come up to college, I become a wild, dissipated, sexually permissive junkie.' She told me, 'My real problem is I do not know which is the real me.' In fact she admitted that even in coming to see me she wondered if she wasn't just adding another role to her repertoire, that of a guilt-stricken penitent, longing for priestly absolution perhaps.

I had a lot of sympathy for that young student. For in one way or another many of us fall into the same trap of inconsistency and unreality in our lives. I explained to her that at least she had one thing on her side. In this pattern of pretence she had woven about herself, at least she was aware of what she was doing; she was suspicious of her motives, she was critical of her insincerity. At least she knew she was play-acting. At least she was still searching for some nobler stance of inward honesty. At least she still wanted above all to her own self to be true, even if she was finding it difficult.

It is a tragedy that it is not always so. There are some who fix the actor's mask so securely to their faces they forget what they really look like. Pretence becomes so habitual they are no longer conscious that it *is* pretence. They practise double standards, they live a double life, they use double talk, and by some extraordinary feat of moral blindness, they feel no pang of guilt about all this duplicity. On the contrary, they frequently contrive to be sanctimonious and self-righteous. They parade themselves as pillars of the church, even as ministers. 'The church is full of hypocrites,' jibes the man in the street. And the tragedy is that so often the reproach is true.

Beware of unreality. There is one person who, while he watches our performance on the stage of life, is never fooled by the false images we present upon it. He sees through the façade of affectation we erect, he observes the hidden inconsistencies, he perceives the false motives, he discerns the secret fraud. He is never deceived, he knows who we really are. He knows what we are really offering, no matter what we pretend to be offering for the eyes of others. So beware of hypocrisy. There is too much of it among us, and it always conceals a secret apathy, a secret contempt for God, a secret lack of real interest in spiritual things.

A lack of responsibility on the part of the professional clergy

'It is you, O priests, who show contempt for my name' (1:6).

'This admonition is for you, O priests' (2:1).

What was wrong with the priesthood?

It might be easier to ask, what was *right* with the priesthood? For a start, the priests were colluding with the people in *the presentation of dubious and polluted offerings*. They accepted the inferior animals without question, placing them on the altar. In so doing of course they were clearly indicating to everybody that they had as little regard for God's name as anybody else.

More than that, there was *their general, shabby personal example*. A priest, according to Malachi, ought to demonstrate what real reverence for God was all about. God's special relationship with the tribe of Levi was conditional upon that. His covenant with Levi meant that life, health and peace would be mediated to the people through their priestly ministries, provided the tribe of Levi showed awe for God's name, and true instruction was found on their lips.

But these priests had violated that covenant. It was transparently obvious to everybody, from the stupefied yawns on their faces and the casual manner with which they did their business, that they were as bored with all this temple ritual as anybody else.

But most important of all, this priesthood had neglected what Malachi clearly regarded as *their chief and most important ministry* – which (perhaps contrary to our preconceived ideas about Old Testament religion) was not offering sacrifices on the altar. The primary role of the priest, says Malachi, is the teaching of God's word.

'The lips of a priest ought to preserve knowledge, and from his mouth men should seek instruction – because he is the messenger of the LORD Almighty' (2:7).

But these priests were not preachers. Oh, no doubt they wore the right vestments, they mouthed the right liturgical words; but their sermons, if they preached any at all, were just empty platitudes. Instead of challenging the general slide towards worldliness and spiritual indifference and apathy, they endorsed it.

'You . . . have shown partiality in matters of the law' (2:9).

Almost certainly Malachi means that there was no consistency, no integrity in what they preached to the people. They bent the truth so that this apathetic, half-hearted people felt secure in their way of life. Their polished sermonettes each sabbath offended nobody and converted nobody. Instead, by their endorsement of the general low standard of spirituality among God's people, they caused them to stumble. No wonder, then, that God says in 1:10 that he wishes someone would close their church doors. By leaving them open they were doing more harm than good. 'Make no mistake about it,' says Malachi, 'God will not overlook this appalling derogation of leadership responsibility. There will be no blessing upon the ministry of such shallow ministers.'

'I will send a curse upon you, and I will curse your blessings' (2:2).

In other words: the benedictions that you priests conventionally announce at the end of the service will have no effect; why should I pay attention to prayers from people who are so uninterested in their mediatorial task? When you pronounce a priestly benediction, it will have the force of a curse on these people, not a blessing. What is more, he says, I will destroy your prestige in the public eye.

'I will spread on your faces the offal from your festival sacrifices' (2:3).

'I have caused you to be despised and humiliated before all the people' (2:9).

It is always the way, of course. The world has ultimately nothing but contempt for clergy who do not live up to the standards of biblical faith and conduct they are meant to represent. We have bishops today who think they are doing us a favour by expressing scepticism about the resurrection of Jesus from the dead. They think they are improving the public image of the church, helping more people to come to church.

But if you ask the person in the street you will discover, quite to the contrary, that all such tactics do is confirm twentieth-century men and women in their utter contempt for the church. The same must be said for the scandals attaching to American TV evangelists that have hit the headlines in recent years. Such things undermine years of evangelistic endeavour. What was it Jesus said? 'If salt loses its saltiness . . . it is no longer good for anything' . . . except to be thrown out and trampled' (Mt. 5:13).

A special word to leaders

We must not underestimate the very special onus God places upon those who are called to be pastors and ministers of his flock. James advises, 'Not many of you should presume to be teachers . . . because you know that we who teach will be judged more strictly' (Jas. 3:1). If there is one thing in the Bible worse than being a sinner it is being a stumbling-block. Better, said Jesus, to have a concrete necklace around your head and be dropped into the ocean, than for a person who has been a stumbling-block to God's people to face God's judgment (cf. e.g. Mk. 9:42). Those are terrifying words on the lips of our Master, but they are words which, if we are Christian leaders, we had better not ignore.

Take heed to your life and your doctrine: that was Paul's advice to Timothy. A Christian leader is not an authoritarian figure who can boss people around. He has only two weapons in his armoury of leadership: personal example (life) and Bible teaching (doctrine). Make sure those two things have integrity.

I am not saying that being that sort of teacher, preacher or pastor will make you popular or successful. It is quite clear there was a lot of pressure on the priests in Malachi's day to be the kind of priests they were. An apathetic church wants apathetic preachers. If you tell people of the cost of discipleship, they will all too often accuse you of religious fanaticism. If you spell out the need for conversion, they will often call you a fundamentalist crank. If you speak of judgment to come, they will call you an intolerant bigot. On the other hand, if you tell people how easy the way is, all too often they will smother you with flattery. Legitimize their sin with your reshaped Christian ethics, and their faces will light up with admiration for your pastoral sensitivity. Abolish hell from your universalist theology, and they will give you university degrees.

Well did the poet Milton say: 'Truth never comes into the world, but like a bastard to the ignominy of him that brought her forth.'

All too often that is the case. But integrity is demanded of us in our personal lives and in our public teaching. Too many of us in the Christian ministry are simply not taking that responsibility seriously. Some of us are spending too much time in the office and far too little time studying. Some of us are offering our people five minutes when their spiritual condition is so appalling it needs at least fifty. Some of us think that by waving our hands over bread and wine once a week we are doing something. Some of us think that when we get into the pulpit we are there to be stand-up comics or chat-show hosts.

No. We are there to be the teachers and exemplars of the word. Our lips and our lives must tell the same message, and it must be the message of the Bible. That is what we owe our people: our holiness and our Bible teaching. If we do not give them that, we are giving them nothing, however well-organized the church is.

I am worried about the standard of ministry in evangelical churches, just as much as I am about that among those who are more liberal in their theological tradition. The trouble with these priests of Malachi's day is not that they were heretics; they were just comfortable preachers. They confirmed people in their preconceived ideas. They were conventional preachers; they never risked their public acceptability by saying anything unpopular. If anybody ever deserved the title 'conservative', these priests did.

That worries me. It worries me when people nod so vigorously in agreement with my sermons; I must be doing something wrong. It worries me, more generally, that so much preaching in our evangelical constituency is boringly predictable, that people come not to be challenged but to be confirmed in what they already know or think. It worries me that so much evangelical preaching is smug and self-assured, that so many evangelical churches are like mutual admiration societies. The real word of God always disturbs, always surprises, always shocks.

What should a priest be? 'The messenger of the LORD Almighty' (2:7). That is an astonishing title. For elsewhere in Malachi, that is his own name: it is the title of a prophet (*cf.* 3:1–5). Clearly, Malachi believes that a real priest should have a prophetic dimension to his ministry. Let those of us who are leaders heed the admonition of Malachi's words. We have a special responsibility for the apathy of the church.

11

Infidelity

Malachi 2:10–16

> Wilt thou have this woman to thy wedded wife, to live
> together after God's ordinance in the holy estate of
> Matrimony? Wilt thou love her, comfort her, honour, and
> keep her, in sickness and in health; and, forsaking all other,
> keep thee only unto her, so long as ye both shall live?
> *The man shall answer:* I will.
>
> ('The Form of Solemnisation of Matrimony',
> *Book of Common Prayer*)

Promises are important to relationships. They are important because
we human beings are so unpredictable. No matter how long or well
you know people, they never lose the capacity to surprise you or
indeed to let you down.

A prophet in the Old Testament once compared the human race in
this respect to a flock of sheep: 'We turn every one to our own way'
(*cf.* Is. 53:6). It's a very appropriate analogy.

A zoologist acquaintance of mine once wrote a doctoral thesis on
'The Normal Walk of Animals'. He set up a course in the laboratory
equipped with various kinds of instrumentation to try to measure
how the gait of animals differed between species. He told me that he
got excellent results from all sorts of beasts except the sheep. No two
sheep ever walked the same way along that course. Indeed, no single
sheep ever walked that same course twice the same way. Sheep
behaviour simply was not reproducible. The sheep is not only
perverse, he discovered, it is individualistically perverse.

According to the prophet, it shares that characteristic with human
beings. Human behaviour is always idiosyncratic; it is not enough
that we go the wrong way; to adapt Frank Sinatra, 'We do it our
way', a way different from everyone else's. We are very original
sinners. That, of course, makes life difficult. People whose behaviour
cannot be predicted cannot be trusted. And without trust, human
relationships are impossible.

Take marriage, for instance. Here is a relationship which, if it can
be terminated on the whim of either partner, can surely never be a
deep and satisfying union. Neither partner can really afford to take

the emotional risk of total self-giving to the other if the thought is there all the time: 'He or she may desert me.' A marriage without promises must always be a marriage with mental reservations, vulnerable to destructive suspicions and doubts. For you dare not commit all your hopes to a person you cannot fully trust, and you cannot fully trust the person whose future responses cannot be reliably predicted.

That is why I say that promises are important to relationships. A promise is a voluntary decision to behave predictably, a way of making my responses dependable without destroying my human freedom of action. 'I will love you, comfort you, honour and keep you in all circumstances of life. I will be totally faithful to you for the rest of my life.' The husband vows this to the wife, the wife to the husband. So the relationship is no longer the victim of fickle passion; it depends now upon the truthfulness of the parties involved. The vital issue is no longer, 'Am I clever enough to predict her future behaviour?' Or 'Am I attractive enough to sustain his future interest?' The vital issue now is: 'Can I rely on my spouse's word?' The promise, by its pledge of constancy, makes possible a relationship of trust, where previously such a relationship would have been foolhardy and presumptuous.

The promises of God

Now one of the most remarkable and important things that the Bible has to teach us is that God makes promises. And those promises are vitally important in our relationship with him, for exactly the reason they are vitally important in a marriage. God's behaviour is not easily predictable either. Of course he is neither capricious nor irrational, still less sinful; but his personality is unfathomably mysterious and his purposes unimaginably complex. As Isaiah says, 'No human being ever guessed what God was up to' (cf. Is. 55:8–9). No, if we are going to depend upon God's future behaviour, it can only be because he has made a promise to us. And the wonderful truth the Bible has to share with us is that he has indeed made such promises.

The Bible calls them 'covenants', and the most important covenant was the one he made when he pledged to Abraham that he and his descendants would be blessed, and through them all the nations of the world would be blessed too. In the years after that promise was given, of course, the children of Abraham, the Jews, encountered all kinds of ups and downs in their historical experience. There were many occasions when God chastened them, when they experienced judgment at his hand. And yet the prophets of Israel never lost their confidence in the special relationship their nation had with God. Why? Because it was based on a promise. They could not always understand what God was doing. But they were convinced that God's relationship with Israel was permanent, because it was based on covenant love.

We have seen an example of that already at the very beginning of this book of Malachi.

' "I have loved you," says the LORD.'

He is not talking there about God's general love for everybody. He is talking about his special, covenant love for the sons of Jacob.

Two things follow from this fundamental revelation in the Bible of God as one who makes covenants. The first is that *God is faithful*. A promise is no use at all if you cannot depend upon it. But God's word can be depended upon. As Moses said in Deuteronomy 7, he is the faithful God who keeps his covenant of love.

The second consequence, which is closely related to the first, is this: that *God requires faithfulness of us*. Faithfulness, that is, in our vertical relationship to him; faithfulness also in our horizontal relationships with one another. That of course is why Jesus, when asked to summarize God's law, said there are just two things involved: love God, love your neighbour. Covenant love works both ways. According to the Bible, we human beings are intended by God to live relationally in a covenant relationship with God and with one another – to love him, to love one another; and to do so reliably. The sure route to all divine blessing and all social harmony, indeed to heaven itself, is faithfulness – behaviour that can be trusted, because it is based on a promise. On the other hand, the sure route to divine cursing, to social anarchy, the sure route in fact to hell, is infidelity – behaviour that cannot be trusted, because it will not be bound by promise.

Sadly, we discover that it was that second route, the route of infidelity, which the Jewish people seemed determined to take in the days of Malachi.

The infidelity of the people

'Have we not all one Father? Did not one God create us? Why do we profane the covenant of our fathers by breaking faith with one another?' (2:10).

Notice that phrase: 'breaking faith'. Look down the chapter and you will find it occurs again and again: in verses 10, 11, 14, 15 and finally at the very end, in verse 16: 'Guard yourself in your spirit, and do not break faith.'

For breaking faith is exactly what Israel was doing. She was sinking in a sea of spiritual half-heartedness and moral declension, and the fundamental reason was that she was not willing to face up to the demands of covenant love. She did not believe in such covenant love towards her from God; and, because she did not believe in it, she was not practising it. Vertically she was being unfaithful to God; horizontally her people were being unfaithful to one another.

Left unremedied, such a situation spelt certain disaster. So, in our passage this morning, Malachi appeals to them to reconstruct this fundamental moral commitment to faithfulness at the centre of their lives. 'Listen,' he says, 'Do you not realize that by very nature we are bound together in a covenant relationship? Have we not all one father?'

Is he speaking of one 'Father' (that is, God), or 'father' (that is, Abraham or even Adam)? Well, the commentators differ. Perhaps he is being deliberately ambiguous, alluding to both the vertical and the horizontal components of this covenant relationship simultaneously. Either way, he is saying this: 'We are a covenant people. We owe a debt, a duty of fidelity to God and one another. Why then are we profaning that covenant by breaking faith?'

He illustrates with two specific examples, and both centre on marriage and family life. The first, in verses 11 and 12, concerns the taking of pagan partners in marriage. The second, in verses 13–16, is about the divorcing of marital partners.

Malachi then is no longer talking about public worship. He is now turning his searchlight upon the much more private, intimate sphere of the home. He is saying, 'Listen – God is just as interested in what is happening in your domestic affairs as in what is happening up at the temple. Don't think you can compartmentalize your life, keeping your religion and your private lives in separate boxes. On the contrary! God insists upon a full integration of your spirituality into every area of your life. So it is no good going up to the temple offering sacrifices, then coming home to a pagan wife and wondering why your sacrifices bring no blessing into your life. It is no good weeping and wailing in prayer at the temple, and then coming back and divorcing your wife. God will not heed or bless those who break faith with him or with one another.'

Unfaithfulness towards God

It needs little imagination to see the immense relevance a passage like this has for us and for our society today. Let us start with Malachi's example of the taking of pagan wives.

> Judah has broken faith. A detestable thing has been
> committed in Israel and in Jerusalem: Judah has desecrated
> the sanctuary the LORD loves, by marrying the daughter of
> a foreign God. As for the man who does this, whoever he
> may be, may the LORD cut him off from the tents of Jacob –
> even though he brings offerings to the LORD Almighty.
> (2:11–12)

Let me tell you about Joe. Joe says, 'It doesn't matter what you
believe, so long as you are sincere.' He is a very liberally minded,
tolerant fellow. He goes to church every Sunday, but he would be the
last person in the world to press his religion on anybody else, least of
all his wife. 'I am sure we will all find our own way to God in the
end,' he confidently affirms. 'The Hindu has his way, the Muslim has
his way, I have mine and my wife has hers. But like lines of longitude
on a globe, eventually we shall find that our paths converge at the
same pole. How could God possibly be so intolerant as to let only
Christians into heaven? What an outrageously narrow-minded idea!
No: it doesn't matter what you believe, so long as you are sincere.'

And there is no denying that Joe's is an immensely attractive point
of view, especially in our modern world where mosques and temples
vie with churches and chapels on the High Street. But is Joe right?

Let us fantasize a little for a moment. Joe, like me, enjoys walking.
One day while out for a walk he meets a hiker.

'Lovely day,' Joe says.

'Great,' replies the hiker enthusiastically. 'I am on a pilgrimage to
Canterbury. They tell me there is an impressive cathedral there.'

Joe considers for a moment. He is pretty sure the road the hiker is
on leads in the opposite direction. But he is not infallible, is he? And
he hates to be a wet blanket on somebody else's religious
enthusiasm. Surely everybody is entitled to their own opinion. If
this chap really wants to get to Canterbury, that road is as good as
any other, he reasons. It doesn't matter what you believe, so long as
you are sincere.

Imagine another scenario. Joe works in a chemist's shop. He is not
a trained pharmacist, but he packs the shelves and serves on the
counter. He has picked up a little bit of knowledge about medicine.
One day an elderly lady comes into the shop, clutching a box of pills.

'My friend gave me these,' she says. 'He says they will cure my
arthritis. But I'm not sure how many to take. Can you help me?'

Joe looks at the unmarked box hesitantly. Privately, he is almost
sure he has seen the pharmacist dispensing pills from the poisons
cupboard that look remarkably similar to these. But then, what does

he know about drugs? And he would hate to discourage anyone in their suffering.

'If you really think they will help you, my dear, you just take as many as you like,' he advises. After all, he reasons with himself, it doesn't matter what you believe, so long as you are sincere.

You may be saying that my imaginary encounters have caricatured Joe's position; that there is all the difference in the world between an attitude of religious tolerance and the kind of irresponsibility that knowingly recommends poisons or gives wrong directions on a journey.

But is there really any difference? At the heart of all those things, you see, there is an issue of truth at stake. To say, 'It doesn't matter what you believe, so long as you are sincere', is nonsense. You might just as well say, 'All roads lead to Canterbury', or 'All pills treat arthritis.' Many world religions teach fundamentally disjunctive and contradictory things about God and the world. They cannot all be true, they cannot all be right. You can hold that they are all true or right only by defying all the normal rules of logic and radically redefining the very nature of truth.

The Bible will not commit such intellectual suicide. Malachi will not. And because he will not, he cannot endorse the marital choices which many of his compatriots were making.

'Judah has desecrated the sanctuary the LORD loves, by marrying the daughter of a foreign god' (2:11).

That is simply an idiomatic way of saying that it was becoming common for Jews to marry pagan women.

It is not difficult to imagine how they rationalized it. Their arguments would be very similar to Joe's. 'A person's religion is their business, that's what I say. My wife has every right to worship whatever god she pleases. It doesn't do to have a closed mind. We'll all get there in the end. I heard the Reverend Levi say so in the temple only last Sunday!' – so plausible, and yet clearly, in Malachi's eyes, so pernicious.

Do not misunderstand. There is no racist prejudice motivating his criticisms. There is no support to be found here for apartheid race laws on marriage, or anything like that. The Old Testament is by no means as ethnocentric as some people make out. Never forget that Ruth, the girl from Moab, married a Jew and became an honoured antecedent of King David. But the point was, she embraced the God of Israel; she was a *converted* pagan. What Malachi disapproves of is the refusal of these men of Israel, who had married pagan women, to bring their homes under the authority of Jehovah.

Their marriages had lost their spiritual and religious dimension and had become mere contracts, based perhaps purely on a goal of sexual gratification. No consideration was given to the implication such an attitude would have for themselves, or for their children or for their nation. They were there in church every sabbath, but they came alone and were content to do so; it did not disturb them. They saw nothing wrong in a marriage that united two bodies without uniting two souls. For Malachi this was just one more mark of the half-heartedness which he could see spreading among the people of God in his day.

See what he calls it in verse 11: 'a detestable thing'. It is a word that is used in the book of Deuteronomy for all kinds of disgusting and disgraceful pagan practices. 'Why,' says Malachi, 'such marriages desecrate the sanctuary.' That is, they make the individual concerned unholy, so that when he comes to offer his sacrifice to God he pollutes the temple area by his presence. Such people, says Malachi, must be disciplined. They must be ostracized from the community, whatever their social standing and no matter how pious they may apparently be.

'As for the man who does this, whoever he may be, may the LORD cut him off from the tents of Jacob – even though he brings offerings to the LORD Almighty' (2:12).

This, of course, is a very tough line. And there are several things that I need to say to you by way of clarification and qualification, if we are rightly to apply these words to our situation today.

Malachi was speaking into a particular historical situation

If you read the book of Nehemiah, particularly chapter 13, you will find that in the days of Malachi (which were also the days of Nehemiah, or just a little after them) the whole Jewish community in Jerusalem was being imperilled by this practice of inter-marriage with pagan women. Everybody was doing it. Nehemiah found himself in a situation where half the children in the city were speaking Philistine, or Ammonite or Moabite. They could not understand Hebrew or Aramaic, because their mothers did not speak it. What is more, many of the most prominent leaders in the community were involved.

That may very well be what Malachi is getting at when he says in verse 12, 'whoever he may be'. There was a real danger that the cultural attrition that these marriages were producing in the Jewish community would go unremedied, because the national leadership itself was hopelessly compromised by the practice.

The governor, Nehemiah, had to take some very draconian actions to remedy the situation, publicly rebuking very senior men, and insisting that Jews separate from their foreign wives. And it is important to realize that these words of Malachi are addressed to that same perilous and extreme historical situation. That is the first thing to note.

Malachi was an Old Testament prophet

The second is that there is something distinctive about the Old Testament period as far as inter-marriage is concerned. At this time, the whole plan of redemption hinged on the purity and survival of a particular nation. It was vital that when Christ came he should be born into a social context where people knew God's law, a place where people had read the prophets and were anticipating the Messiah the prophets had promised.

This was the very purpose of Israel in God's plan, that she should provide the arena in which the Saviour of the world would be born. But all that could be lost if Israel became dissolved in the cultural melting-pot of the ancient world. That is why, 'theologically' if you like, God supports Nehemiah and Malachi in this very strong line against inter-marriage; because inter-marriage was perilous for the whole plan of redemption. The survival of the people of Israel as a culturally intact, pure people was essential to his cosmic purpose.

Inter-marriage in the New Testament

When we come to New Testament times, this negative appraisal of inter-marriage is still there, but it is far less strident. There are two reasons. The first is that the historical situation has changed and the second is that the theological situation has changed. The historical situation is different, because now there are many, many Christians who are legitimately and unavoidably married to non-Christians. Some of these were converted from Gentile homes and families. They were already married to pagans when they became Christians. There was no way they could avoid that situation. More than that, the social structure of the first century meant that marriages were often arranged by parents, so a young Christian may well find he had no choice but to marry a young pagan woman, because his parents insisted upon it. Such people simply could not be blamed for the marital partners they finished up with. The church was bound to have many such mixed marriages in it; the more successful its evangelism, the more it would be faced with this problem.

But not only has the historical situation changed in the New Testament; the theological situation has changed too. In the New Testament God's purpose is no longer dependent upon the survival of a particular ethnic group, with a particular cultural background. The church now comprises people of all nations and cultures. For this new covenant, which Jesus Christ has inaugurated, is no longer based on a genetic pedigree. It is based now on a spiritual affiliation – one generated not by physical birth, but by the birth of the Spirit. Thus it is that when Paul has to wrestle with this situation of mixed marriages in the New Testament, he treats it far less severely than Malachi does.

You do not find, for example, the apostles throwing people out of the church because they are married to non-Christians. Rather the contrary. In 1 Corinthians 7:12–16, Paul deals with some who, perhaps under the influence of Old Testament teaching, were saying: 'We should divorce our pagan partners.'

Paul's response is a negative one. 'No, that's not what you should do,' he says. 'In these New Testament days, there is no desecration of the church as a result of a mixed marriage as there was desecration of the temple in Malachi's day. Our situation is different. Rather, the unbelieving husband or wife is sanctified by the believing wife or husband. For the believer does not bring contamination into the church because at home he or she has an unbelieving partner. No; believers take a holy, sanctifying influence back into their homes from the church. That is how you must look at it,' says Paul.

This is very important, of course, for any of you involved in one way or another with a mixed marriage. Whether by choice or by an unavoidable divine providence, your spouse is not a Christian. I would not wish you, if that is your situation, to be unduly dismayed in consequence. In Malachi's day a pagan spouse represented a defilement of the sanctuary and a great peril to the destiny of God's people, but in the New Testament a pagan spouse is regarded as an opportunity for evangelism. Paul says, in 1 Corinthians 7, 'Think about it, maybe you will be the means of saving your unbelieving partner. Do not divorce him or her.' It is a view that Peter supports in his first letter. 'If your husband does not believe the word,' he says to the Christian woman, 'then go out of your way to be a good and faithful wife. Maybe he will be won over to the faith by the purity and reverence of your life' (cf. 1 Pet. 3:1–2).

If you are involved in a mixed marriage, that must be your unceasing hope and prayer. Do not treat your marriage as some kind of spiritual handicap that condemns you for ever to God's second best. It is not so. By the presence of the Holy Spirit in your life you bring a sanctifying influence into your family, which can only be for their good.

But – and it is a very big but – that does not mean that in the New

Testament, the apostles encouraged mixed marriages in the church. They did not; in 2 Corinthians the apostle Paul also warns of the danger of being unequally yoked with unbelievers (2 Cor. 6:14). And it may very well be that marriage is one of those unequal yokes that he is talking about. Certainly, when in 1 Corinthians 7 he discusses a person who is free to choose her marital partner (as, in the ancient world, a widow was), he insists that the one she marries 'must belong to the Lord' (1 Cor. 7:39); that is, he must be a Christian.

So those of you who are single must not interpret the New Testament's more moderate attitude to mixed marriage, in comparison with Malachi's very tough line, as an invitation to contract marital relationships with non-Christians as if such things were innocuous. It is not so. The spiritual danger of mixed marriage is still there, because God's covenant is still there. The difference is that when you marry someone who is not a Christian, you are not imperilling the church, in the way that these people were imperilling Israel. But you are still imperilling your own spiritual well-being personally, for you are diminishing that covenant relationship with God which ought to come first in your life. You are breaking faith with him.

If you do not believe that a mixed marriage can do you spiritual harm, go and talk to people who are involved in mixed marriages. You will not find them telling you, 'Oh, it's OK! You go ahead. No problem.'

No; they will tell you it is hard. All kinds of conflicts of loyalty arise within a mixed marriage, which the Christian couple does not have to face. And there are temptations to spiritual backsliding which may well prove irresistible, and which, in far too many cases, do prove irresistible. Every pastor can tell you the sad tale of young men and women who seemed to show such potential for Christian service, but have finished up as casualties because their hormones got the better of them. They started by going out with non-Christians, because of course they wanted to 'witness' to them; they finished up by getting married to them.

Be sure of this, God is interested in whom you marry. Your vertical relationship with him demands that you make that choice wisely and prayerfully, for that relationship with him can be irreparably damaged by a foolish and rebellious choice. In that sense, Malachi's words here are just as relevant to you as a Christian as they were to those Jews. Do not marry the daughter of a foreign god. To do so deliberately is to court disaster; it is to break faith with the God who loves you and has called you to be his own. It is to break faith with Jesus, every bit as much as these Jews were breaking faith with

Jehovah. And that brings us to the second kind of unfaithfulness which was being exhibited in Israel.

Unfaithfulness in marriage

In Britain every day of the week, thousands of marriages break up, many in savage pain. One partner walks out on the other, usually into the arms of someone else: 'I know you will understand,' says the farewell note on the mantelpiece. But the truth in many cases is, of course, that they do not understand. Because when someone you love leaves you for someone else, it hurts. Few things in this world hurt more.

It is popular today to treat that old commandment 'You shall not commit adultery' as the vestigial remains of an outdated moral straitjacket. We are in the post-permissive society. Extra-marital sex is not even naughty any more, it's normal. To suggest sexual continence as a possible solution to the Aids problem is to invite ridicule. It is almost as bad as recommending the reintroduction of chastity belts. Opinion polls prove conclusively that the majority of men and women today expect to experience sexual intercourse with several partners during their lifetime.

Indeed, some sociologists argue that we are technically no longer a monogamous society. It would be closer to the truth to describe the marital situation in the western world today as serial polygamy – the convention of having only one sexual partner at a time. As someone has put it, 'It is not so much a case of "Marry in haste and repent at leisure" as "Marry in haste and repeat at leisure".'

Something very similar was happening in Malachi's day (2:13–14). As we said on our first morning, these Jews were treating divorce as casually as they would trading in an old car. A man looked at the wife he had married some years ago, and noticed that she was beginning to sag a bit in the suspension and that her bodywork was deteriorating. 'It's time for a new model,' he thought to himself. And that was it; no thought that marriage was a covenant, a promise. No thought that this was a one-flesh union, sealed by God himself. 'Everybody is doing it. We will remain good friends, won't we? I have just discovered, after fifteen years of married life, that we are incompatible. That's all.'

As far as Malachi was concerned, all the excuses collapsed when confronted with one single sentence in verse 16: ' "I hate divorce," says the LORD God of Israel.' In my book, God says, divorce is as serious a crime as murder: I hate it as implacably as I hate a man 'covering himself with violence'. To tolerate divorce in the complacent way you people have been doing, therefore, is just one more symptom of your spiritual half-heartedness, one more proof of your faithlessness.

Now once again we need to make some careful qualifications, if we are to avoid causing unnecessary hurt. Let me give you three.

1. Divorce is not impossible

Malachi knew perfectly well that divorce was actually permitted in God's law, and that Moses made provision for it in Deuteronomy 24:1–4. You may ask, why did God do such a thing if he hated divorce so much? The answer is given to us from Jesus' own lips. He said, 'Moses permitted you to divorce your wives because your hearts were hard' (Mt. 19:8). Sometimes God has to make concessions to the fallenness of human nature. We cannot keep his law perfectly, and so it is occasionally a lesser evil to permit his moral law to be broken in, as it were, a regulated fashion that minimizes the consequent damage, than to enforce that law rigidly and uncompromisingly. That is what Moses' divorce law was all about, says Jesus. It was a concession to our hard hearts, but it was not what God really wanted. He knew that keeping a couple together who were determined to break up was just unrealistic; it would do more harm than good. So the law had to make some provision for divorce as an inevitable fact of life in a fallen world. In that sense, divorce is possible – but that does not mean God likes it. On the contrary, he hates it.

2. In some divorces there may be an innocent partner

Malachi does not deny it. Indeed he suggests that the majority of divorces happening in his day did involve such an innocent partner. The abandoned wife was being deserted by her husband for no good reason at all, he said. She was an innocent partner in the affair.

No doubt there are two sides to every story. But the Bible does make a clear distinction between the sort of behaviour which undermines marital happiness and the sort of behaviour which breaks a marital bond. Jesus, in his teaching on divorce in the gospels, seems quite clearly to recognize for instance that adultery constitutes grounds for divorce, and that a husband or wife separating from a partner in such circumstances is not sinning (see Mt. 5:31–32). Similarly in 1 Corinthians 7 Paul seems to regard desertion by an unbelieving partner as grounds for divorce (see 1 Cor. 7:15). These are areas of controversy, as I am sure many of you are aware. Not all evangelical interpreters would endorse all that I have just said. But Malachi is certainly not denying that in many divorces there is an innocent partner, who experiences the pain of the break-up without deserving it.

3. Divorce is not an unforgivable sin

Malachi is not saying here that a divorcee, even if he or she is partially or totally responsible for the marital breakdown, has committed an unforgivable sin. God hates all sins. But no sin is unforgivable, except the repudiation of the work of God the Holy Spirit in our lives. Forgiveness is always available (see for instance Ps. 51). In fact, God has a wonderful way of repairing lives shattered by divorce, and every pastor can tell you stories of that. But that is not to say that there are no painful consequences in our lives as a result of divorce. Divorce leaves debris – hurt feelings which may take years to heal.

Often, of course, there are children to be considered. Verse 15 is unfortunately almost untranslatable from the Hebrew. But Malachi seems to be acknowledging in it that one of God's purposes in marriage is godly offspring. That is one reason he is so concerned about the sanctity of marriage; because the emotional and moral stability of children hinges on their experience of the faithfulness of the marriage bond. If they do not observe their mother and father being faithful to one another, they will not learn how important it is to be faithful in human relationships generally.

It should cause no surprise that the moral behaviour of children and young people gives such cause for concern in our society today. Any society in which almost every other marriage ends in divorce is going to be a society saturated with children who have suffered emotional and moral damage to their lives. It is an inevitable consequence of our shabby example of love. The murder of a little child by two ten-year-olds, the rape of a teacher by a teenage pupil – of course such stories horrify the nation; but it is no good beating our breasts and saying 'Bring back the cane' or 'Rebuild the Borstals', as if that were going to change the situation. We are beginning to experience the moral fallout of our statistics of broken marriages. And we have not seen a fraction of it yet.

Nevertheless, our situation is not without hope. Christ can repair lives which divorce has blown apart – the lives of the divorcees themselves, and the lives of the children. He can work in that situation of brokenness and evil and turn it to his good, by his overruling purpose and grace. I am sure that some of you here can testify to such a miracle. So we do not need to despair in a situation of divorce, as though we have committed an unforgivable sin that can never be resolved.

God hates divorce

Nevertheless, having said all these things – that divorce is possible; that there is an innocent partner sometimes; and that divorce can be forgiven – it would be irresponsible of me this morning if I did not draw your attention to the unequivocal language with which God expresses his outrage concerning divorce.

'I hate it,' he says.

Why? Because of the hurt it causes to the partner? Of course. Because of the damage it does to the children? Of course. But most of all, he hates it because it is one more example of broken faith, of promises not kept. Relationships depend on promises; and to treat divorce as casually as these Jews were treating it was to invite a collapse in relationships and therefore in society generally. There could be no deep and satisfying commitment of one person to another in a world that did not understand the importance of faithfulness. And of course it is just such a society that we are generating for ourselves.

Listen to these words from Christopher Lasch, in his book *The Culture of Narcissism*:

> Our society . . . has made deep and lasting friendships, love affairs, and marriages increasingly difficult to achieve. As social life has become more and more warlike and barbaric, personal relationships . . . take on the character of combat. Some of the new therapies dignify this combat as 'assertiveness'. Others celebrate impermanent attachments under such formulas as 'open marriage'. Thus they intensify the disease they pretend to cure.

People in our world today are lonely, and getting lonelier – because, as Hosea says, there is no faithfulness, no love, in the land (Ho. 4:1). People cannot trust each other any more, because they will not keep a promise.

Erich Fromm, in his books *The Art of Loving* and *The Sane Society*, blames it all on the economic system. Capitalism, he says, reduces all relationships to self-interest. It makes real love impossible by its cultivation of individualism. Men and women do not really love one another any more in a capitalist society; they just use each other for the fulfilment of their individualistic needs, rather as a car owner uses a mechanic to service his car.

Other sociologists draw attention to the effects of eroticization of modern society by the media. Forty years ago the publication of

D. H. Lawrence's novel *Lady Chatterley's Lover* was sufficient to scandalize the nation and bring about a court action. Now we have soft-porn videos, thinly disguised as sex-education courses, on sale in Woolworth's. We have girlie magazines, that would once have been found only in some curtained Soho dive, on public display in the High Street newsagent's. And our advertisers seem incapable of marketing even so ordinary a consumable as a bar of chocolate without turning it into an object of phallic fantasy. Expectations of sexual athleticism in one's partner, and of sexual ecstasy in oneself, have risen to extraordinary heights. I suspect that not since the closing days of the Roman Empire has the general level of sexual arousal in a society been quite so high as it is in ours. And in such an environment, it is not surprising if the boundary between love and lust gets rather blurred.

So is capitalism to blame for the shallow quality of our relationships? Or is it the exploitation of sex by the media? I do not deny that those things play a part, but I suggest to you that it is Malachi who has the deepest insight: at the root of our problem is unfaithfulness, an unwillingness on our part to be bound to anybody by promise.

In the 1980s a group of sociologists at the University of Berkeley in California carried out a very interesting study which was published as *Habits of the Heart*. One of the most important questions they addressed concerned contemporary attitudes to feelings. They found that people holding traditional ideas took the view that feelings should always take second place to duty. So they placed a higher value on virtues such as self-control, self-denial, self-discipline and self-sacrifice. Marital love was seen as fundamentally a commitment of the will, which one ought to honour irrespective of one's personal feelings about it, whether good or bad.

But these researchers discovered an interesting thing; that the traditional view was rapidly being displaced in the West by another attitude, which they characterized as the 'therapeutic attitude'. On this view, feelings take priority over everything else. The important thing is not what restrains the expression of the self, but rather what liberates it. Honesty and openness are what count, not self-discipline or self-denial or self-control. Self-realization, self-fulfilment, self-acceptance, self-actualization – these are the buzz-words of the therapeutic attitude. 'The spontaneous sharing of feelings between authentic expressive individuals' – this is the therapeutic definition of love.

Long-term commitment does not necessarily feature at all in such relationships. According to the therapeutic attitude, if my emotional needs are not being met by my partner I am entitled to ditch him or her. The therapeutic attitude denies all forms of social obligation and replaces them simply by the ideal of open and honest communication between people. The only thing therapeutically liberated lovers owe their partners is to share their feelings fully with them. Emotional independence and self-sufficiency are the goal; and a personal relationship is seen merely as a device for achieving those essential individualistic ends.

Now I am not saying that the therapeutic attitude is all bad. Undoubtedly, it does do some a great service by helping them to get in touch with their own wants and needs, and emancipating them from the artificial constraints of a social role which is inappropriate to them. But it has to be said that, carried to its extreme, this sort of attitude is desperately corrosive of the marriage bond, because it destroys faithfulness. As far as the Bible is concerned, the key thing that makes us human is our ability to form relationships, and there can be no relationships, either with God or with our neighbour, unless we are able to be faithful to one another.

Love is not just a feeling intended for our private enjoyment. It is a covenant that binds two people together. Love is not a passion; it is a promise. You know the reason most people shy away from marriage today, why they do not even bother getting married, let alone divorced? They are scared of it. Those vows are just too permanent. Promise to love somebody for better for worse, for richer for poorer, till death us do part? 'Why,' says our twentieth-century Romeo or Juliet incredulously, 'you cannot possibly expect me to make an unconditional commitment like that. If they cannot do it in the Royal Family, how can they expect me to do it? Life-long promises are out of place where your feelings are concerned. Nobody knows how I am going to feel about someone else in ten hours' time, let alone ten years. There's no controlling Cupid. He is a capricious and arbitrary imp. He makes no promises, so how can I?'

'You fall in love, you fall out of love,' asserts our Romeo. 'It is sentimental measles; you catch it, you recover from it. Certainly you cannot rely on it. Those who gamble on love lasting for ever are backing a horse that regularly falls before the first fence. Where relationships are concerned, the wise keep their options open. Do not put all your eggs in one basket. Enjoy it while it lasts!'

But the Bible insists that that is all rubbish. There is a stronger kind of love than that, a dependable love. How do we know it? We know it because God has shown it to us. He is a faithful, covenant God. 'I have loved you,' he tells them. There is a cross on a hill, where the blood of God was shed to make a covenant with us. There is his promise written indelibly and by his own hand for the universe to see. 'I love you and I do not intend to stop loving you. I will give my very self for you.'

That is the kind of love he expects us to emulate. Not a passing whim, born of romantic sentiment or sexual lust, but a strong, endurable covenant. That's what God means by love. Not a feeling, but a promise.

So, says Malachi, guard yourself in your spirit and do not break faith. Watch those wandering eyes, control those illicit fantasies. Settle it in your heart, he says, that you will not break faith: not with your marital partner, not with your God. 'Be faithful, even to the point of death,' God says, 'and I will give you the crown of life' (Rev. 2:10).

12

Cynicism

Malachi 2:17 – 4:6

When I was a young Christian, the question of rewards gave me a lot of trouble. It seemed rather discreditable to me that God should offer Christians incentives. It appeared to pander to the acquisitive spirit. The essence of the Christian ethic is unselfishness and altruism, so surely if people are going to serve God, let it be because he is worthy of it, not because they think they are going to get something out of it.

I was a great admirer in those days of a hymn by Francis Xavier which we used to sing at school:

> My God, I love thee, not because
>   I hope for heaven thereby;
> Nor yet because who love thee not
>   Are lost eternally.
>
> Not with the hope of gaining aught,
>   Not seeking a reward . . .
> Solely because thou art my God
>   And my most loving King.

Noble words, and bang on target, I thought. If God be God, then the matter of following him was an utterly thankless task with no hint of personal advantage. Integrity surely demands I honour him. Faith is not a bargain I strike on the basis of some calculated profit margin. Faith is my unconditional surrender to the irresistible claim of God's truth upon my conscience.

Or so I thought in those early days. And in many respects I still think like that. I do not approve, for instance, of evangelists who try to gain converts by offering inducements; by promising healing to the sick or prosperity to the poor, rice to the hungry – or visas to the refugees, come to that. Such tactics are simply bribery, and those who respond to such appeals are likely to have no more true faith in them than a mercenary has true patriotism. No, the highest motive for becoming a Christian is that we want God in our lives, not the blessings that God may give us. Francis Xavier's hymn is a masterly expression of that sentiment.

But as the years go by I have to confess that my youthful idealism has been moderated somewhat on this matter. I have discovered just how difficult it is to sustain the Christian faith in this broken and unhappy world in which we live. There are an awful lot of things around that contradict a breezy confidence in God, are there not? There are crime, war, natural disaster and sickness; tragedies of a dozen kinds are reported in our newspapers daily.

And such things quite clearly happen in a way that makes no distinction between good people and bad people, between Christians and non-Christians. Adversity is undiscriminating and arbitrary – at least, so it seems. The innocent suffer just as much as the guilty; indeed, sometimes, the innocent seem to suffer far more than the guilty. The guilty, precisely because they are unscrupulous and self-centred, all too often get away with murder. Do you know this little rhyme?

> The rain it raineth on the just
>   And also on the unjust fella:
> But chiefly on the just, because
>   The unjust steals the just's umbrella.
>   (Baron Bowen Charles, 1835–94)

It is precisely this unfairness which Malachi's compatriots are complaining about in this final section of his prophecy. 'What is the point of religion?' they ask. 'It's all very well for preachers like Malachi to pontificate about a God of righteousness, but he has created an unjust world.'

It is not hard to feel some sympathy for such complaints. I think we have to acknowledge that the most serious objection that could be raised against the theistic faith of the Bible is the problem of evil in the world. Other religions can adopt the dualistic solution. They can say, 'Well, there are equal and opposite powers of good and evil in the world, locked in a never-ending struggle. All the good things that happen derive from the good force, from God, and all the bad things that happen derive from the bad force – that is, the devil.'

It is a very convenient theory. But unfortunately, the Bible cannot endorse it. No, it says; God is an absolute sovereign in his universe. Nothing happens outside his control. The devil is no more than a malevolent rebel spirit, a creation of God, and far inferior to him in both power and knowledge. The book of Job tells us that he has no ability to harm human beings, except as God gives him permission to do so.

In many respects this doctrine of divine omnipotence is very

208

comforting, but it inevitably invites the question: 'Well then, why does this sovereign God give the devil so much rope?' Again, other religions can take refuge in monism. The monistic solution to the problem of evil says that God is in everything, both 'good' and 'evil'. All distinctions of that sort in the universe are really illusory. For there is no evil except as we choose to call it so. Christian Science comes very close to this when it tells us that pain is all in the mind.

> There was a faith healer of Deal
> Who said, 'Though I know pain ain't real,
>   When I sit on a pin
>   And it punctures my skin,
> I dislike what I fancy I feel.'

Convenient as the monistic solution to the problem of evil is, once again the Bible cannot accept it. It insists that God is good, that he loves what is just and right, that he stands over against all forms of evil, that he does not enjoy the pain or suffering of his creation in any way; and that is why goodness really matters, because it matters to him.

But once again, reassuring though a doctrine of divine righteousness is, it invites the objection: 'If God hates all this evil and suffering so much, why does he go on tolerating it?' So the Christian feels exceptionally vulnerable on this issue of evil. The Bible forces us to tread a difficult path between dualism and monism, to believe in an almighty God who for some reason is allowing things to go on in his universe to which he is thoroughly opposed. It is not difficult for atheists to ridicule such an idea. Bertrand Russell said, 'I can imagine a sardonic demon making us for his amusement, but I cannot attribute to a God who is almighty and benevolent the appalling weight of misery and degradation which has so marred the history of mankind.'

Malachi's compatriots were basically expressing the same scepticism; with less erudition, and in a rather sulkier tone perhaps, but it was essentially the same point they were making.

'All who do evil are good in the eyes of the LORD, and he is pleased with them' (2:17).

'Look,' they were saying, 'there is brother Eliezer over there; everyone knows he has a mistress on the other side of town. It does not seem to diminish his business profits, does it? And then there's Jonah the rent collector over there, crooked as they come. He always wears a very nice suit, you notice. As for caring for the weak in society, the widow, the orphan and the refugee – forget it. That's a mug's game. Don't you know we are in the middle of a recession, Malachi? Look after number one, that's the only sensible policy. If God is so concerned that we Jews should keep his law, how come all the pagans have got all the money?

'No, religion is just a big confidence trick. What is the point of performing all those religious rituals, praying all those prayers? It's the proud and the oppressors who get on in life, not the meek and the lowly ones. People can defy God, even curse him to his face, and nothing happens to them.'

'It is futile to serve God. What did we gain by carrying out his requirements and going about like mourners before the LORD Almighty? But now we call the arrogant blessed. Certainly the evildoers prosper, and even those who challenge God escape' (3:14–15).

To Malachi this is undoubtedly the most difficult aspect of his people's spiritual declension with which he has to deal. Their apathy in worship and their infidelity in personal relationships he can counter by appeal or by admonition. But at the root of this aspect of their spiritual half-heartedness lies not just laziness, indiscipline or sensuality, but a profound doubt about the goodness and dependability of God.

And that is what makes the situation so serious and dangerous. Kenneth Clark in his great book *Civilisation* writes: 'We can destroy ourselves by cynicism, just as much as by bombs.' He is absolutely right about that, of course, for the cynic has lost confidence in values. The cynic says that it is an unjust world, that virtue is triumphant only in theatricals and that once a people has surrendered to that kind of radical pessimism and cynicism, then moral anarchy, social decadence and pandemic despair are the inevitable consequences. That sort of cynicism is just as devastating as war, and there are plenty of civilizations that have fallen prey to its self-destructiveness.

The reply to cynicism

How was Malachi to address such a pernicious cancer in his society? There is really only one way. It is the Bible doctrine of rewards. Malachi cannot deny the negative and demoralizing aspects of human experience, of which these cynics complain; but he *can* insist that it is only one side of the story, a passing hiccup, an ephemeral blip in the moral order of the universe. 'No,' he says, 'it is *worth* serving God. Those who do not serve him will be losers in the long run. It is worth pursuing goodness. Those who do not do so will pay a price for their wickedness, in the last analysis.'

That hymn of Francis Xavier is all very fine and noble – but it is also naïve and sentimental. 'My God, I love thee, not because I hope for heaven thereby' – but if there is no heaven to hope for, how on earth can any love for God survive in this sin-sick world in which we live?

The whole point about the Christian faith is that it offers the final vindication of the goodness of God. No matter how dispassionate our quest for religious truth may be, no matter how high-minded our spiritual aspiration may be, there is no way a faith like that can be rationally sustained in the face of present evil without a doctrine of rewards. That is why there is no embarrassment in Malachi's recourse to that doctrine here in order to counter the embittered cynicism of his society. Reward is not some bait on his evangelistic hook by which he is unscrupulously enticing the people of his day to believe. Rewards, for Malachi, are the necessary consequence of that victory over sin which God must win if there is to be any gospel for the evangelist to proclaim at all.

If we do not believe in rewards, how can we any longer believe in God? It is not because the Bible loses its veracity in the absence of rewards for goodness; but because, if there are no rewards for goodness, the victory of God about which the Bible speaks loses its credibility.

Some of us perhaps have been moved by our studies in Malachi. We have made resolutions to be less apathetic, less indifferent, more committed. And it is a good thing to make such resolutions; but I tell you this – they will not endure a month, perhaps not even a week, battling in the gale of adversity, fighting the tide of rampant wickedness in our world unless we are convinced it's all going to be worth it – unless we are convinced that God must win, and that because he must win, we shall be winners too. How does Paul put it? 'We share in his sufferings in order that we may also share in his glory' (Rom. 8:17).

The rewards of commitment

What are these rewards for whole-heartedness, to which Malachi draws our attention in these closing chapters? There are two kinds. In 3:6–12, Malachi teaches us that there is a reward for godliness in this world, in the here and now. But in 3:1–5 and in 3:13 – 4:6 he points also to rewards that lie in the future, that belong to the last day.

Present rewards

' "Bring the whole tithe into the storehouse, that there may be food in my house. Test me in this," says the LORD Almighty, "and see if I will

211

not throw open the floodgates of heaven and pour out so much blessing that you will not have room enough for it"' (3:10).

It is clear from 3:10–12 that one of the ways in which the half-heartedness of the Jewish community was revealing itself in Malachi's day was the lack of funds in the temple treasury. The people simply were not giving generously to God. It is no surprise: people who are too mean to give a good animal sacrifice are hardly likely to put their hands in their pockets for cash any more readily. But the verdict which Malachi passes on this parsimony may come as something of a shock, nevertheless.

'Will a man rob God? Yet you rob me . . . You are under a curse – the whole nation of you – because you are robbing me' (3:8–9).

Malachi's point here is that in the Old Testament, people were required by law to donate one tenth of their annual income to the temple. It belonged to God by right according to the law. So to withhold it, said Malachi, is nothing short of larceny. 'Is it any wonder, then,' he says, 'that there is an economic recession? Is it any wonder there is no food in the shops, that Israel's reputation internationally is at an all-time low? Why on earth should God bless a den of thieves? It is not as though he deserves such treatment.'

All through history, says Malachi (verse 7), Israel has been abandoning the Lord, kicking him in the teeth, refusing to do things his way; when all through history God has been faithful to his covenant, he has never given up on us. 'That,' says Malachi, 'is why we are here in Jerusalem today. "I, the LORD, do not change" – that is why you descendants of Jacob are not destroyed.

'If he has denied us economic affluence, then, he is only fulfilling the promise he made to Moses. He told us in his law that if we as a nation ignore his moral rules, we will forfeit his economic blessings. But he also told us that if we repented of our sins, he would restore our prosperity' (cf. 3:6–7).

'Isn't it about time', asks Malachi, 'that we broke this habitual cycle of apostasy? God invites us to do so. He never stops wanting us to do so.

"Return to me," he says, "and I will return to you." The promises of the covenant and the prosperity that goes with them are there waiting to be claimed by you. And', says Malachi, 'there is a very simple way to prove it.

'If you want to return, do so in your tithes and offerings,' says Malachi. 'Put my covenant promise to the test,' says God; 'see if it is not true that those who honour me, I will honour. The measure you give will be the measure you get. See if it is not true that I will open the floodgates of heaven and pour out so much blessing on you that you will not have enough room for it. There is a reward for a whole-hearted commitment to me in the here and now. And once I see the sign of your restored whole-heartedness in those tithes and offerings, you shall receive it. You have only yourselves to blame for your current economic austerities. You will never discover the prosperity God wants you to enjoy while your mean fists are grasping your wallets so tightly whenever you come to church' (*cf.* 3:10–12).

It is a very bold challenge, is it not? How do you think we should apply that to our contemporary situation? Is Malachi proposing a kind of prosperity doctrine? Give to God and he will give back to you, just like that? There are plenty of preachers, of course, who have interpreted this text in exactly that way. There are countless churches that invite you, not to give, but to 'invest' in their work; the implication is that you will get a return with interest. And who has not heard the testimony of those Christian business people who assure us that it was only when they started to tithe that, miraculously, commercial success began to be their lot?

But I want to suggest that it would be a mistake to read this passage as an endorsement of that kind of prosperity teaching.

The promise is to a nation

First, we see that Malachi's words are directed to the nation as a whole, not to individuals; because, of course, the law of Deuteronomy was addressed to society generally. That law promises economic blessing to the people that obey God, but the Bible is far more chary about individualizing those material rewards. Scripture gives us for example the story of Job, a good man who obeyed God's law completely and yet who experienced poverty rather than wealth.

Let us be as realistic about this as the Bible is. For every Christian business person who testifies to the prosperity God has brought his or her way, there is another silent in the pew, broken by bankruptcy. I am not saying that God does not bless us as individuals materially. Undoubtedly he does, but there is no mechanical and inevitable link between the amount of money I put in the offering bag on Sunday and the amount of money in my pay packet on Friday. The blessings of which Malachi speaks here concern the macro-economy of the national, rather than the micro-economy of the individual.

Malachi is an Old Testament prophet

Secondly, just as in the case of inter-marriage which we examined yesterday, the Old Testament location of Malachi's words makes a vital difference. In his day, the people of God were a political entity and the temple of God was a national institution. But in New

Testament days the church is an international community and the temple has been replaced by the spiritual solidarity of the body of Christ. It follows then that the blessings and rewards of Christian faithfulness of which the New Testament speaks tend to be spiritual rather than material, eternal rather than temporal.

Now, it is true that there are compensations promised by Jesus to offset the cost of discipleship. But there is nothing in the gospel to suggest that the Christian disciple should expect to be wealthy. In fact the reverse is true. Sell what you have and give to the poor, and you will have treasure in *heaven* – that was Jesus' emphasis. He certainly said, 'Seek first God's kingdom and your material welfare will be taken care of' (*cf.* Mt. 6:33), but he was talking about food and clothing, not Aston Martins and caviar.

So how should we apply Malachi's challenge to his people, to ourselves and to our present day? Let me offer just a few hints.

I think that first of all, a careful application of his words can be rightly directed to *our nation*. Does this mean that the Archbishop of Canterbury should be recommending to the Chancellor of the Exchequer that the way out of the recession is to put 10p on income tax, and devote the resulting revenue to the refurbishment of the Church of England and the remuneration of its clergy? At the risk of disappointing my Anglican friends, I have to say no, I have no confidence in such a policy at all. But I think the passage can be applied in this sense – that we, the body of Christ, as a prophetic community in our nation, should be as courageous as Malachi is in drawing the connection between economic decay and moral ills in our community.

Secondly, I think this is a passage that can be rightly applied within *our churches*. Does this mean that the pastor should insist upon 10% tithing of income as a requirement of church membership? No. That would be a legalistic measure, out of place in the New Testament church. But the principle of giving to God's work regularly a proportion of our wealth, prayerfully determined, as Paul said in 2 Corinthians 8:11, in keeping with our income, seems to me a principle the New Testament fully endorses. We should be teaching our churches that if our people give in that kind of committed way, then we, as the community of God's people, will find he opens the floodgates of heaven and pours out blessing upon us. Paul says something with which Malachi would have agreed, when he says, 'Whoever sows sparingly will also reap sparingly, and whoever sows generously will also reap generously' (2 Cor. 9:6).

And I think there is a sense in which these words do rightly apply to *us as individuals* too. Do you want to return to God? Have you been touched by God's word, and are you seeking some way of responding to the challenge, to be 100% for God in future? Well, Malachi here is suggesting one way you can do it: a simple, practical, concrete way of consolidating that resolution. Christian discipleship begins in the head, as we understand what God's word demands of us. Christian discipleship proceeds to the heart, where we respond willingly to the demands God places upon us. And between the head and the heart, Christian discipleship passes through the pocket. If it does not, it is not real; that is what Malachi is saying. If you really mean that you want to return to God, the offering basket will be fuller next Sunday.

Put God to the test, then. There are rewards for the whole-hearted believer. Giving is good for you, not an onerous duty. It is a joyful privilege; it is a pathway to blessing. Malachi is convinced you cannot out-give God, but he does invite you to try.

Future rewards

There are present rewards for the faithful believer, then, but there are even greater rewards yet to come!

> 'See, I will send my messenger, who will prepare the way before me. Then suddenly the LORD you are seeking will come to his temple; the messenger of the covenant, whom you desire, will come,' says the LORD Almighty (3:1).

One of the most characteristic features of our contemporary world is its loss of hope. It was Woody Allen who made the remark that the future is not what it used to be. He was right. Optimism about the destiny of the human race has collapsed in our century. That vision of Utopia, the fire and political idealism of an earlier generation, lie wrecked under the carnage of a dozen bloody wars and revolutions. All those predictions of technological progress that motivated the scientific enterprise have been shrouded in the mushroom cloud of Hiroshima and the pollution of Chernobyl.

A few still cling to the old Utopian dreams of a man-made paradise on earth. They talk of a New Age now, the Age of Aquarius. But the vast majority of thinking people today are no longer wearing rose-tinted spectacles of such a discredited humanism.

Kenneth Clark, in the book *Civilisation* which I mentioned earlier, says this: 'Confident articles on the future are, to my mind, the most disreputable of all public utterances.' And as the millennial year of AD 2000 approaches, I suspect that global insecurity will become more and more acute.

Malachi's compatriots seem to have been interested in the idea of a Utopian new age too. They loved to speculate about the prophetic predictions of a coming Day of the Lord when God would intervene miraculously and establish Jerusalem as the capital of the entire world. That dream had fired many of them as they returned to Jerusalem from Babylon. They were like some Zionists today; they believed the kingdom of God was imminent. They had come home to get Jerusalem ready for the Messiah, for the Lord's coming.

But Malachi has some words of caution to offer them in respect of that eschatological enthusiasm of theirs.

God will come in judgment

But who can endure the day of his coming? Who can stand when he appears? For he will be like a refiner's fire or a launderer's soap. He will sit as a refiner and purifier of silver; he will purify the Levites and refine them like gold and silver. Then the LORD will have men who will bring offerings in righteousness, and the offerings of Judah and Jerusalem will be acceptable to the LORD, as in days gone by, as in former years. (3:2–4)

The Day of the Lord is certainly going to arrive, he says. God will come. In fact shortly he will send the prophetic forerunner to prepare for that day, the one he calls in 3:1 'my messenger', and in 4:5 'the prophet Elijah', whom 'I will send . . . before that great and dreadful day of the LORD comes'. But are you really sure you want that Day to come? For let's face it, says Malachi, you are a half-hearted people. Your public worship is apathetic, your lives are selfish and sinful, and your attitudes are just thoroughly cynical. There is no way that coming day is going to be a pleasant experience for people like you. 'Who can endure the day of his coming? Who can stand when he appears?' (3:2).

For it is going to be a day of judgment, a *refining* judgment, first of all purging the clergy of their compromise up there in the temple. 'He will be like a refiner's fire or a launderer's soap. He will sit as a refiner and purifier of silver' (3:2–3). Whom is he going to purify? Not the pagans, not even the people in the pew – the Levites. 'He . . . will refine them like gold and silver. Then the LORD will have men who will bring offerings in righteousness, and the offerings of Judah and Jerusalem will be acceptable to the LORD, as in the days gone by, as in former years' (3:3–4).

It is going to be a retributory judgment too, punishing a sinful, morally degenerate society.

'So I will come near to you for judgment. I will be quick to testify against sorcerors, adulterers and perjurers, against those who defraud labourers of their wages, who oppress the widows and the fatherless, and deprive aliens of justice, but do not fear me,' says the LORD Almighty' (3:5).

There are countless sins that bear no penalty in our statute book. But God will execute judgment against them all. The sorcerers, the perjurers, the adulterers, the oppressers – God will execute judgment against them all.

But most significant of all, for this cynical audience of Malachi's, it is going to be a *discriminating* judgment. The books are going to be opened, and the real people of God are going to be revealed. All lives will be assessed, and then it will be seen who has 'feared the LORD and honoured his name' (3:16).

'You will again see the distinction between the righteous and the wicked, between those who serve God and those who do not' (3:18).

'"Surely the day is coming; it will burn like a furnace. All the arrogant and every evildoer will be stubble, and that day that is coming will set them on fire," says the LORD Almighty. "Not a root or a branch will be left to them"' (4:1).

I do not like the idea of hell any more than you do. But, you see, *unless Malachi can speak of such a final judgment, the cynics are right.* Unless God imposes some ultimate sanction against the wickedness of the human race, his righteousness is a farce. Hell is not an embarrassment to heaven. God is glorified in judgment. For in judgment, he affirms his righteousness over against everything that denies it. And heaven is glad about that.

God will bring his reward with him

But not only will the wicked perish; there is a positive side to this Day of the Lord too. Those who fear the Lord and honour him '"will be mine," says the LORD Almighty, "in the day when I make up my treasured possession. I will spare them, just as in compassion a man spares his son who serves him"' (3:17).

'For you who revere my name, the sun of righteousness will rise with healing in its wings' (4:2).

All the darkness which clouds our faith and makes it hard going to believe in God at the moment is going to be dispelled when the sun of his justice finally sends those clouds scudding away. And then there will be no more suffering and pain for the righteous, only healing and mercy.

'You will go out and leap like calves released from the stall' (4:2).

Have you ever seen an animal released after being confined and frustrated by its cramped environment? It gambols all over the field in its new-found freedom. And in the same way, says Malachi, the true people of God who are struggling right in the frustrating confinement of this sin-sick world will find liberation. As Paul puts it, 'We ourselves, who have the firstfruits of the Spirit, groan inwardly as we wait eagerly for our adoption as sons, the redemption of our bodies' (Rom. 8:23). That groaning is not going to last for ever. The day of emancipation is coming, says Malachi; a day which will make all the suffering we have had to endure pale into insignificance by the radiance of its glory.

And when that day comes, ' "you will trample down the wicked; they will be ashes under the soles of your feet on the day when I do these things," says the LORD Almighty' (4:3).

No, heaven is not embarrassed by hell, and you and I will not be either. It will not spoil heaven for us to know that God has judged the wicked. We will understand that it is the only way that heaven can remain heaven.

Recapturing the dream

I ask you: can you survive in this world of ours without a hope like that?

There is so much cynicism today. A young American student at Cambridge who expressed it to me in words I have never forgotten. He said, 'We Americans used to trust the generals, but Vietnam changed all that. We used to trust the politicians, then Watergate changed all that. We used to trust the scientists, but Three Mile Island changed all that. We used to trust the economists, but recession changed all that. Now we know there is no-one to trust.'

He predicted, 'The 1990s will be years of cynicism.' And so they have proved. The optimism of the past seems almost laughable. Experience has revealed it to be a fantasy of infantile human political imagination, as far removed from reality as Disneyland is from Hiroshima. And, I have to say, that disillusionment is most tragic. That does not mean that I grieve because the intoxicated expectations of the early socialists and the early humanists have been sobered by a few bucketfuls of cold political reality. I do not mourn that; it was very necessary. Nor does it sadden me that people are becoming more wary of technological advance. Scientific hubris is dangerous. As long as we do not plunge back into medieval superstition or Luddite paranoia, a little more ecological sensitivity and caution will be all to the good in our use of scientific discoveries.

No, what worries me is that mankind in the West has lost its dream.

We have lost the hope, the vision that gives meaning to our existence. It is not enough that we human beings should just survive; we need hope and a purpose. Without some incentive like that we languish into apathy – yes, and cynicism; and ultimately into despair. Take away everything that people have to live for, and they put a bullet through their brains. And we can see the signs of that suicidal apathy, cynicism and despair all around us in our contemporary society. People are shutting the future out of their minds in myopic self-indulgence. 'Let us eat, drink and be merry, for tomorrow – who knows? Enjoy yourself while you have a chance.' This is a world that has lost its hope.

Such a world is doomed. Slowly but surely, such pessimism tears the guts out of a culture. People have nothing to work for, nothing to save for, nothing to live for beyond the immediate satisfaction of their desires. That, it seems to me, is exactly why the West is finding it so hard to advance economically right now. High interest rates are a consequence of the desire for instant gratification. You have to penalize people for consuming, in order to stop them. But it does not matter how high a penalty you impose on consumption, a hopeless generation will go on buying to comfort itself for its lack of future.

Where is our society to turn for hope, in days like ours when secular dreams have lost their credibility? Christians have an answer. Indeed we should be more conspicuous on this ground than perhaps on any other – not just because we maintain habits of religious worship in a secular age, or just because we maintain standards of moral behaviour in a permissive age.

At the turn of the twenty-first century, the most obvious thing about Christians may be that we still have hope, that we have not surrendered to cynicism, that we still believe in the victory of goodness, that we are still looking forward to the future.

Why are we able to do that? Because the messenger of the covenant has come just as Malachi said he would, with John the Baptist as his prophetic forerunner. And now he stands at God's right hand, clothed in victory.

Dr David Cook tells a lovely story of an Oxford undergraduate who, in his final year, somewhere around June or July, wrote a letter to his parents.

Dear Mum and Dad,
   I know you haven't heard much from me in recent months, but the fact is this. A few weeks back, there was a fire in the flat and I lost all my possessions. In fact I only escaped with my life by jumping out of a second-floor

window. In the process of doing so I broke my leg, so I finished up in hospital. Fortunately, I met the most wonderful nurse there. We immediately fell in love, and, well, to cut a long story short, last Saturday we got married. Many of our friends say this was over-hasty, but I am convinced that our love will more than compensate for the difference between our social backgrounds and ethnic origins.

By this time, Mum and Dad, I suspect you may be getting a bit worried, so let me tell you straight away that everything I have written in this letter up to now is false. I made it up.

The truth is, two weeks ago I failed my final exams. I just want you to get this in the proper perspective.

Certainly there is evil and suffering in the world. We Christians cannot deny it. And if you want to allow it to make you cynical, you can. But Malachi wants you to get it in the right perspective. 'Surely the day is coming' (4:1). There is a reward for those who seek the face of God. Do not doubt it!

So we come to Malachi's final words. They constitute a postscript, not only to his prophecy, but to the whole Old Testament.

Obey the inspired word of God. Do not neglect it. 'Remember the law of my servant Moses, the decrees and laws I gave him at Horeb for all Israel' (4:4).

Be ready for the coming day of God. 'See, I will send you the prophet Elijah before that great and dreadful day of the LORD comes' (4:5).

Love one another earnestly, like members of a huge family. 'He will turn the hearts of the fathers to the children and the hearts of the children to their fathers' (4:6).

And *never, never surrender to that doubt which says the God of justice will not judge the world.* 'I will come and strike the land with a curse.'

THE CHURCH IN THE MODERN WORLD
Acts 16 – 20

13

Acts 16

Dick Dowsett

I wonder why you have come here this week? I hope that it is because you do not want to be a passive Christian. You want to move with God, and you want to move out with God. You want to go places for, and with, the Lord. But you do want to be sure that it is with him, and in accordance with his will.

At least, I hope that is why you are here. If so, we are going to learn some important lessons in these studies as we travel to Philippi and find out more about the church that was established there.

Walking into God's plans (16:6–10)

Paul and Luke and the rest of their team were a group that wanted to move with God and for God: to go places, to count for something for him in a spoilt world. And we ought to look at them closely, for by the end of this passage they were clearly quite sure that they were walking in the will of God (verse 10).

The first thing I want you to see is that for them, *what they learnt of the principles of God was enough to get them moving.* Verse 6, 'they travelled'; verse 7, 'they tried to enter' another place. Why? Not, I suggest, because they were taking time off from their quiet times and just doing their own thing. Rather, they were planning to be biblical. In his letter to the Romans, Paul gives us an insight into the mindset that led him to try to enter different provinces of Turkey. 'I do want to come to Italy', he says, 'because I do want to reap an Italian harvest' (*cf.* Rom. 1:13). Later (15:24) he says, 'I'm planning to go to Spain.' If you had asked him why, he would have explained, 'Well, I've been reading in Isaiah recently that God's purpose is that those who haven't heard the gospel will hear it' (*cf.* 15.:21).

What was the apostle Paul doing? He was learning the principles of God's word, and in the light of those principles he was making plans. And as we study together this week and interact together, this is very important for us to understand. God does not teach us his principles so that we can put them into cold storage until we are suddenly zapped, but so that we can be enabled to get up and go. Somebody once said, 'A disciple is not just a learner or a student, he's a learner or a student *with legs*.' And this is what we see demonstrated in the early verses of this paragraph.

So our first point is that if we are going to get up and go with God, then as we learn God's principles this week we have got to make decisions on the basis of those principles.

Secondly, we see that *the plan of God for the group was not instantly revealed*. The door into Asia was temporarily closed (verse 6); they couldn't go there. They were not allowed to enter into Mysia (verse 7). Are you prepared to be confused for a while? God does not give you all the answers at once, does he? And he did not do so even for the apostle Paul. Nor is there any hint that Paul was not having his quiet time in those days!

But do you see? He began to move in line with the principle of God – that he had to go and make disciples of the nations – and he found the Lord putting roadblocks in the way. He did not merely say, 'Well, I've got the Bible and I've got my mind, so that's it.' He was also concerned to walk in the Spirit, and to keep in a day-by-day relationship with the Lord himself.

It was not to be simply a relationship with the Lord's book. A Muslim once said to me, 'My Christian friends do not have the same sort of relationship with God that I have. I have a relationship with God's holy book the Qur'an, but my Christian friends have something more than that.' Well – I hope you do. We have an infallible book, but we also have a living God who inspired and wrote that book. Sometimes people say, 'I've got the principles in the Bible, and I went a particular way, and there was an open door: so it *must* be God's will.' But a door can open to a lift-shaft! So we find Paul deciding on the basis of Scripture, walking with God and walking in the Spirit, and keeping those lines of communication open.

Thirdly, we see *the call of God was clarified in Paul's vision*. One night Paul was zapped with a vision for Greece. He saw a Greek man, who said, 'Come over and help us.' I do not know what you think of visions. Some of you would probably be scared out of your wits if you had one, while for others visions are very desirable. But if you get visions – or hunches, or urges, or ideas – where do they come from? Perhaps you had a vision of a Greek man because you ate too much moussaka last night. Or maybe it's because you would like to be warmer and you are hankering to go to Greece. Or maybe it was because God is so using you here that the devil is determined to get you to go to Greece instead.

Or maybe it was God.

You see, visions, ideas, hunches and 'thoughts' come from many sources. They can come from your stomach, they can come from your wishful thinking, they can come from the pit – or they can come from the Lord himself.

So what did Paul do when he got a vision? Well, Luke gave us a clue in verse 10: 'We . . . concluded that God had called us.' He shared it with those who really meant business with God. And that is tremendously important too. As we come here we need to be open to the living God, to deal with us, to zap us, to speak to us in whatever way he chooses; but if an idea comes into your head, or if you have a wonderful dream tonight, share it with others who mean business with God. Test it out! And Paul's friends concluded together that it wasn't the moussaka, it was God. And so they started to go to Greece in response to the vision. But they made the decision – or chose – to stop in Philippi.

Let me summarize what we have learned so far, by means of an illustration that may help you as you go on studying what God's plan is for you.

The Scripture tells us that in our relationship and our duties towards God we are 'stewards' of the gospel. We do not talk about stewards these days, we talk about 'junior managers'. A junior manager is entrusted with a product that he is to market creatively. He is given the company principles, and he also has a telephone line to the managing director. It is the job of the junior manager to develop the markets creatively in line with company principles. Sometimes the managing director will get on the phone and say to him, 'Listen, lad, you're doing well – now would you develop the markets over here?' Now: there are two types of junior manager who are disasters. Those who will not do a thing unless they get a personal phone call from the managing director – and those who so enjoy being creative and doing their own thing that they unplug their telephones.

Look at the pattern we are given in this first paragraph. We are junior managers, entrusted with God's answers for a lost world. We are expected to be creative, to develop the markets in line with company principles: the Bible. And woe betide the junior manager who will only act when he gets a special, individual, personal phone call from the managing director who has already written the principles and commissioned him or her to the task! But equally, woe betide the junior manager in this 'Jesus business' who unplugs the phone. The managing director, our Lord of heaven and earth, is

alive. And he may well want to get through to you, to redirect you –
in all sorts of ways that will blow your mind.

We obey and plan on the basis of the word, but we also cultivate a
personal relationship with the Lord of the word. And notice, when
Jesus mobilized them and they ended up in Philippi, the Lord came
too. Whatever he's going to ask you to do, he is not going to sit in
heaven and fold his arms and watch you make a fool of yourself.
Where the Lord calls, the Lord comes.

So it was in Philippi. It was the Lord who opened Lydia's heart so
that she could hear (verse 14).

The people the Lord touched through Paul (16:11–37)

Look now at the different people whom the Lord touched through
the ministry of Paul and the rest of the team that travelled with him.

Lydia (16:13–15)

First, he went to the place of prayer where the women were gathered
to pray. (I could make some caustic comments about men here!) A
woman called Lydia, who ran a store selling expensive material, was
praying. She was committed to, and understood, much of the truth
of the Old Testament – the Scripture that, Paul wrote in the Holy
Spirit, is able to make us 'wise unto salvation' (2 Tim. 3:15, AV). She
had those Scriptures; she was talking to God; but she needed the
gospel. She needed the Saviour, Jesus. Her religion, for all its fine and
splendid points and the fact that indeed it pointed to Jesus, was not
enough. She needed our Saviour.

How important that is for us, as we are confronted in our
pluralistic society with many different religions. Perhaps we admire
– I hope you do – our Muslim neighbours who have a quiet time five
times a day, and have so many answers and seem to believe more
about the Lord Jesus than certain notorious bishops! We may admire
our Jewish neighbours with their commitment and their prayers. We
may admire our Catholic neighbours with their devotions and
commitment and so many doctrines that we all affirm. We may
admire our nominal Protestant neighbours with their reformed, or
not so reformed, truths.

But the question is not, 'How many answers have they got tucked
under their arm?' Or even, 'How many times do they say their
prayers?' The question is: 'Do they know the Saviour?' Religion does
not save. Jesus does. And we need to hold on to that.

We need to hold on too to the awesome fact that it took a miracle to get Lydia to listen. Sometimes you meet nice, decent, religious folk and you think, 'Well – they are terribly convertible!' Don't you believe it. The Lord Jesus looked at Nicodemus, who was a sort of Old Testament elder of the church, if you like; and he said to him, 'Listen, Nicodemus – if you're not switched on from above, you're not even going to see this thing, let alone get in' (cf. Jn. 3:3.5). And this was exactly Lydia's situation. But the Lord opened her heart so that she heard the gospel and she knew it was for her. We need to hold to that in these days, when people will tell us that if only we mastered certain techniques people would fall over themselves to become believers. They will not, unless they are born from above. Unless the Lord opens people's hearts, our evangelism will be but fruitless talk.

Lydia was saved. And from the first day, she became a partner (Phil. 1:5). She didn't go on a basic course, not to be trusted with anything until she had at least graduated from a three-year or four-year course and been to Bible school. She was part of the outgoing work of mission, because that day she trusted Jesus.

The demonized woman (16:16–22)

The next person whom the apostle encountered was a demonized woman; a woman who, the text suggests, had committed herself to the worship of a snake. As a result she had an alarming testimony. People went to her to find out about the future because what she said, happened.

She had a testimony. Indeed, when she testified, 'These men are servants of the Most High God, who are telling you the way to be saved' (verse 17), she obviously knew more about them than most of the local people did; and she was absolutely right.

It was the devil trying to get in on the act. He knew that the people were going to turn to Jesus, but he thought, 'If only they can carry on dealing with the spirits for the practical affairs of life, if only they can still read the horoscopes to find out about their future, that's going to be fine. They can have Jesus – as long as they keep me as well.'

Now, notice here something that is alarming but important for us to understand. *It isn't just Christians who have testimonies.* The devil is a good businessman. He gives discounts to gain regular customers. That's why things work in religions, why things work among the powers of darkness. But, you see, this person needed to be delivered. And what happened now is very fascinating. The authority of Jesus was and still is quite enough to deal with this demon problem.

There are all sorts of fashions regarding the demonic these days, which I find rather alarming. We do not find the apostle Paul here galloping round to everybody he set eyes on and saying, 'You've got a demon problem, and I'm going to cast it out.' Actually, he was rather slow to get involved: it was only when this girl really got up his nose that he started dealing with the problem.

The second thing that we find is that *Paul did not seem to feel that he needed to be in the business of binding all the demons in Philippi.* Why not? It seems to me, from the very simple way that he dealt with the problem, that he had discovered that it is the Lord Jesus who has authority and commands the evil spirits, and they do as they're told. But more than that, and most important, on the cross Jesus disarmed the 'powers and authorities', triumphing over them (Col. 2:15).

In other words, Paul did not need to bind. Jesus did the binding on Calvary. The earth is full not so much of wandering demons as of the glory of our Saviour; and Paul capitalized on this when he was confronted by someone who was demonized. There was, and still is, deliverance in the name of Jesus. So we are not cold-blooded rationalists who think that demons are only part of mythology; neither are we baptized animists who find a demon under every chair and talk no longer about sin but only about possession. We take seriously the powers of darkness, and the many people in this world who have been brought up to deal with spirits and do not know that there is one who is mightier. Such people need deliverance too.

The jailer (16:27–37)

There is a third person ministered to: the jailer. I see him as part of the organized opposition to the gospel.

For here is somebody who had beaten Paul up. Here is somebody who was an agent for the suppression of Christianity. Are you the sort of person who says, 'I'll go and take the gospel so long as the people welcome me and are nice to me'? But those who do not welcome you, who are nasty to you, need Jesus as well. And the extraordinary thing, as this story testifies, is that a hardened thug can be broken in an instant; can in this case be about to commit suicide, and yet may – extraordinarily! – then be at the point where he is asking exactly the right question: 'What must I do to be saved?' Suddenly a man was broken, and the man of God was there, loving him – loving him and his family.

Have you noticed something quite amazing here?

Look at Lydia. We do not know if she was married or single, but she was not living alone. And we find that when she showed interest in the gospel, immediately the apostle Paul was interested in her household. 'Who are these people who live with you – who share your flat with you?' (*cf.* verse 15). And he went back to her home.

Look at the jailer. He asked, 'What must I do to be saved?' He was highly traumatized, he was about to commit suicide – and the apostle Paul said, 'By the way, can we talk about it with your family?' It's so un-British, isn't it? We're so besotted with one-on-one evangelism that it is often we, rather than the gospel, who split families. You who are in women's Bible studies: when you get a woman who is seeking, how about saying, 'Can I come home and talk to your husband and the kids about it as well?' Maybe you're talking to a student: 'Can I come back to your flat and talk to the rest of your flatmates?' You say, 'Oh no, we couldn't do that! We like to do it very personally.' But do we like to do it *biblically*?

It's interesting that the apostolic practice was to go for the families wherever possible. And as Paul went for the families, there was joy in that thug's family in Philippi and the rest of his household.

For the sake of a lost world

Let me ask you one more question. Are you prepared to be like Paul for the sake of a lost world? As we read this story we see a person who was open to what God is doing. I find the story very amusing, because, as you remember, the apostle Paul was brought up in the synagogue to thank the Lord daily: 'O Lord, I thank thee that thou hast not made me a slave, a Gentile or a woman.' And then he went into Europe and won a woman, a slave and a Gentile for Christ . . .

He was open to doing not what he was brought up to do but to moving where God was on the move, and to establish the work that way. Not only was he open to what God was doing, he was prepared for Satan's attacks. Today many people seem to think that if God is in some enterprise, if God wants you to do something, then it is sure to go well. If God calls you out of your work into the ministry, then you really are going to be blessed, people are going to get zapped through your ministry, and things are going to go right. If God calls you to go overseas, if God tells you to do something that is awkward through his word, you think, 'Well – if I do it, it's all going to turn out lovely!'

But you see, it was not like that for Paul. When he went over to Macedonia he was confronted by a noisy spirit. Then there was a racist reaction: 'These people are Jews – so they're not like us.' Then there was the reaction of the crowd: 'These people are socially disruptive, advocating alien and illegal customs.' Everything went wrong.

That is the world we live in. The word does not proclaim that if only you follow Jesus, everything in the garden will be lovely. As the apostle Paul said: 'If in this life only we have hope in Christ, we are the most miserable people there are' (*cf.* 1 Cor. 15:19). Won't it be great to get to heaven? If we go with God, we will expect the devil to throw things at us on the way.

Therefore the question for you and for me is, 'Have I learnt what it is to go with God when it all goes wrong?' Does it not strike you as absolutely magnificent that in the prison in Philippi at midnight, when Paul was experiencing insomnia (and so would you, if you'd been beaten up under the Roman law), he sang hymns and praised the Lord? And do you notice that it says that the other prisoners were listening? That's not what I do when my son is playing pop music at maximum decibels, while I am addicted to Radio 3. It does not mean that the other prisoners wished they would shut up so that they could have a normal night's sleep! It means that they wanted to hear what made these men tick; to discover that they'd got something to sing about and somebody to rejoice in, when they had just been beaten up.

As I study the Scriptures, and as I think particularly about the work of God in Asia where I have a particular concern, I observe that there is a principle here. *The gospel advances on disasters and suffering.*

You may say, 'Why has God allowed this to happen to me?' But when everything goes well, who listens? If they listen at all, they just say, 'Well, you have your path and I have mine.' Then everything starts to go badly, and they see that in that fragile clay pot that you are, there is a treasure that they cannot explain. They look up, and they say, 'What have you got that we have not got?' The answer is, Jesus. For he has said, not 'Everything will go well if you live by the Bible', but 'Never will I leave you; never will I forsake you . . . The Lord is my helper' (Heb. 13:5–6). And that is all he guarantees.

Are you going to walk with God? Are you going to move out for God? He will not let you down.

So as you go into this week, for the sake of a lost religious world, for the sake of a lost demonized world, for the sake of a world organized against Christ, plan to do what you learn and walk with the living God. It may be tough; but he will shine through, and he will not fail.

14

Acts 17

David Cook

Our address this evening is two parts. In the first, I want to look with you at Acts 17 which tells the story of Paul in Athens, because I believe that we have there a model for how to communicate the gospel into any and every context. Then I want to step back from that particular biblical understanding and model, and to reflect with you a little on the nature of our own context, our secular world, so that we can understand it and understand how best you and I can communicate the gospel to our neighbour, to our society and to our world.

Occasionally Paul was between missions. It happens to the best of us. And here Paul was waiting for Silas and Timothy. I imagine he was totally frustrated, doing absolutely nothing. But still, there are worse places than Athens in which to do nothing. People speak of 'the glory that was Greece', and though Greece was in decline, it wasn't ancient ruins in Paul's time; it was alive and reasonably well. The Parthenon, the tower of the winds – there was so much to do, so much to see in this centre of intellectual thinking and of spirituality! The Greeks were very flexible; they had a whole pantheon of gods, and when the Romans came and Rome was in the ascendant, the Greeks simply took over the Roman gods and made them their own. And there was the extra twist of eastern spirituality, eastern mysticism, that drifted in to the heart of Athens.

Paul could have been a tourist, even in the midst of Athens in decline. But he was no ordinary tourist. He wandered round, he looked and he was greatly distressed. The word is one often used to describe an epileptic. Paul had a fit, we might say; he was disturbed, provoked, stirred to fury, angry, exasperated. I don't think he was merely gnashing his teeth. I think he was expressing a feeling which in the Old Testament is described as being jealous for the living God. He was offended because God was being abused. He was offended because God, and God's name, were being taken lightly.

So what offended Paul in Athens? He found a city full of idols. There was a veritable forest of them. It was idol-ridden, not just in the sense that there were many idols there, but that the people were under the power of idols.

Paul's feeling led him to embark on a typically Pauline plan of action. Beginning in the synagogue with the religious people – Luke describes them as 'God-fearers' – he moved into the market-place; and from there into formal settings, as was Paul's way, whether it be governments, or rulers, or those in authority.

Luke says that Paul talked with anybody and everybody who happened to be there. He did it day after day. This was no flash in the pan. Of course it led to opportunities to speak before the Areopagus. We read that Paul reasoned, that Paul argued, that Paul proclaimed, that Paul preached. We read elsewhere that Paul debated, he engaged. It wasn't simply a matter of saying, 'Let me share my faith with you.' Paul's method was critical. Here was something that passed a judgment on people's ideas. Here was Paul arguing. 'Not a very Christian thing,' we think; but we've lost something of that New Testament desire to engage in critical thought, judgment, debate and argument, reasoning and proclaiming God's word.

But Paul was also able to draw on the culture in which he sought to minister. He drew from the poetry, the philosophy, the cultural ideas, the literature. What amazes me is that Paul, that busy workaholic, is nevertheless concerned enough to read the literature, understand the ideas and come to grips with the philosophy. Why? So that he can minister more effectively the grace, the word, the power of God, into situations.

A right view of God

And that's exactly what happened. Paul was confronted with the philosophers of his day, the Epicureans and the Stoics. The Epicureans believed that if there was a God, he was remote. What was important was the here and now, the material world. 'Therefore,' they argued, 'enjoy pleasure, but be tranquil about your pleasure-seeking.' The Stoics believed in Nature. They held that the best pattern for men and women was to live according to the paths of Nature, to be detached from the ordinary world, and to put one's passions and feelings in some kind of good order.

Paul argued with them. He reasoned, preached and proclaimed, and they said, 'This man is a babbler.' The word is the one used for a scavenger, like a magpie that wanders around picking things up. A modern picture might be a tramp, picking up a cigarette stub and smoking it. That was what they thought Paul was. 'He talks, he advocates foreign deities.' He was hauled in front of the Areopagus, which most commentators think was the education commission.

To teach in Athens you had to be properly qualified. When I moved to Oxford they didn't recognize my degrees from Arizona

State University and Edinburgh University. So I was given an MA – it was the easiest degree I ever earned, no work at all! – so that I could teach in the University of Oxford. Paul, before he could teach, had to satisfy the men of the Areopagus, the men who lived on lectures and were filled with intellectual curiosity; the men who loved nothing but the latest fashion in ideas. The men, because, of course, the slaves and the women were out doing all the work.

Men of Athens loved new ideas. They had open minds in Athens, but of course the completely open mind is the completely empty mind. These men loved what was strange. They wanted to know what something meant, but the problem was that they wanted intellectual titillation. Their interest in ideas was not genuine. They loved to talk and listen, they loved idle chatter and discussion, but it wasn't a discussion based on need. It's a bit like hens and pigs having a discussion about bacon and eggs; hens make a little contribution but the pig is totally committed! But the problem in Athens was, they weren't totally committed.

Your God is too small (17:22–23)

Paul begins by accentuating the positive, which is an important evangelistic device. He was particularly good at doing it just before he put the boot in.

'I perceive that you are a very religious people,' he tells them. 'You're a very superstitious people.' It was true. And yet there's an element of irony and sarcasm here. There was a religiosity and a superstition all around the area of Athens. They needed to worship and that religiosity was there. And yet somehow it hadn't produced the right kind of response. Paul says, 'As I was wandering backwards and forwards I found an altar. It was an altar to an unknown god' (*cf.* verse 23). It's rather like the reference to the Samaritans in John 4:22, 'You Samaritans worship what you do not know.' The Athenians bothered so much about making sure that all religions got an honourable mention that they even had an altar for 'an unknown god'.

'Now,' Paul says, 'I've come to proclaim the one whom you worship without knowing. Now I've come to make him known.'

Other religions worship, and for them it's a genuine worship. But it's not a worship of the true God, and it is not what God really wants. The mark of proper God-worship is that it's properly fulfilled in the nature of God and in the nature of Jesus. That is really the theme of the second part of Paul's address to the men on the Areopagus hill. We might take as a title for that sermon the phrase that J. B. Phillips coined: 'Your God is too small'. And I believe that

Paul would say these words not only to the Athenians but also, perhaps, to people at Word Alive.

God is the Lord (17:24–28)

Of course, what we have in Acts 17 is not a full sermon. Otherwise Paul would be famous for his brevity! We are given the highlights, the headings. So we do not have the whole gospel expressed, but we do have a clear understanding that 'God . . . is the Lord'. That's how Paul begins this second part, as he attempts to express who God is. God 'made the world and everything in it'. He is the Creator and Lord of the whole earth.

How Paul longs for the men of Athens! In any circumstances, Paul's desire is always that people should have a proper view of God, that they should put God first, recognizing that he is the Creator. And he is not only the Creator; he is *self-sufficient*. He 'does not live in temples built by hands. And he is not served by human hands.' So away with temples and sacrifices! God needs none of it.

But God is also *the maker and giver of life*. Paul wants to emphasize to the Athenians that there is a fundamental basis on which the whole of reality, the whole of human knowledge and being, is based: that God the maker of humanity is the giver of life and breath. Through one man, through one blood, there is a common humanity of which the root and basis is God himself. And every nation, and humanity as a whole, everything that 'inhabits the whole earth', comes from God who made humanity.

And God is *the Lord of history and the Lord of time*. Paul illustrates this by the fact that God has determined for humanity 'the exact places where they should live. God did this so that men would seek him and perhaps reach out for him and find him.'

God is *the sovereign one, who gives purpose to human beings*. Human beings were built to have a relationship with God, to seek him and perhaps reach out and find him who is 'not far from each one of us'. There is a purpose for human beings: that we should find a living relationship with God. Men and women without that relationship are not fulfilling God's purpose. They are not fulfilling the reason for which God made us all.

Acts 17 shows us other religions seeking but never quite finding, until and unless God reveals himself. And that's Paul's task and ours: to proclaim the good news that the real God – the Creator, the giver of life, the maker of the earth, the maker of humanity – God, the Lord, the sovereign one, is near. He is ever-present. He is nearer to us than our hands and feet, nearer than breathing. He is present with us now, present in every situation.

God is the Father (17:28–34)

Now Paul reminds the men of Athens that God is the Father who creates human beings: 'For in him we live and move and have our being . . . We are his offspring.'

My two children carry two burdens. One is that they live with me and the other is that they look like me. They're made in the image of their father. Paul was reminding the Athenians that they were made in the image of God, their Father.

But God was not only the Father of humanity. God was a God who could not be captured in the form of a statue or an idol, even one made out of silver or gold. There was no way of encapsulating God, of making him so small that human beings could understand all of him.

Nothing created by human beings, no act of idolatry, will bring men and women into a relationship with God. For this God who is near, who is the Father, who is the God who rejects idols, is also a God of grace.

This God, in the past, overlooked our ignorance (*cf.* verse 30). 'Overlooked' – there's the grace of God, of which Paul writes in Romans 3:25: 'The forbearance of God' (AV). That's how gracious God is. He puts up with me, he puts up with you.

But this gracious God makes demands. God commands 'all people everywhere to repent'. Paul is not afraid to bring people from an understanding of the grace and the goodness of God to the reality that God is a demanding and jealous God. God creates an authority and that authority says, 'Repent.' He is a God of judgment. We don't like talking about judgment and we don't like preaching about it. In an age of tolerance the idea that all of us will be judged is not popular. But Paul emphasizes the fact of judgment.

He emphasizes, too, that the God who passes that judgment is a just God. Sometimes when a tragic suicide happens, the family asks me, 'What's happened to the person who committed suicide? Will our loved one go to hell?' And I tell them that God is a just God. He doesn't judge that one last moment over and against all the other moments. God is just and fair in his judgment and we can trust that justice and judgment.

But there *is* a judgment. Paul says, 'God has set a day.' That's how precise it is. God has even appointed a man, the man-God Jesus, who will be the Judge. The Son of Man is the one who comes in judgment. And who better to judge us, than the one who became flesh? Who better to judge us, than the one who has been tempted in all points as we are, yet without sin? The one who knows from the inside what human existence is like? Jesus is the Judge. And the God who is near, God the Father, God rejecting idols, the God of grace, the God who makes demands, the God of judgment, the God who is all-powerful – this God, Paul says, raised this man Jesus from the dead (*cf.* verse 31). There he presents us with the clear status of Jesus. And, of course, in Luke's ten-minute summary it may appear that Paul is putting all his emphasis on the resurrection. But I don't believe that Paul preached about the resurrection without making clear the death of Jesus, the cross of Jesus.

Paul was confronted by a culture, an intellectual climate and a world that all needed the gospel. What did he do? He gave a clear picture of God. And what was the result? Well, some sneered; some said, 'Let's hear this man again'; a few, just a few, gladly believed and became Christians – Dionysius and Damaris and a few others. Oh, there were results. Who knew what the results would be? Certainly there was no church founded. That is why some have said, 'Paul was not very successful in Athens.' Notice that the church very often took root and grew when there was persecution. Isn't it sad that so often we do not respond to God and obey him until the hard times come?

Some would say that when Paul went on to Corinth he said, 'Enough of this foolishness to the Greeks; let's concentrate on knowing nothing but Christ crucified; let's become nothings, so that God can be everything.' But I don't believe that Luke would have given such a detailed, accurate account of all that happened in Athens unless he intended you and me and generations of Christians to recognize that the gospel must be communicated into the context. We need to proclaim and defend the Christian faith in a real and a living way.

It is of course a problem that missionaries have always faced. How much of the foreign culture do you take, how much of it do you use in communicating the gospel? What do we use, and what do we confront? What do we accept, and what do we throw away? But the reality is that we are all missionaries. We live in a secular culture. So we are all missionaries, or should be, whether it's to our family (as Dick Dowsett was saying in our study of Acts 16), to our neighbours, to the nation, or to the whole world. How are we to proclaim the gospel in our context? Well, we need to have not just a right view of God, but a right view of our context.

A right view of our context

So how can we understand our secular world, as Don Carson urged us to do in our studies in Philippians?

A visual context

One of the nice things about working in a 'vicar factory', as I did for many years, is that you meet such a nice class of person. Sometimes they would say, 'Come and spend a weekend with us.' When I first left Nottingham I spent many a free weekend enjoying hospitality! Now the problem is that when you are a guest you have to fit in with the way other people live. I remember one family in a very nice part of the country who held a special sort of observance on Saturdays. It began at 12:30 and it lasted until 5:00 and it was called *Grandstand*. We watched everything. On the Saturday I was visiting them the main event was weightlifting. I have to confess that I'm not really interested in weightlifting, but as weightlifting goes it was very interesting. It was a competition between the Czechs and the Russians, and oh how they loved one another! The Czechs won and everybody was delighted except the Russians, particularly the Russian super-heavyweight – a huge, hulking brute of a man who came staggering back into the stadium and demanded that the judges allow him one extra lift, which he hoped would reverse the whole result.

They gave in (if I'd been a judge I'd have given in too!) and let him have another chance. He lifted the weight, got the bar right up to his chest, and stopped. Then he did his special breathing. So there he was panting away, and then, just before he pushed his arms up in the air for a proper lift, the bones in his thighs came shooting through his kneecaps and he collapsed.

I'm telling you a story, but I have a picture in my mind, a slow-motion replay of that man's legs breaking, again and again and again. It's imprinted in my mind; I can't erase it, even though I want to. A picture is worth a thousand words and we live in a visual society which gives us many pictures. They come into our homes and they carry values and opinions with them. And you and I and our families open our eyes and mouths and we swallow them whole. How can we proclaim God's word in a visual age, a visual society?

John writes, 'The Word was made flesh, and dwelt among us, and we beheld his glory' (Jn. 1:1, AV). The incarnation, I believe, is a way of responding to our context.

A pleasure-seeking context

It is a visual context, but it is also a pleasure-seeking context, in which people want to enjoy themselves. 'Eat, drink and be merry – for tomorrow we diet!' We live in a society where people are interested in happiness and pleasure, in fulfilment. It affects the

235

church too. I've been involved for twenty years in selecting men and women for all kinds of ministries. And I've seen a change. Twenty years ago you'd say to someone, 'Why do you want to go into the ministry?' They would respond, 'I want to serve Christ, I want to serve the world, I want to serve humanity, I want to be a servant.' It was a great motive for going into the ministry. Today when you ask the same question the response is often: 'It will fulfil me. It will give me an opportunity to exercise all my gifts and my talents.'

That is what makes the difference between so many ministries today: a move away from service to fulfilment. We are a society of pleasure-seeking individuals. That's why people are interested in drugs, alcohol abuse and sexual expression.

It affects the church, but of course it also affects all of us in the wider society. What satisfies men and women? Does pleasure satisfy? Or is long-lasting satisfaction to be found in Christ alone? And the pleasure motif doesn't just affect individual men and women as they make their moral choices in society and live out their lives; pleasure also becomes a basis for decision-making in government. Why does the present government pursue the economic policies it pursues? Because they believe that in the end it leads to the greatest happiness of the greatest number. And time and again in politics, whether it's the local NHS deciding how to allocate the budget between heart transplants and kidney replacement, between Aids prevention and care for the elderly; or whether it's governments deciding on what kind of economic policies, what level of taxation – the aim so often is the greatest happiness of the greatest number.

A secularized context

We've become a pragmatic, secular society interested in pleasure for the individual or the community. If Martians were to arrive and look at our western world they'd describe it as secular. The word 'secular' is misleading because it means two different things. Secularization, as Don Carson has well described, is a process; one where religion is no longer central in popular thinking but moves to the periphery. It's marginalized, and we are in a secularized world. It is not only Christianity, but the Muslim faith too – all faiths are being secularized in that sense.

But there's another form of the secular which is a particular philosophy: secularism. It's a philosophy that attacks Christianity and Christian truth, and it's important that we understand it.

We need to understand, first of all, that *this secular philosophy is fundamentally anti-authority*. My wife used to be called a head-mistress; you're not allowed to call her that any more. Now she's a 'head teacher'. But she was trained to teach infants. When I used to go into her infant class it was chaos. I was told it was 'organized chaos'; this was the 'integrated day'. Here was Johnny in the Wendy house; here was Gemma in the sand; here was somebody else thrashing the living daylights out of another child; here was total chaos . . . it was 'organized'. If they survived that, there was even a moment at the end of the day called 'choosing'. Every child was allowed to choose to do his or her own thing.

And if they do well in nursery school and primary and secondary school, then they can come to university. At Oxford, parents save up and send their kids to us. After eight weeks we send them home for the vacation. Then the telephone calls and letters arrive.

'What have you done to John [or Jean]? Before he left home he was a lovely person. He always did exactly what he was told. His room was always immaculate. He always dressed very tidily. Whenever he went out he told us where he was going. Whenever he came back he told us where he'd been. You could always have a nice conversation. But since he went to university, he lies in bed all day. When he crawls out of the pit he looks like a tramp, his hair is all over the place. He wanders out – never tells us where he's going. He comes back at all hours, he never tells us where he's been. Then if you sit down and try and have a conversation with him, what does he do? He criticizes us all the time. *What have you done to him?*'

And I reply, 'Well, what we've done is we have educated these people'!

But what is the heart of education in our western, secular world? It is to question every authority. The father of Hector, one of our students, died and left him a theological college. It was a lovely thing to have; the only difficulty was that Hector didn't know any theology. So he was sent to Nottingham and I was given the task of teaching him theology. I gave him a book. 'Read the book, Hector, and write me an essay.' And he did. I have to tell you, the essay was copied almost word for word from the book. I said, 'Hector, this is fine, but you don't tell me whether this book is right or wrong. You don't tell me whether this is a good argument or a bad argument. You don't tell me what *you* think.'

He answered, 'Dr Cook, this book has been written by a professor of theology. He's a very intelligent man. I don't know anything about theology. How can I criticize this man?'

I said, 'Hector, unless you learn to criticize you'll never get a degree.'

We teach people to criticize and we make them into experts in criticism. They don't switch off their criticism when they go home.

They don't switch off when they go into church. We teach people how to take things apart. We never teach them how to put things together again.

We live in a world of critical, destructive, anti-authoritarian thinking, and behind it all is the idea that men and women make their own rules. They call it autonomy, the rights of the individual, the rights to make our own laws and follow our own wishes. I've just come back from the United States where they're talking about the 'entitlement generation'. That is, people who believe that they're entitled to everything, who recognize no responsibility or limits on their freedom, who want to be able to do everything.

But there are limits on freedom. I drove here; I had to wear a seat-belt, not because I want to but because I'm not free to do whatever I want with my own body. A group of homosexuals got together to have a party in which they intended to engage in sado-masochistic practices. They recorded the party on video, and after the party was over some of them ended up in hospital and the video fell into the hands of the police. The police charged them with causing grievous bodily harm. The defence was that everybody knew what kind of party it was, attended it voluntarily and took part willingly. Nobody complained. But they were sent to prison, because we are not free to do whatever we want with our own bodies.

Ours is an anti-authoritarian society and it is *a subjective society*. We emphasize the individual – doing our own thing, individual rights, individual truth. Truth is no longer something objective but something personal and purely subjective. We've separated the world of facts from the world of values, and religion has drifted over into that realm of personal subjective opinion.

It is made worse by the fact that we live in *a pluralist world*, a global village where travel and communications allow us to see the rest of the world instantly, in our own home. We live with difference in our midst. And that variety creates questions. The consequence is what is called 'relativism', the idea that there are no absolute standards, no absolute truths, no absolute moral standards. It holds that the words 'right' and 'wrong', 'good' and 'bad', 'true' and 'false' vary in their meaning from time to time, from place to place and from person to person. There are no absolute standards.

In order to cope in a pluralist and relativistic world the secularist says, 'Be tolerant, live and let live.' As Christians we need to respond to that challenge of relativism. We need to show God's absolute standard. We need to show in practical ways, as well as in 'principle' ways, that truth is something objective, that moral standards are good for people, good in themselves, good in practice and good in principle. We need to respond to the problems of tolerance.

As we conclude, I wish we had had time to look at what is called 'post-modernism'. Our post-modernist secular world celebrates diversity. It celebrates mystery and holisticism and allows aromatherapy and a kind of spiritism. We might have looked, too, at the way our society is becoming increasingly anti-mind, anti-intellectual. Remember, this is a people to whom God says, 'Love the LORD your God with all your heart, all your soul, all your mind, and all your strength.' I wish we'd time to talk about violence, about crime, about environmental concerns, and the threat to all our well-being. I wish we'd time to talk about the breakdown of the family unit, the destruction of marriage and the impact which that has on families and communities. I wish we'd time to reflect on the complexity of life and how we cope with that; the pace of life, the loss of meaning and how all of us as human beings in our secular society are faced with economic pressures.

But as I leave you I want to emphasize that in spite of all the problems and difficulties, in spite of the need to give a critical analysis of our secular society, there is a universality of human need. And more than that, there is a universality of God himself, the Creator, the maker of life, the giver of life, the sovereign Lord, the Father, the one who will not accept idols, the gracious, saving, judging God, the God who is able not just to do exceedingly abundantly above all that we ask or think, but is able to take our secular world and impact it, to transform it. A handful of men and women turned the world upside down; and we can do the same again.

As I was preparing for this evening, I remembered the first convention in which I ever took part. It was in Scotland. I was ten years old and I was invited to read a lesson at a Christian Endeavour convention. I was moved at the end of the convention, because they sang 'Scotland for Christ'. I believe that we at Word Alive, we at Spring Harvest, wherever we're meeting, need to say not just 'Scotland for Christ', not just 'the United Kingdom for Christ', not just 'Europe for Christ', but 'the world for Christ'. For the world's sake, for Christ's sake, and for God's sake. Amen.

15

Acts 20

Alec Motyer

Wherever we open our Bibles, we find something that tells us that this is the faithful word of God. The more we read, the more impossible it becomes not to believe and be convinced by what we find. Wherever we look we discover veracity, the unvarnished truth of God. You may have wondered why, when you read the story of that great giant of faith Abraham, you find stories of his failures in faith. But the Bible is like that; it paints its portraits 'warts and all'. That's its faithfulness, its truthfulness to the reality of which it speaks. That's why David, the man after God's own heart, is described as losing his heart to Bathsheba.

The Bible is real; it proclaims its reality and its veracity to us wherever we open it. That's why on the mount of transfiguration we see the Lord Jesus Christ surrounded by as prize a group of failures as ever you might meet. Moses, whose failure denied him entrance to the Promised Land; Elijah with his nervous breakdown; Peter, who simply didn't know what was going on and as usual put his great foot in it; James and John who were presently to forsake Jesus and flee. How real it is! You couldn't have a much better picture and symbol of the church: a prize crowd of failures, gathered round a lovely and glorious Saviour.

It will help us if we keep that in mind as we move into this passage in Acts. For here also we find that the word of God is speaking to us, really and truthfully and accurately, out of the situation it presupposes; directly from that moment when Paul gathered the Ephesian elders and began to instruct them. It's a very different sermon from any of the others in Acts. I suppose the closest comparisons are Peter's sermon in Acts 2 to that huge Jewish gathering, and Paul's sermon in Acts 13 delivered in a Jewish synagogue; both were preached to similar congregations.

But how different is Peter's sermon in Acts 10! It's even written differently. I believe that as Peter walked from Joppa to Caesarea, on the way to see Cornelius, he found a stub of pencil and on the back of an envelope scribbled a few notes as he went. And later when Luke said to him, 'By the way, have you any memory of what you said to Cornelius on that wonderful day?' Peter replied, 'Well actually, I have that envelope in my sermon file. I'll give it to you.' And it became Acts 20. The chapter reads just like that: scribbled jottings, from which he preached to Cornelius. How real the Bible is!

So we come to the only sermon in Acts preached to Christians. What an occasion, and what a preacher! Look at our dear brother and apostle Paul with me, in all his devotion. He's looking back to the time he was at Ephesus, a period marked by what Acts 19 says were most unusual occurrences, spiritual phenomena entirely out of the ordinary. But as Paul looks back to that time and picks out what he wants them to remember, there's no mention of all that. There's only mention of dogged, daily, public and private telling and teaching. That's what he remembers, and that's what he wants them to remember. There it is in verse 20: 'I have not hesitated to preach [or proclaim] anything that would be helpful to you but have taught you publicly and from house to house.' That's our Paul. That's real! That's what he was like.

Preaching and teaching; making the truth heard and making the truth plain; telling, teaching. This was Paul's great concern as with tear-filled eyes he ran after Jew and Gentile alike, bringing them the gospel of the grace of God, calling them to repentance and faith. We can enter into the situation being described and say, 'That's real, that's the Paul we know and love.'

At the end of the passage, he spread out his hands to them. 'You yourselves know', he said, 'that these hands of mine supplied my own needs and the needs of my companions' (20:24) That's Paul – ever responsible for his own support, ever generous to those who are with him.

Do you feel, with me, that we are brought right into that situation, that for Paul it is always Jesus first, Jesus last and Jesus at every stage in between? Paul starts his record of his time in Ephesus in verse 19: 'I served the Lord.' The Greek actually says 'slaving to the Lord'. And at the end of the sermon he's back focused on 'the words of the Lord Jesus himself'. How lovingly he dwells on Jesus! And then all through the sermon: verse 21, 'faith in our Lord Jesus' – Jesus as the object of personal, trusting faith; verse 24, the Lord of the harvest – the one who has given him a race to run and a ministry to fulfil, 'the task of testifying to the gospel of God's grace'. And, marvellously, verse 28, 'the church of God, which he bought with his own blood'. Or as we might translate it, 'which he bought with the blood of his One and Only'. If the reference is to the great God himself, then he did not spare his only Son and the only Son did not spare himself. Yes, we're right in the presence of Paul: that's why the sermon is so special.

Unlike the other evenings in this series, we are not now watching an apostle go out into the world to win the world for Christ. We're not being instructed by precept and example how to tackle the thought-forms and situations that are presented to us in the world. This is something quite different. This is the wonderful Paul speaking to the church, telling us about ourselves, nourishing us, establishing us, making us straight and strong for what Jesus may want of his church in the coming days.

For this is literally Paul's 'upper room'. Just as Jesus gathered his own into an upper room the night he had to tell them he was leaving them, so Paul is here speaking as one going away, never to be seen again. Verse 25: 'Now I know that none of you among whom I have gone about preaching the kingdom will ever see me again.' We are in the upper room together. And this what gripped them, so that we find in verse 38 just after the end of our passage today, 'What grieved them most was his statement that they would never see his face again.' As we overhear Paul, and as the word of God and its living reality make our situation into that situation, we are listening to that apostolic upper-room sermon.

The sermon sits on a dividing line in church history. On one side is the apostolic period when these unique men, raised up and appointed by the Lord Jesus Christ, taught and led and extended the church; that unique period, the apostolic age. And now we're going across the dividing line, and Paul is showing us how to look forward, to a time without any apostles alive. What will be your situation then? What are you going to do? How very apt this passage of Scripture is to you and to me, and indeed to the whole church of our Lord Jesus Christ, because we are over that line. The apostles are gone. How are we placed? What are we to do? What are our resources? What are we to aim at?

The easiest way to come to grips with what he's saying to us is to examine the structure of his sermon. In verse 18, he explains that he's going to look back to his time at Ephesus. He reminds the elders that he's telling them something they know already: 'You know . . .' Now look forward to verse 33: 'I have not coveted anyone's silver or gold or clothing. You yourselves know . . .' He begins and ends his sermon by telling them what they already know. There's a 'you know' passage at the beginning and at the end. Now, verse 22: 'And now, compelled by the Spirit, I am going to Jerusalem, not knowing . . .' He looks forward into the future, and he finds the future unknown. But in contrast to that, look at verse 25: 'Now I know . . .' He's going to describe now the future – not his own, about which he is uncertain, but the future of the church after his time. 'I know that none of you among whom I have gone about preaching . . . will see me again.' He's going to tell them about their future, and he does know it. And in verse 29, 'I know that after I leave, savage wolves will come . . .'

Are you beginning to sense the shape of the sermon? We can divide it into four or five sections, framed by the beginning and ending 'you know' passages and including the intervening part where he doesn't know what's going to happen to him but he does know what's going to happen to them.

Right! Come, step with me into Paul's sermon, and I'll do my best to use his sermon notes and preach his sermon to you.

Character (20:18–21)

What is Paul saying to us in this, the first of the 'you know' passages, looking back at his time at Ephesus?

He's saying that *character is the basis of testimony*: 'You know how I lived . . .' That's his starting-point: 'You know what sort of person I proved to be when I was with you.' He's going to go on and talk about a most impressive slavery to our Lord Jesus Christ from verse 19 onwards: 'slaving to the Lord' (in the NIV it is watered down a little: 'I served the Lord'). Paul tells us four things about a true slavery.

First of all, it's marked by *humility*. The word means 'humble-mindedness'. The slave has first of all a humble estimate of his own position and abilities. Secondly, he tells us of *tears*. The slave has a real, heartfelt, weeping concern for the needs of other people. Thirdly, he speaks about *trials*. 'I was severely tested by the plots of the Jews . . .' but he still went on; a slave has durability when life turns difficult. And finally the fourth side of the slave quadrilateral of reality: to himself, humility; to other people, concern and tears; to circumstances, durability and persistence – and now *testimony*. 'You know that I have not hesitated to preach anything that would be helpful to you but have taught publicly and from house to house. I have declared to both Jews and Greeks that they must turn to God in repentance and have faith in our Lord Jesus' (verses 20–21). The first thing, says Paul, is the sort of person you saw me to be. Character comes first.

Commitment (20:22–24)

As we move now into the second stage of Paul's sermon I share with you from his sermon notes that *commitment is the overriding value in life*. When he knows so much, how can he say in verse 22, 'I don't know'? The answer is that he knows details of what will happen to him, but the outcome has not yet been revealed. He's got to walk blind into a difficult, threatening and challenging situation, a situation that would make a strong man flinch, never mind Paul with all his tears and weakness, fear and trembling – all that made the merciful Lord Jesus draw near to him in Corinth and say, 'Do not be afraid' (18:9)

When the group around Paul heard this word of the Holy Spirit coming in yet another city, 'we and the people there pleaded [that he] would not go up to Jerusalem' (21:12). It was enough to make anybody flinch. But there was something more valuable than comfort, something more valuable than preserving his life and his skin. That greater value was this: 'I consider my life worth nothing to me, if only I may finish the race and complete the task the Lord Jesus has given me – the task of testifying to the gospel of God's grace' (verse 24). Commitment to the Lord Jesus – oh, how lovely that name and title are in all their simplicity! Not the full, formal title of 'the Lord Jesus Christ', but that lovely simplicity: 'the Lord Jesus'.

'If only I can do what he wanted me to do,' says Paul. 'If only I can run my race and complete my task and share this lovely, lovely gospel of the grace of God. If only I can do that, that's the overriding value, that's more important than anything else.'

Self-care (20:25–28)

Now we have the first 'I know' passage. Here Paul is looking forward, into the future of the church. 'Now I know that none of you among whom I have gone about preaching the kingdom will ever see me again. Therefore I declare to you [I testify to you] that I am innocent of the blood of all men. For I have not hesitated to proclaim to you the whole will of God' (verses 25–27).

'Do take care of yourselves' (a better rendering than NIV's 'Guard yourselves') 'and all the flock in which the Holy Spirit has made you overseers. Be shepherds of the church of God, which he bought with his own blood.' What's he saying to them? He has said to them that his own ministry has been a faithful one, perfectly discharged; but as he says, 'I know what the future will hold', what does he say to them about the future of the church? He says that self-care is the first duty of the minister.

Oh, the ministry was important – super-important. According to verse 17, they were *elders*. That was their seniority and maturity in the church. But when we come to verse 28 we find that they are *shepherds in the flock*. They have a caring, guarding, ministry. And also we discover that they are *overseers*. That is to say, they have a responsibility to keep all the flock of God constantly under their eye, and that flock of God is such a precious thing because God bought it as his very own possession by the blood of his very own Son. There's value!

Explore with me for a minute the words that we have in verse 28: 'which he bought', 'which he made to be his own personal possession'. The ancient kings theoretically owned everything. But as with millionaires today, it's very easy to have everything, but actually to have very little at your own disposal. For those ancient kings, actually owning something meant putting their possessions in their treasure chest. That's the word that Paul uses here. The church is that which God, who owns everything, has put in his treasure chest. His very prize possession; so prized, so valued, that he was willing to purchase it with the blood of his One and Only.

Now, beloved, how important self-care must be if it takes priority over that! Do look after yourselves. I speak to my brothers and sisters in ministry, do look after yourselves. The thing that's given first place in importance is often the thing that is first to go in the busy-ness of life. The besetting sin of ministers is to sacrifice the best to the good; to spend every day of every week fully involved in good things, lovely things, God-honouring things, things that respect and care for the church, the task of shepherding and the task of overseeing – to the neglect of their own vineyards, their own walk with God and the welfare of their own souls. Then the day comes when we have nothing to give, because we have nothing in store; and the flock of God goes unfed because the minister is undernourished. Self-care has the priority in ministry.

The powerful apostolic word (20:25–32)

Paul now explains, with a second 'I know', that persistent, directive teaching is the safeguard of the church. He is looking forward, in verses 25–29, into the future. He speaks of dangers from outside, verse 29: 'After I leave, savage wolves will come in . . .' And he speaks about dangers from inside, verse 30: 'Even from your own number men will arise . . .' He is quite clear the church is an endangered species. It is endangered from the world outside and it is in danger from the false church inside; it's endangered by invasion and it's endangered by apostasy, by those who would come in to destroy and by those who pretend to be in already and are equally destructive. The world will seek to destroy the church. Savage wolves will come in, not sparing the flock.

In John 10:12, the Lord Jesus in his 'good shepherd' illustration spoke about the wolf coming and scattering the sheep. Paul doesn't quite say that. He's not talking about individual sheep being endangered, but the flock being endangered. And that tells us what the enemy from outside wants to destroy. The flock, as we have just seen, is the blood-bought possession; and the one thing that the world around us cannot stand is the shedding of the blood of God's Son. They cannot stand a church that affirms an atonement by the blood of Christ. They cannot stand the church as a blood-bought possession. And pressures from outside, from the world around, will constantly try to diminish the atonement content of the Christian message.

And those from inside will distort the truth too. What *they* cannot stand is a church that rests four-square upon Holy Scripture. They will distort the norms. They will tell you that the Bible is not speaking the truth, or that it doesn't mean what it says, or that in order to understand it you must have specialist knowledge and training. And one way or another, that apostate professing church will take the Bible out of the hands of the true church and the true believer. It says that they will try to 'draw away' the disciples. It is not that they are anxious to create a party to draw away disciples after themselves, but that they are anxious to diminish the number of those who stand as disciples of Jesus, the true reality of the actual church of God. And they will draw away the disciples, it says, 'after them'.

Where did you hear that word last? In the gospels. It's Jesus' word. 'Come,' he said to Peter and James and John, 'Come after me.' And these 'wolves' don't want that. They want a church that is astray from Scripture, and for disciples who belong to Jesus to cease to follow him. They want to give the church a replacement Jesus.

And the safeguard? The safeguard, says Paul, is not new experiences; it's not new powers; it's not new structures. *The safeguard is the old apostolic model.* 'What did I do among you for three years?' he asks. 'Remember that for three years I never stopped warning you' (verse 31). The word means more than 'warning'; in fact, it's rather a positive word. It means bringing out the truth of God gently, caringly, persuasively, and applying that truth to people. Look it up in the concordance. You'll find that it means the ministry of the word of God, the counselling exercise, which brings the word of God home to the people of God. That's the safeguard.

And so he goes on to say, in verse 32: 'I commit you to God and to the word of his grace, which is able [it's a much stronger word than the NIV's 'can'], to build you up and to give you an inheritance . . .' This is your resource against the wolves from outside and the apostates from inside; the powerful word which can guard you, and build you, and secure your inheritance.

Personal submission to the word of the Lord Jesus Christ (20:33–35)

The truth in these final verses is as clear as daylight; I want to share it with you. Paul lived as he did, earning his own living, supporting his companions, not because no other lifestyle was permissible or possible for him, but because he had a clear word of Jesus which he intended to obey. It was he himself who said it. So the fifth heading of his sermon is: personal submission to the word of the Lord Jesus Christ. And this last section could not be a more apt summary of what he has been saying all the way through. Remember, we're standing on the dividing line. The apostles are gone. We're facing the task of being apostolic Christians without living apostles. How are we to do it?

I can tell you what this passage means to me, and please God it means the same to you. It means the all-sufficient Lord Jesus and his all-sufficient word – not one or the other, but both together. It means the irreplaceable centrality of Jesus Christ our Lord and the irreplaceable centrality of his holy word – not one or the other but both together. Hasn't everything in this sermon come back to rest on Jesus? Are we slaving to the Lord, are we converted? It was because we put our trust in the Lord Jesus. Are we in the ministry? We have received that ministry from the Lord Jesus. Is it a matter of the atonement? Atonement is by the blood of God's One and Only. Is it our discipleship? Then we have pledged ourselves to come after him and to refuse to go after anybody else. Is it our obedience? Then we will be obedient to the words of our Lord Jesus.

Everything comes back to him, to the incomparable, total sufficiency of the Lord Jesus for the church when the apostles are gone. For us! Turn your eyes upon Jesus, and keep them there.

But also, everything in this sermon issues from what we do with our Bibles. For though Paul speaks of the word of God in many ways, the Bible I hold in my hand is the form of the word of God in which we are privileged to possess it. Is preaching it our ministry? Then we mustn't play tricks; we mustn't trim the word of God to suit what people want to hear. Do we want to please Jesus by fulfilling our ministry? The Bible is the gospel of the grace of God. Is our ministry that of countering error and those who would depart from the norm? Well then, that means counselling, teaching, advising and directing out of that 'word of his grace' which alone has power – this is the only place in the whole sermon where Paul talks about power – to build up, to safeguard and to secure our inheritance. And in our daily living, too (verse 35), we are to remember the words of our Lord Jesus Christ.

I want to leave with you two lines from different hymns. The first is, 'Thou, O Christ, art all I want.' Sometimes hymnwriters, in order to get the rhyme, have to choose the wrong word! What Wesley meant was, 'Thou, O Christ, art all I *need*.' And the other line, from a different hymn, is a prayer: 'Make thy word my guide to heaven.' The irreplaceable centrality and sufficiency of the Lord Jesus and the irreplaceable centrality and sufficiency of the word of God. Not one or the other, but both together.

Notes

Chapters 1–4

1. 'Direct' is not perhaps the happiest term, but I cannot think of a better word at the moment. We might say that packing pork to the glory of God has *indirect* eternal significance, in that it honours the God of eternity and prepares me for eternity. But it does not have the same *direct* eternal significance that, say, fruitful evangelism or prevailing intercessory prayer does.
2. The Greek future tense commonly signals expectation rather than mere futurity.
3. James Paton (ed.), *John G. Paton: Missionary to The New Hebrides. An Autobiography*, (Edinburgh: Banner of Truth Trust, 1965), p. 56.
4. The last few decades have witnessed the rise of another interpretation of Philippians 2, an interpretation that has found its way into many commentaries. I am persuaded it is wrong, and in any case I cannot deal with it here. One of the best treatments of the exegetical questions that are at stake is in the commentary by Peter T. O'Brien, *Commentary on Philippians* (Grand Rapids: Eerdmans, 1991), pp. 186–271.
5. As usual, I am citing from the NIV, but I would not want to mislead someone by giving the impression that I care nothing about anachronisms. At the time, of course, the English Bible that both I and my friends used was the Authorized Version: 'Be imitators of me, as I also am of Christ.'
6. *Engaging with God* (Leicester: Apollos, 1992).
7. A. W. Tozer, *The Pursuit of God* (Harrisburg: Christian Publications, 1948), pp. 45–46.

Chapters 5–8

1. David F. Wells, *God in the Wasteland: The Truth of Reality in a World of Fading Dreams* (IVP, 1994), p. 88.
2. Published by St Matthias Press.